FIERCE

SELF-
COMPASSION

FIERCE

SELF-
COMPASSION

HOW WOMEN CAN HARNESS
KINDNESS TO SPEAK UP,
CLAIM THEIR POWER AND THRIVE

KRISTIN NEFF, PhD

PENGUIN LIFE

AN IMPRINT OF

PENGUIN BOOKS

PENGUIN LIFE

UK | USA | Canada | Ireland | Australia
India | New Zealand | South Africa

Penguin Life is part of the Penguin Random House group of companies
whose addresses can be found at global.penguinrandomhouse.com.

First published in the United States of America by Harper Wave 2021
First published in Great Britain by Penguin Life 2021
002

Printed and bound in Great Britain by Clays Ltd, Elcograf S.p.A.

The authorized representative in the EEA is Penguin Random House Ireland,
Morrison Chambers, 32 Nassau Street, Dublin D02 YH68

A CIP catalogue record for this book is available from the British Library

ISBN: 978-0-241-44865-6

www.greenpenguin.co.uk

MIX
Paper from
responsible sources
FSC
www.fsc.org   FSC® C018179

Penguin Random House is committed to a
sustainable future for our business, our readers
and our planet. This book is made from Forest
Stewardship Council® certified paper.

To my beloved son, Rowan,
and to all women everywhere

CONTENTS

CONTENTS

PART I

WHY WOMEN NEED FIERCE SELF-COMPASSION

INTRODUCTION
CARING FORCE

One thing is certain. If we merge mercy with might,
and might with right, then **love** becomes our legacy and
change our children's birthright.

—*Amanda Gorman, U.S. National Youth Poet Laureate*

There's something in the air. Every woman I talk to can feel it. We're fed up, angry, and ready for change. Traditional gender roles and societal power structures restrict the ability of women to express the full range of who we are, at great cost both personally and politically. Women are allowed to be soft, nurturing, and tender. But if a woman is too fierce—if we're too angry or forceful—people get scared and call us names (witch, hag, shrew, and ball-breaker are some of the milder insults that come to mind). If we're ever going to move beyond male dominance and take our proper place at the tables of power, we need to reclaim the right to be fierce. That's how we'll make a difference in the issues facing our world today: entrenched poverty, systemic racism, a failing health-care system, and climate change, to start. This book is aimed at helping women do just that.

A valuable framework for understanding how women can make productive change is self-compassion. Compassion is aimed at alleviating suffering—it's the impulse to help, an active feeling of concern, the palpable instinct to care for those who are struggling. Although most people naturally feel compassion for others, it's harder to direct this instinct inward. The last twenty years of my career have been devoted to researching the psychological health benefits of self-compassion and teaching people how to be kinder and more supportive toward themselves. Along with my close colleague Dr. Chris Germer, we've developed a training program called Mindful Self-Compassion that's taught around the globe. But in order to realize the full benefits of self-compassion, we need to develop both its fierce and tender side.

This is a recent realization for me. When leading self-compassion workshops in the past, I often told a funny and true story designed to illustrate how mindfulness and self-compassion can help us work with "difficult" emotions like anger.

The story goes like this: When my son Rowan was about six, I took him to see a bird show at the zoo. Once we got settled, Rowan, who's autistic, started being a bit disruptive—not screaming-and-flailing disruptive, but talking-out-loud and standing-on-rather-than-sitting-in-his-chair disruptive. The woman in front of us, her two perfectly behaved little girls sitting next to her, kept turning around to shush Rowan. Rowan wouldn't be shushed. I tried to help him keep quiet, but he was so excited he couldn't control himself. After about her third failed shooshing attempt, the woman turned around and with a crazed look in her eye exclaimed, "Will you please be quiet, we're trying to hear the show!"

Rowan was confused. He turned to me and asked in a frightened voice, "Who's that, Mommy?"

If anyone does anything at all threatening or aggressive to *my* son, I turn into Momma Bear. I was furious. So, I told him, "That's a . . ." Well, let's just say I used a word that started with "B" and it wasn't bear—you can use your imagination. The bird show ended shortly thereafter and the woman turned around to face me.

"How dare you call me that!" she said.

"How dare you give my son the evil eye!" I spat back. And we started going at it. *Two moms with their little ones by their sides, in a shouting match at a bird show!* Luckily, I was practicing a lot of mindfulness at the time (yes, I see the irony) and said relatively calmly, "I am so angry right now." The woman responded, "Tell me something I don't know." But for me it was a pivotal moment, because instead of being lost in my rage, I was able to be mindfully aware of it, de-escalate, and leave.

It's a great teaching story because it illustrates how skills like mindfulness can help pull us back from the edge when we're being swept away by our reactive emotions. But for years I failed to fully appreciate the importance of what happened: that instinctive arising of fierce Momma Bear energy. I took for granted that moment of protective anger and assumed it was a problem when it was actually remarkable and awe-inspiring.

The Marvel Comics writer Jack Kirby was so astounded after witnessing a car accident and seeing a mother lift a three-thousand-pound vehicle to save her baby trapped underneath that it moved him to create the Incredible Hulk. This fierce aspect of our nature is far from problematic; it's a superpower. Something to be celebrated rather than merely "accepted" with mindful awareness. And not only can we use this force to protect our children, we can also use it to protect ourselves, meet our needs, motivate change, and engage in the work of justice. This book is designed to help women tap into our fierce inner warrior, so we can rise up and change our world.

CARING FORCE

Women still live in a male-dominated society, and we need all the tools we can get our hands on to emerge triumphant but also healthy and whole. One of the most powerful weapons in our arsenal is caring force. Tender self-compassion harnesses the energy of *nurturing* to alleviate suffering, while fierce self-compassion harnesses the energy of *action* to alleviate suffering—when these are fully integrated, they manifest as caring force. Our force is more effective when it's caring because it combines strength with love. This is the message taught by great leaders of social change such as Mahatma Gandhi, Mother

Teresa, Nelson Mandela, and Susan B. Anthony. It's what Reverend Martin Luther King Jr. articulated in his call to end the Vietnam War: "When I speak of love I am not speaking of some sentimental and weak response. I am speaking of that force which . . . [is] the supreme unifying principle of life."

Fortunately, caring force can be turned inward as well as outward. We can use it to propel our personal journey of growth and healing at the same time that we fight for justice. After all, social activism is an act of self-compassion (not just other-compassion) because we're all interconnected, and injustice impacts us all.

Although I used to believe my own fierceness was a character flaw I needed to overcome, I now realize it's what has allowed me to succeed in life. In 2003, I published the first theoretical paper defining self-compassion, and I created the Self-Compassion Scale (SCS) the same year to measure it. My initial studies demonstrated that people who score higher on the SCS have greater levels of well-being. While for the first few years I was the primary person conducting research on self-compassion, since then the field has exploded and now includes well over three thousand scientific journal articles, with new studies being published daily. I doubt I would've had the courage to enter this uncharted territory without the same warrior energy that sometimes gets me into trouble (like calling a complete stranger names in front of my child at a bird show).

COMING FULL CIRCLE

Unpacking the fierce as well as tender sides of self-compassion is the latest development in my work, and something I've yet to write extensively about. At the same time, it draws on threads that have run throughout my career. I did my Ph.D. in the area of moral development with a scholar named Elliot Turiel at the University of California, Berkeley. He'd been a student of Lawrence Kohlberg, the famous theorist who proposed that morality developed through three main stages. According to Kohlberg's model, the first stage (occurring in childhood) focuses on meeting personal needs, the second stage (found in adolescence) focuses on care and meeting the needs of others, and the final stage (reached in adulthood if at all) focuses on justice and equitably considers everyone's rights and needs. Kohlberg's research, conducted mainly in the 1960s, found that women tended to make moral decisions based on care, whereas men more often made decisions based on rights and justice. This was interpreted to mean that women were less advanced moral thinkers than men.

Many feminists were rightfully angered by this position and saw it as biased. Carol Gilligan, author of the influential book *In a Different Voice*, countered that care and justice were two different ethical lenses through which one can see the world. A woman's way of knowing was connected, rather than autonomous, but not inferior to a male perspective. Although her theory was intended to thwart the view that women were less moral than men, it ironically portrayed women as not valuing justice!

I disagree with both these positions, finding each of them sexist in their own way. Turiel resolved the argument by demonstrating that males and females at all stages of development make moral judgments based on autonomy, care, and justice depending on the context. Almost everyone, regardless of age, gender, or culture, judges that it's better to care for and help rather than harm others, that people should be able to make autonomous decisions about certain personal issues, and that justice matters. In fact, one of the first moral judgments little kids make is "that's not fair!" Turiel's research also shows that social power plays an important role in how each type of reasoning is expressed. Dominance grants more autonomous decision-making, and subordination demands more care for others. By definition, a central feature of having power is the ability to do what you want, and part of what defines subordination is having to meet the needs of those with power. Equal power is necessary to ensure that everyone's needs are considered fairly. I spent a year in India to conduct my dissertation research on how culturally embedded beliefs about gender hierarchy influence reasoning about these issues in marital conflicts (more on this later).

It was only after returning to Berkeley to write up my dissertation that I learned about self-compassion. As I wrote about extensively in my first book *Self-Compassion*, my journey to self-kindness was a painful one. Just before embarking on my research abroad, I left my husband for another man (much to my horror and shame given that I considered myself a highly caring and moral person), who was supposed to join me in India. But that man didn't leave his partner for me and never showed up. Not only that, when I came home I found out he'd developed brain cancer and died shortly after my return.

I wanted to learn meditation as a way of picking up the pieces of my shattered life. I started practicing with a group that followed the teachings of Thich Nhat Hanh, a Vietnamese Zen Master who emphasizes the need to be compassionate to ourselves as well as others. I read books by pioneering Western Buddhist teachers, like Sharon Salzberg's *Lovingkindness* and Jack Kornfield's *A Path with Heart*, which also stress the importance of including ourselves in the circle of compassion.

As a result of my reading and meditation practice, I tried to be warmer to myself and more supportive. Instead of beating myself up about what I'd done—just so I could convince myself I was a good person for hating what a bad person I'd been; this is how convoluted the mind gets—I tried to be more understanding and forgiving. Admittedly it was a bit awkward at first. When I tried telling myself, "Human beings make mistakes," another voice would pop up and say, "You're just making excuses." But eventually the voice of objection quieted, as I learned to acknowledge the pain of the harm I'd caused while being kind in the process. I told myself, "I know you would have done it differently if you could have, but you weren't capable at the time. You were frustrated in your marriage and were trying to find happiness. Everyone wants to be happy." Rather than obsessing about myself and my misdeeds, I began to appreciate my imperfect humanity and the way it connected me to the larger whole. I would put my hands on my heart and say, "I know you're hurting, but it will be okay. I accept you exactly as you are, flaws and all." Doing so allowed me to take full responsibility for what I'd done, painful as it was, without flagellating myself in the process. With practice, I learned how to hold my shame with love, and it radically changed my life for the better.

After graduating, I did two years of postdoctoral study with a professor at the University of Denver named Susan Harter who was one of the country's leading researchers on self-esteem, a concept that had dominated psychologists' conceptions of well-being for decades. Self-esteem can be defined as a positive evaluation of self-worth. Researchers were starting to understand that although judging yourself positively makes you happier, it can lead people into traps and dead ends like narcissism and continual comparison with others. Furthermore, self-esteem too often depends on social approval, or looking attractive, or succeeding rather than failing. Self-esteem is a fair-weather friend. It's there when things go well but deserts you when things go badly, just when you need it most. Self-compassion is a perfect alternative to self-esteem. It doesn't require feeling better than others, it isn't contingent on other people liking you, and it doesn't require getting things right. All you need to have self-compassion is to be a flawed human being like everyone else. It's a constant source of support and refuge.

When I took a faculty position at the University of Texas at Austin, I initially continued my research on how power impacts autonomy, care, and justice in relationships. But I was also developing my ideas on self-compassion and wrote about it as a healthier alternative to self-esteem. I became so enthralled with self-compassion that I dropped all other lines of study; it's been my primary focus ever since. Only recently have I revisited my early research interests in the context of self-compassion. When we relate to ourselves with tender self-compassion, we care for and nurture ourselves. When we relate to ourselves with fierce self-compassion, we assert our autonomy and stand up for our rights. When fierce and tender self-compassion are balanced, we can be fair and just. Power and gender expectations also play a role in the expression of self-compassion, with male dominance emphasizing fierceness, female subordination emphasizing tenderness, and the drive for gender equality demanding that we integrate both. The previously disparate lines of my work have now come together, like puzzle pieces clicking into place.

WHY THIS BOOK IS WRITTEN FOR WOMEN, AND WHY NOW

Self-compassion is useful for anyone, and most of what I've written about in the past has been gender neutral. But I believe that self-compassion is especially necessary for women at this moment in history. Women have had it with mansplaining and being treated as if we were incompetent. It's time for us to be paid fairly and to have equal power and representation as national leaders in business and government. Fierce self-compassion, especially when balanced with tender self-compassion, can help us fight for our rights and counter the harm done by centuries of being told to keep quiet and look pretty.

I was also inspired to write this book as a consequence of the #MeToo movement. For far too long women swept sexual harassment and abuse under the rug. We feared people wouldn't believe us if we revealed the truth. It would bring shame upon us, or it would only cause more harm. But this changed in 2017 as hundreds of thousands of women used the hashtag #MeToo to share their experiences of sexual harassment and assault. Suddenly, the men were the ones leaving their jobs with their reputations in ruin.

As I will discuss in detail later, my story resonates with those of countless other women around the globe. Despite being a well-known mindfulness and compassion teacher, I was fooled and manipulated by someone who turned out to be a sex predator. A man I trusted and supported was actually harassing and abusing countless women without my knowledge. My self-compassion practice is what allowed me to cope with the horror of revelation after revelation. Tender self-compassion helped me to heal, and fierce self-compassion spurred me to speak up and commit to not letting the harm continue.

The women's movement gave us access to the professional realm, but to succeed in it we've needed to act like men, suppressing tender qualities that are devalued in a man's world. At the same time, we're disliked for being too aggressive or assertive. This leaves us with a false choice: to succeed and be scorned or to be liked and remain disempowered. Women have more pressure to prove ourselves at work, but are also subject to sexual harassment and lower pay. The bottom line is this: the current setup isn't working for us anymore. I believe that by developing and integrating fierce and tender self-compassion, women will be better equipped to realize our true selves and make needed changes to the world around us. Patriarchy is still alive and causing great harm. We're being called by the pressing issues of the day—sexual harassment, pay inequality, rampant prejudice, health disparities, political division, our dying planet—to claim our power and take action.

Because I'm a White, cisgender, heterosexual woman, undoubtedly there will be unconscious biases in what I write. Although I'll try as best I can to address the diverse experience of people who identify as women, my efforts will surely fall short. Please forgive me. It's my hope that this book will lay out general principles that can speak to the experience of people with differing intersections of identities in a meaningful way. All women are not the same and all suffering is not the same. But I believe that fierce and tender self-compassion are relevant to all people and are key to the fight against sexism, racism, heterosexism, ableism, and other forms of oppression.

SELF-COMPASSION AS A PRACTICE

Self-compassion isn't just a good idea. It's something we can *do*. We can train our brains and build new habits to respond to our mental, physical, and emotional pain with compassion. Research shows not only that we can learn to be more self-compassionate, but that it radically changes our lives for the better. This book will introduce concepts, discuss research, and help you develop both tender and fierce self-compassion. It will teach you how to combine them to create a caring force that can be used in key areas of your life like relationships, caregiving, and work.

Throughout the book I'll provide tools to help you understand what you're reading firsthand. Sometimes I'll present empirically validated assessments of traits such as self-compassion, gender stereotypes, or relationship styles that are commonly used in research, so you can conduct that same research on yourself! I'll also include concrete exercises to help you develop your self-compassion muscles. (Guided audio versions of many of these practices are available at FierceSelf-Compassion.org.) And while there will be a few meditations, this is not a meditation guide. I'm not a spiritual teacher, I'm a scientist, but when self-compassion goes deep it can be a spiritual experience.

Most of the practices included in this book are adapted from the empirically supported Mindful Self-Compassion (MSC) program that I developed with Chris Germer. You can take an MSC course online at www.CenterforMSC.org or go through the program yourself using *The Mindful Self-Compassion Workbook*. MSC isn't therapy, but it can be highly therapeutic. Rather than focusing on healing particular wounds from the past, MSC helps us adopt a more self-compassionate approach to everyday life. In an early study of the effectiveness of MSC, we found that eight weeks of training led to a 43 percent increase in self-compassion. Participants reported they were also more mindful and compassionate to others; less depressed, anxious, stressed, and emotionally avoidant; as well as happier and more satisfied with their lives. Most significantly, the resource of self-compassion was a steady friend from then on. The increased self-compassion and improved well-being gained from MSC was demonstrated to last for at least a year.

The amount that people benefitted from the program was also linked to how much they practiced. For this reason, I encourage you to practice self-compassion intentionally for at least twenty minutes per day. Although research shows that these self-compassion tools work, the only way you'll know for sure is if you give them a try.

TEST YOUR LEVEL OF SELF-COMPASSION

If you want to get a sense of how self-compassionate you are, you can fill out this brief version of the Self-Compassion Scale that is used in most self-compassion research. For fun, you may want to record your score now and then take the SCS again after finishing the book to see if your level of self-compassion has changed. You'll notice that the SCS does not differentiate between fierce and tender self-compassion. While I might refine the scale to reflect these two sides of self-compassion in the future, currently the SCS is a general measure of the trait.

Instructions

Please read each statement carefully before answering. To the left of each item, indicate how often you behave in the stated manner. Answer according to what really reflects your experience rather than what you think your experience *should* be.

For the first set of items, use the following scale from 1 (almost never) to 5 (almost always), or some point in between:

_____ I try to be understanding and patient toward those aspects of my personality I don't like.

_____ When something painful happens, I try to take a balanced view of the situation.

_____ I try to see my failings as part of the human condition.

_____ When I'm going through a very hard time, I give myself the caring and tenderness I need.

_____ When something upsets me, I try to keep my emotions in balance.

_____ When I feel inadequate in some way, I try to remind myself that feelings of inadequacy are shared by most people.

For the next items, use a scale from 1 (almost always) to 5 (almost never), or some point in between. Notice that the scoring system has been reversed, so that higher scores indicate lessened frequency:

_____ When I fail at something important to me, I become consumed by feelings of inadequacy.

_____ When I'm feeling down, I tend to feel like most other people are probably happier than I am.

_____ When I fail at something that's important to me, I tend to feel alone in my failure.

_____ When I'm feeling down, I tend to obsess and fixate on everything that's wrong.

_____ I'm disapproving and judgmental about my own flaws and inadequacies.

_____ I'm intolerant and impatient toward those aspects of my personality I don't like.

Total (sum of all 12 items) = _____

Mean self-compassion score (Total/12) = _____

In general, you can interpret a score ranging from 2.75 to 3.25 as average, below 2.75 as low, and above 3.25 as high.

GOING SLOWLY

As you go through this book, you'll likely encounter difficult feelings, which naturally arise whenever we practice compassion. When we give ourselves love, we may immediately remember all the times in the past when we were unloved, or thoughts may come up about all the ways we're unlovable. For instance, when you try to care for yourself by drawing boundaries with a male coworker who comments inappropriately about your figure, you may remember being shamed by your father in adolescence for how you dressed. Or when you try to comfort yourself when grieving a failed romantic relationship, you may be deluged with old fears about not being funny enough or attractive enough or exciting enough. These are actually good signs. They show you're opening your heart. It means that old pain stuffed down into the recesses of your unconscious is being released into the light of day. When given space and held with warmth, the pain can start to heal.

However, these feelings may sometimes be overwhelming. You want to practice self-compassion in a way that feels safe, or else you're not being self-compassionate! Especially for women with a history of trauma, it's important to go slowly and at your own pace, pulling back whenever you need to by disengaging from the practices and coming back to them later, perhaps even with the guidance of a therapist or other mental health professional. We can't learn new things if we feel overwhelmed, so allow yourself to stop if you feel a particular exercise or practice is too difficult or destabilizing. *Please take responsibility for your own emotional safety and don't push yourself to do something if it doesn't feel right in the moment.*

This book is designed to help you unlock the potential of self-compassion in both its fierce and tender forms. The two are often unbalanced, and it's important to learn how to integrate them. Self-compassion will allow you to access your inner power so you can thrive and be happy. It will help you to be more authentic and internally fulfilled, so you can be an effective agent of progress in society. The world is transforming rapidly, and women are being called to take the lead in making sure things change for the better. With caring force, anything is possible.

CHAPTER 1

THE FUNDAMENTALS OF SELF-COMPASSION

We need women who are so strong they can be
gentle . . . so fierce they can be compassionate.

—*Kavita Ramdas, former head of the Global Fund for Women*

Self-compassion isn't rocket science. It's not some rarefied state of
mind that takes years of meditation practice to achieve. At the most
basic level, self-compassion simply requires being a good friend to ourselves. This is heartening news, because most of us already know how
to be a good friend, at least to others. When someone close to us is
feeling inadequate or is facing a difficult life challenge, we've learned
over the years what to say: "I'm so sorry. What do you need right now?
Is there anything I can do to help? Remember I'm here for you." We
understand how to soften our voice, use a warm tone, and relax our
bodies. We can skillfully use touch to convey the fact that we care, perhaps giving the person a hug or holding their hand. We're also familiar
with taking fierce action for our loved ones when needed. We've felt
that Momma Bear energy arise within us when someone we care about
is threatened and needs protection, or when they need a little kick in
the butt to tackle a challenge. We've earned the wisdom needed to
understand what steps are called for in the moment.

But, sadly, we don't treat ourselves with nearly the same degree of compassion when we struggle. Rather than pausing to ask what we need in the moment so we can comfort or support ourselves, we're more likely to pass judgment, get absorbed in problem-solving, or simply freak out. Let's say you get in a car accident on the way to work because you spilled coffee and were distracted. A typical inner conversation might be: "You're such a stupid idiot. Now look what you've done. You better call the insurance company right away and tell the boss you'll miss the meeting. I bet you'll get fired." Would you ever talk this way to someone you cared about? Probably not. But we often treat ourselves this way and think it's a good thing. We can be downright mean to ourselves, even harsher than we are to those we dislike. The golden rule says: *Do unto others as you would have others do unto you.* An addendum should be: *Do NOT do unto others as you do unto yourself, or you'll have no friends.*

An important first step in becoming more self-compassionate is to examine how we treat ourselves when we struggle compared to how we treat those we care about. The best context for examining this is a close friendship—because let's face it, sometimes we're not as compassionate as we might like to be with our children or partners or family members: they're too close. We tend to have more space in our reactions with our friends, and we take them less for granted since these relationships are voluntary. This means we're often our best selves with our close friends.

HOW DO I TREAT MY FRIENDS AND MYSELF IN DIFFICULT TIMES?

It can be really eye-opening to consider the degree to which you display compassion with your friends compared to yourself. We begin the MSC program with this examination to set the stage for learning self-compassion. This is a written exercise, so please take out a pen and paper.

Instructions

Think of various times when you had a close friend who was suffering in some way. Consider different types of situations: perhaps she was feeling bad about herself for a mistake she made, or was being bullied at work, or was exhausted by caring for her kids, or was afraid of a challenging task. Now write down your answers to the following questions:

- How do you typically respond to your friends in these types of situations? What do you *say*? What *tone* do you use? How is your *posture*? What *nonverbal* gestures do you use?

- How do you typically respond to yourself in similar situations? What do you *say*? What *tone* do you use? How is your *posture*? What *nonverbal* gestures do you use?

- Do you notice any patterns of *difference* in how you respond to your friends versus yourself? (For instance, maybe you catastrophize with yourself but have more perspective with friends.)

- What do you think it would be like if you started to treat yourself more like you treat your friends? What impact could it have on your life?

When doing this exercise, many people are shocked at the difference between how they treat themselves versus their friends. It can be a bit disconcerting to realize the degree to which we sell ourselves short. Luckily, we can use our vast experience of compassion for others to inform how we relate to ourselves. It's a template to build upon, though at first it can feel a bit odd to treat ourselves the way we'd treat a friend. That's just because we're in the habit of treating ourselves like an enemy. Over time it becomes more natural. We mainly need to give ourselves permission to turn these well-honed skills of compassion inward.

Of course, there are stumbling blocks that get in the way; habits of self-criticism and feelings of unworthiness and shame can be hard to shake. There are also fears that maybe self-compassion isn't so good for us, that it will turn us into lazy, selfish, self-indulgent losers. I'll try to address these blocks in the chapters that follow, although some may want to read *Self-Compassion* or *The Mindful Self-Compassion Workbook* in order to go deeper into how to overcome barriers.

Still, practice makes perfect, or as we like to say in the self-compassion world, practice makes imperfect. We can become more skilled at accepting our human limitations, and at the same time we can learn how to take action to change things for the better. As Jack Kornfield says, "The point of spiritual practice isn't to perfect yourself, but to perfect your love." Love is the driving force of both fierce and tender self-compassion.

THE THREE ELEMENTS OF SELF-COMPASSION

Although self-compassion involves treating ourselves with the same kindness we'd naturally show to a good friend, it takes more than kindness alone. If it were just about being kind to ourselves, we could easily become self-absorbed or narcissistic. Kindness is not enough. We also need to be able to see our flaws, admit our failures, and put our own experiences into perspective. We need to connect our own struggles to those of others, moving beyond our small selves to realize our place in the larger scheme of things.

According to my model, self-compassion is comprised of three main elements: mindfulness, common humanity, and kindness. These elements are distinct but interact as a system, and all three must be present in a self-compassionate mindset to make it healthy and stable.

Mindfulness. The foundation of self-compassion is the ability to turn mindfully toward our discomfort and acknowledge it. We don't suppress our pain and pretend it's not there, but we don't run away with a dramatic story line about it either. Mindfulness allows us to see clearly when we've made a mistake or failed. We turn toward rather than run away from the difficult emotions that accompany our troubles: grief, fear, sadness, anger, uncertainty, regret. We pay attention to our present moment experience, aware of our ever-changing thoughts, emotions, and sensations as they unfold. Mindfulness is essential to self-compassion so we can know when we're suffering and respond with kindness. If we ignore our pain or are completely lost in it, we can't step outside ourselves to say, "Wow, this stressful, I need a little support."

While mindfulness is simple, it can be challenging because it goes against other natural tendencies. Neuroscientists have identified a set of interconnected brain regions called the default mode network, which is located down the midline of the brain, from front to back. It's called our default mode because it's the normal state of brain activation whenever we aren't actively focused and engaged in a task. The default mode performs three basic functions: (1) it creates a sense of self, (2) it projects that self into the past or the future, and (3) it scans for problems. And so, instead of being present with what is, we get lost in worry and regret. This is beneficial from an evolutionary point of view so that we can learn from our past difficulties, and anticipate future threats to our survival and imagine how we might do things differently. However, when we're suffering in real time, this means we often don't have the presence of mind to *know* we're struggling. Instead, we get lost in stories of the past or future as we try to solve our problems. The intentional focus of mindfulness deactivates the default mode, meaning that we can be present with our own pain as we're feeling it.

Like a clear, still pool without ripples, mindfulness mirrors what's occurring without distortion so that we can gain perspective on ourselves and our lives. We can then wisely determine the best course of action to help ourselves. It takes courage to turn toward our pain and acknowledge it, but this act of courage is essential if our hearts are to open in response to suffering. We can't heal what we can't feel. For this reason, mindfulness is the pillar on which self-compassion rests.

Common humanity. Also central to self-compassion is recognition of our own humanity. In fact, this is what differentiates self-compassion from self-pity. The word *compassion* in Latin means "to suffer" (*passion*) "with" (*com*). Connectedness is inherent to compassion. When compassion is turned inward, it means we acknowledge that all humans are imperfect and lead an imperfect life. While this may sound obvious, we often fall into the trap of believing that things should go well and that something has gone wrong when they don't. We irrationally feel like everyone else is just fine and it's only me who slipped and broke the glass, cutting a nerve in her thumb and having to wear something resembling a giant pink wedge of cheese on her upright hand for three months while it healed (true). This adds insult to injury, because not only are we in pain, but we also feel alone and isolated. This sense of disconnection is terrifying because, as they like to say in evolutionary biology, a lone monkey is a dead monkey.

When we remember that pain is part of the shared human experience, we escape from the rabbit hole of self-pity. Instead of crying "woe is me," we honor the shared nature of suffering. The circumstances and degree of suffering is different, of course. People who are oppressed by systemic injustice or entrenched poverty suffer more than those with privilege. But there's also no human being who completely escapes physical, mental, or emotional hardship.

Compassion is predicated on the idea that all conscious beings are intrinsically worthy of humane treatment. When we deny compassion to ourselves but extend it to others, or when we value the needs of one group over those of another, we're undermining the basic truth that we're all part of a larger interdependent whole. Your actions impact mine just as mine impact yours. The idiom "don't sh*t where you eat" may be vulgar, but it conveys this idea well. How I treat myself affects my interactions with everyone else I come in contact with, and how I treat others similarly affects all my interactions. The consequences of not understanding interdependence can be seen everywhere: racial, religious, and political tensions that breed violence; immigrants fleeing to the United States from countries where American policies helped to sow economic despair; and a planet that is warming so quickly that it will soon be uninhabitable. The wisdom of recognizing our common humanity allows us to see the larger picture and realize that we're all in this together.

Kindness. The motivational core of self-compassion is kindness—the desire to alleviate suffering. This caring urge is experienced as the felt impulse to help. It's a warm, friendly, and supportive attitude toward ourselves as we wade through the mud of life. Too often when we struggle, we're more likely to beat ourselves up than put a supportive arm around our own shoulder. Even people who are unfailingly kind to others often treat themselves like crap. Self-kindness reverses this tendency so that we are genuinely good to ourselves.

When we recognize we've made a mistake, self-kindness means that we're understanding and accepting, encouraging ourselves to do better next time. When we get bad news or smash head-on into life's problems, we actively open our hearts and allow ourselves to be emotionally moved by our own pain. We stop to say, "This is really difficult. How can I care for myself in this moment?"

We can't be perfect. Our lives will inevitably involve struggle. But when we respond with benevolence and goodwill to our pain, we generate feelings of love and care that make a positive difference. Self-kindness provides the resources to cope with hardship and makes it more bearable. It's a rewarding and fulfilling emotion, the sweetness that counters the bitterness of life.

THE BENEFITS OF SELF-COMPASSION

Thousands of studies have examined the association between self-compassion and well-being. Research on self-compassion is typically conducted in one of three ways. The most common method uses the Self-Compassion Scale (SCS) to determine if higher scores correlate with higher levels of positive outcomes like happiness and lower levels of negative outcomes like depression. A second way to study self-compassion is to induce a self-compassionate frame of mind experimentally, often by having people write to themselves about a life difficulty while invoking mindfulness, common humanity, and kindness.

Participants are randomly assigned either to this self-compassion condition or to a control condition, where participants will write about something neutral instead, perhaps a particular hobby they enjoy. Then the groups are compared in terms of behaviors like motivation to study for an exam. A third and increasingly common method is to train people in self-compassion through programs such as MSC, to see if their well-being changes after training. All three methods of research tend to produce the same findings.

The research literature on the benefits of self-compassion will be discussed throughout this book, but I'll briefly sum it up here. People who are more self-compassionate tend to be happier, more hopeful, and optimistic. They're more satisfied with their lives and grateful for what they have. They're less anxious, depressed, stressed, and fearful. They're less likely to contemplate suicide or abuse drugs and alcohol. They're wiser and more emotionally intelligent, and can regulate their negative emotions more effectively. They have a more positive body image and are less likely to develop eating disorders. They're more likely to engage in helpful behaviors like exercise, eating right, and seeing the doctor regularly. They're physically healthier—they sleep better, get fewer colds, and have stronger immune systems. They're more motivated, conscientious, and take more responsibility for themselves. They're more resilient when faced with life challenges and have more grit and determination to reach their goals. They have closer and more functional relationships with friends, family, and romantic partners and report more sexual satisfaction. They're more forgiving, empathetic, and able to take others' perspectives. They're more compassionate to others but are also able to caretake without burning out. Not a bad set of perks for something as simple as treating yourself as you would a good friend.

Self-compassionate people also have higher levels of self-esteem, but don't fall into the traps laid by the quest for high self-regard. Self-compassion is not linked to narcissism the way high self-esteem is. It doesn't lead to constant social comparison or ego-defensiveness. The sense of self-worth that comes from self-compassion doesn't depend on looking a certain way, or being successful, or having others approve of you. It's unconditional. This means that the sense of worthiness that comes from self-compassion is more stable over time.

The tremendous benefits of self-compassion, combined with the fact that it's a skill that can be learned, help explain why so many researchers have begun to study this mindset. My good friend and fellow researcher Shauna Shapiro, who wrote a great book on mindfulness and self-compassion called *Good Morning, I Love You*, likes to say that self-compassion is the secret sauce of life. It makes everything better.

THE PHYSIOLOGY OF SELF-COMPASSION

As I said earlier, most people aren't nearly as compassionate to themselves as they are to others, especially when they fail or feel inadequate. Part of the reason for this has to do with the automatic reactions of our nervous system. When we make a mistake or encounter hardships in life, we instinctively feel threatened. All is not well. So, we react to our perceived peril with the "threat-defense response" (sometimes known as our reptilian brain), the quickest and most easily triggered reflexive reaction to danger. When our brain registers a threat, the sympathetic nervous system is activated. Our amygdala springs into action, we release cortisol and adrenaline, and get ready to fight, flee, or freeze. The system works well for protecting against threats to our physical bodies such as a falling tree or a snarling dog, but can be problematic when the threat stems from thoughts such as "I'm such a loser" or "Do I look fat in this dress?"

When our self-concept is threatened, the danger is an inward one. We are both the attacker and the attacked. So, we fight ourselves with criticism, hoping it will get rid of the weakness by forcing us to change. We psychologically flee from others by shrinking in shame, withdrawing into the oblivion of worthlessness. Sometimes we freeze and get stuck in rumination, repeating our negative thoughts as if somehow thinking it through for the thirty-ninth time will make the problem go away. This constant state of reactivity is why being hard on ourselves is so bad for our health, leading to stress, anxiety, and depression. It's important that we don't judge ourselves for these reactions, as they stem from the innocent desire to be safe.

But we can learn to feel safe another way—by tapping into the mammalian care system. The evolutionary advantage of mammals over reptiles is that mammalian young are born very immature and have a longer developmental period to adapt to their environment. Compared to all other mammals, human beings take the longest to mature: it takes twenty-five to thirty years for the prefrontal cortex to develop due to our remarkable neuronal plasticity. To keep vulnerable youngsters safe during this long developmental period, the "tend-and-befriend" response evolved, which prompts parents and offspring to stay close and find safety through social bonding. When the care system is activated, oxytocin (the love hormone) and endorphins (natural, feel-good opiates) are released, which increases feelings of security.

Although the tend-and-befriend response is instinctually activated when caring for others, we can also learn to turn it inward. We can tend to and befriend *ourselves* to provide a sense of safety, security, and well-being. When we do this, the parasympathetic nervous system comes online, increasing heart rate variability (so that we're more open and relaxed) and reducing sympathetic activity (so that we're less tense). In fact, the three components of self-compassion—kindness, common humanity, and mindfulness—directly counter the self-judgment, isolation, and rumination that occur as part of the threat-defense reaction. In effect, we're changing the balance between these two highly evolved, instinctive behaviors, both designed to ensure our safety, increasing one and decreasing the other simultaneously.

Because self-compassion happens physiologically, physical touch is a highly effective way to demonstrate care for ourselves. Our bodies respond to physical touch almost immediately, quickly helping us to feel supported. Touch taps into the parasympathetic nervous system, which calms and centers us. The human body is exquisitely designed to interpret touch as a signal of care. Just as during the first two years of life, parents convey a sense of safety and love to their infants through touch, we can do the same for ourselves.

SOOTHING AND SUPPORTIVE TOUCH

We teach soothing and supportive touch as a foundational self-compassion practice in the MSC program. When we are upset, sometimes we are too overwhelmed to remember to speak to ourselves kindly. The act of dropping out of our heads and into our bodies by moving our attention away from our thoughts to focus on a physical sensation such as touch can be incredibly helpful in difficult moments.

Instructions

Try out some different types of touch to see how they make you feel. Linger for about fifteen seconds with each type of touch and let yourself really sink into the experience. Check in to see the effect on your body. It's good to find one touch that can help you feel soothed and comforted and another that helps you feel strong, empowered, and supported. People are different, so experiment until you find what works best for you.

Some tender soothing options include:

- One or two hands over your heart

- Cradling your face in your hands

- Gently stroking your arms

- Crossing your arms and giving a gentle squeeze

- Hugging yourself and rocking softly back and forth

Some strong supportive options include:

- A fist on your heart with the other hand over it

- One or two hands on your solar plexus, your energetic center (which is located right below your ribcage and about three inches above your belly button)

- One hand on your heart and one on your solar plexus

- Squeezing your own hand

- Two arms planted firmly on your hips

The idea is to find a "go-to" touch that you can use automatically in stressful or difficult situations. Choose a couple for now and try using them whenever you are feeling emotional or physical discomfort. Sometimes our minds are too overwhelmed to think straight, but you can use touch to communicate compassion to your body. It's an easy and surprisingly effective way to care for and support yourself.

DIFFICULTIES WITH SELF-COMPASSION

Some people are naturally more self-compassionate than others, in part due to the way we're raised. If our parents consistently nurtured and were kind to us as children, so that our mammalian care system became fully responsive and well-functioning, we'll be more likely to internalize this supportive attitude as an adult. If they harshly criticized us, or were neglectful or abusive, it can be more challenging to be self-compassionate.

The level of security that we felt with our parents is called our attachment style. People with secure attachment—meaning those whose parents were consistently warm and caring, and who met their needs—tend to feel worthy of comfort and support, and are consequently kinder to themselves as adults. Those whose parents were inconsistent—sometimes emotionally available and sometimes not—or who were neglectful are more likely to feel they are unworthy and unlovable. This makes it more difficult to have self-compassion. And for those whose parents were emotionally, physically, or sexually abusive, fear can become intermingled with signals of care. In this case, it can actually be scary to give yourself compassion.

My colleague Chris Germer, a clinical psychologist and author of the insightful book *The Mindful Path to Self-Compassion*, frequently observed this pattern in his patients. The label he came up with for it is "backdraft," a firefighting term. When a fire has been raging in a closed or poorly ventilated room, firefighters are careful about opening doors to combat the blaze within. If the oxygen inside has been used up by the fire and doors are suddenly opened, fresh oxygen rushes in, igniting the fire even further. It can be dangerous and explosive. The same thing can sometimes happen with self-compassion. If we had to tightly shut the doors of our hearts to deal with early childhood pain, when we start to open our hearts the "fresh air" of love comes in, bringing awareness to the suffering trapped inside. This can sometimes burst out in disturbing ways and become overwhelming. It's not just people with trauma histories who experience backdraft, either. Anyone who's used shutting down and closing themselves off as a way to manage difficult emotions can experience backdraft when first starting to practice self-compassion. This is actually a good sign because it means the healing process has begun.

Another slightly less scary metaphor is when our hands freeze and go numb while shoveling snow, then hurt like hell when we go inside and warm up. Just like our hands, we want our frozen hearts to thaw—it's a good thing, even though it hurts. But we don't want to move too quickly. One of the reasons firefighters carry those picks is so that they can poke holes in the perimeter of a burning building, allowing the air to come in more slowly. Sometimes we need to do this with ourselves: bring the compassion in slowly so it's not so intense. In other words, we need to practice self-compassion in a way that is self-compassionate.

When we ask ourselves what we need, sometimes the answer is to focus on something else for a while. We can find another, more indirect way to care for ourselves, like taking a bath, going for a walk, petting the dog, drinking a cup of tea. Doing so is actually an act of kindness. It's a way of caring for ourselves and meeting our needs, and therefore helps build the habit of compassion. Once we feel more stabilized, we can come back to the practice of opening our hearts more explicitly.

Mindfulness is very effective when working with backdraft. Anytime we focus our mind on a single object, it has the effect of settling us down. This is one reason why taking a conscious breath is calming, because we're focusing on something other than our thoughts. Another effective practice is to simply feel the soles of our feet on the floor, helping to stabilize our awareness and ground ourselves to the earth.

SOLES OF THE FEET

Research finds that this practice helps people self-regulate and center themselves when they are emotionally distraught. It's the central practice we teach in MSC to work with backdraft. While it's typically done standing, it can be modified for a sitting position.

Instructions

- Stand up, and begin by noticing the sensations—the sense of touch—in the soles of your feet on the floor.

- To better feel sensation in the soles of your feet, try gently rocking forward and backward on your feet, and side to side. Then try making little circles with your knees, feeling the changing sensations in the soles of your feet.

- Feel how the floor supports your whole body.

- If your mind starts wandering, just return to feeling the soles of your feet.

- Now begin to walk, slowly, noticing the changing sensations in the soles of your feet. Notice the sensation of lifting a foot, stepping forward, and then placing the foot on the floor. Now do the same with the other foot. And then one foot after another.

- As you walk, appreciate how small the surface area of each foot is, and how your feet anchor your entire body. If you like, take a moment of gratitude for the hard work that your feet do for you, which we usually take for granted.

- You can imagine that the ground is rising up to support you with each step.

- Continue to walk, slowly, feeling the soles of your feet.

- Now return to standing again, and expand your awareness to your entire body—letting yourself feel whatever you're feeling, and letting yourself be just as you are.

SELF-COMPASSION AIN'T FOR SISSIES

Culture tends to provide a false narrative about self-compassion. It tells us that self-compassion is an indulgence that will take away our drive and make us soft. I remember when the first big *New York Times* article came out about my work, I was really surprised that many of the reader comments were negative. One in particular really stands out: "Great, just what we need, a nation of sissies." I began to see that most people don't understand the powerful nature of self-compassion. They assume that it's weak or passive because it's associated with care and tenderness. But compassion can also be forceful and dynamic. For example, first responders may endanger their lives while rescuing people from the path of a hurricane, parents may juggle multiple jobs to put food on the table for their children, or underpaid teachers may keep toiling in inner city placements to help students break out of the cycle of poverty. These are tremendous acts of compassion.

In Buddhist teachings, this powerful action-oriented aspect of compassion is called "fierce compassion." It's the force that stands up to harm or injustice. Sharon Salzberg talks about it as a type of tough love that brings together kindness, clarity, strength, balance, and action. The Buddhist scholar Bob Thurman describes it as "a strong, powerful energy of heat force [that] can be used to . . . develop inner strength and determination." In order to alleviate our own suffering, in order to give ourselves what we truly need in the moment, we want to call on the full range of responses available to us—fierce or tender. A helpful metaphor we can draw upon to understand these two sides of self-compassion is yin and yang.

THE YIN AND YANG OF SELF-COMPASSION

The concept of yin and yang comes from ancient Chinese philosophy. It posits that there are two aspects of a universal energetic principle that are in constant dialectic. Yin represents stillness and yang represents movement. Yin is a soft, yielding, receptive, nurturing energy while yang is a firm, forceful, commanding, goal-oriented energy. Yin has historically been associated with the feminine and yang with the masculine, but both are considered essential aspects of being human, regardless of gender. Because yin and yang are complementary expressions of qi, or vital life force energy, each plays a crucial role in health and well-being. In fact, from this perspective, sickness stems from the imbalance of these two energies. As seen in the familiar symbol of yin and yang, the dark represents yin and the light yang, negative and positive polarities, although each has an element of the other, representing a fundamental nondualism. This metaphor of yin and yang closely reflects the core distinction between fierce and tender self-compassion. Though self-compassion isn't typically discussed from this perspective and I'm certainly not an expert in Chinese philosophy, it's a helpful framework that I draw upon with respect and humility.

The yin quality of tender self-compassion involves "being with" ourselves in an accepting way. It entails comforting ourselves, reassuring ourselves that we aren't alone, and being present with our pain. This is the healing power of self-compassion. A good example of tender self-compassion is a mother cradling and rocking her crying child. When we feel hurt or inadequate, we're there to soothe ourselves, validating our pain and embracing ourselves as we are. We tap into the caring energy that flows easily to those we cherish and turn it inward. One way to describe what it feels like when we embody tender self-compassion is *loving, connected presence*, corresponding to kindness, common humanity, and mindfulness. When we embrace our pain with kindness, we feel loving. When we remember our common humanity, we feel connected. When we're mindful of our pain, we're present. With loving, connected presence, our pain becomes bearable and begins to transform.

The yang quality of fierce self-compassion is associated with "acting in the world" to alleviate suffering. It looks different depending on the action required, but tends to involve protecting, providing for, or motivating ourselves. The dynamic energy of compassion is metaphorically like a Momma Bear who ferociously protects her cubs when threatened, or catches fish to feed them, or leaves a territory where the resources have been depleted to find a new home with more to offer. Just as tenderness can be turned inward, the fierce energy of Momma Bear can also be turned inward. We can stand up for and protect ourselves, we can nourish and provide for ourselves, and we can motivate the changes necessary to thrive.

The quintessential question of self-compassion is "What do I need right now?" and more specifically "What do I need to help alleviate my suffering?" The answer to this question changes depending on the circumstances. Sometimes what we need is to accept ourselves in all our human imperfection; in this case tender self-compassion is called for.

However, when we need to protect ourselves from potential harm, the elements of compassion have a different expression. Self-kindness in this case is *brave*. We find the courage needed to draw boundaries, say no, be as strong as steel. Common humanity helps us recognize that we aren't alone in our fight, that all people deserve just treatment. We are *empowered* by joining with others and standing up for what's right. Mindfulness enables us to act with *clarity* and decisiveness—seeing and speaking the truth. When self-compassion is aimed at protecting ourselves from harm, we embody *brave, empowered clarity*.

When our goal is to provide for ourselves, to give ourselves what we need to be happy, the form shifts yet again. In this case, self-kindness means we *fulfill* ourselves emotionally, physically, and spiritually. We take action to meet our own needs, knowing that they matter. Common humanity allows us to satisfy ourselves and others in a *balanced* and equitable fashion. We aren't selfish, but we don't subordinate our needs either. We respect everyone's desires—including our own. Mindfulness facilitates our ability to be *authentic*, to actually know what we need, deep down, so that we can give it to ourselves and stay true to our values. When self-compassion is aimed at providing for ourselves, we embody *fulfilling, balanced authenticity*.

Finally, when our aim is to motivate ourselves to reach a goal or make a change, yet another form of self-compassion is required. Self-kindness demands that we *encourage* and support ourselves to do something different—the way good coaches motivate their athletes or parents motivate their children. Constructive criticism and feedback are used to help ourselves do our best. Recognition of common humanity enables us to learn from our failures. We employ *wisdom* to determine how to take corrective action, understanding that we'll naturally make mistakes and hopefully grow from them. And mindfulness provides the *vision* to realize what needs to be done, to acknowledge what isn't serving us and to pursue actions that would serve us better. We see our next steps clearly and stay focused on our goals. When self-compassion is aimed at motivating ourselves, we embody *encouraging, wise vision*.

EXPRESSIONS OF SELF-COMPASSION			
Purpose	Self-Kindness	Common Humanity	Mindfulness
Tender (Be With)	Love	Connection	Presence
Fierce (Protect)	Bravery	Empowerment	Clarity
Fierce (Provide)	Fulfillment	Balance	Authenticity
Fierce (Motivate)	Encouragement	Wisdom	Vision

The Buddhist goddess of compassion, Avalokiteshvara (which means "the one hears the cries of the world"), has many arms, each holding a different instrument to alleviate suffering. The table above displays some of the different forms of self-compassion that we can draw upon. Each of these ways of caring for ourselves will be explored in detail in the following chapters, so don't worry if it's too much to take in right now.

Some people wonder why there are three forms of fierce self-compassion and only one form of tender self-compassion. That's because "being with" our pain implies stillness. It requires accepting things as they are with an open heart, and therefore has one main form. Although we may express this open heart in slightly different ways (physically soothing, saying kind words, etc.), it all falls under the umbrella of compassionate presence. Taking action to alleviate our suffering has more varied forms. In fact, there are likely many more than three, and the manifestation of self-compassion in action is as varied as our human needs. However, the three main forms of protecting, providing, and motivating capture some of the most essential ways we can use self-compassionate action to alleviate our suffering.

GESTURES OF SELF-COMPASSION

The three elements of self-compassion feel different when used to meet different needs, and we can actually experience their energies in our body. We teach this practice in the MSC program to help participants get a felt sense of fierce and tender self-compassion. This exercise is best done standing up but can also be done sitting down.

Instructions

You are going to be making a series of gestures that will help you feel the various expressions of self-compassion in your body. To start, it's important to explore what the lack of self-compassion feels like:

- Clench your fists and squeeze them close to your body. See what *emotions* arise when your fists are clenched. You might notice that you feel tense, or tight, or stressed, or constricted. This is a metaphor for *self-judgment and resistance*—what it feels like when we fight ourselves or resist our pain or ignore our needs, and we do that unconsciously much of the time.

Now you can explore what tender self-compassion feels like:

- Open your palms, turned upward. How does this make you feel, especially in contrast to having your fists clenched? Many people notice that they feel more relaxed, peaceful, calm, accepting. This is a metaphor for *mindfulness* in tender self-compassion—what it feels like when we accept what's happening with open, spacious awareness. It allows us to be with and validate our pain.

- Now extend your arms outward, symbolically reaching out to others. You might imagine giving a hug to a friend or loved one. How does this make you feel? You might feel a sense of connectedness, togetherness, or expansion. This is a metaphor for *common humanity* in tender self-compassion—when we go beyond our separate selves and include others. It's what it feels like when we reassure ourselves that we aren't alone.

- Now place one hand over the other, and slowly bring them both to the center of your chest. Feel the warmth and gentle pressure of your hands on your heart. Breathe gently. How does this make you feel? Often people say when they make this gesture it feels safe, soothing, warm, relaxing. This is a metaphor for *self-kindness* in tender self-compassion—how it feels when we give ourselves love. It can feel really good (unless you're experiencing some backdraft, and that's okay too).

- Then all together as a single movement, hold your palms up, reach out, and then bring your hands to your heart. This is what tender self-compassion feels like as a whole—*loving, connected presence*.

Fierce self-compassion manifests differently, and how it shows up depends on its purpose.

- Stand up if you can and adopt what's called a "horse stance" in martial arts. Put your feet hip-width apart, bend your knees slightly, and tilt your pelvis forward. (You can also just sit up straight.) A horse stance is a balanced, stable posture with a low center of gravity. From this position we can take whatever action is needed in the moment.

Sometimes we need to protect ourselves:

- Stretch one arm out firmly in front of you with palm raised, and clearly and loudly say, "No!" Do this three times.

- See if you can sense the energy of this movement moving up and down your spine. How does it feel? People often say strong, powerful, courageous. With this form of fierce self-compassion, we embody *brave, empowered clarity*.

Sometimes we also need to provide for ourselves, to give ourselves what makes us happy:

- Stretch your arms out and pretend to gather up whatever you metaphorically need, bringing your hands in to rest on your solar plexus, your energetic center. As you bring your hands inward, say, "Yes!" Do this three times.

- See if you can sense how this affirmation energizes your body. How does it feel to stake your claim in this way? It might feel silly, but perhaps also satisfying. With this form of fierce self-compassion, we manifest *fulfilling, balanced authenticity*.

Sometimes we need to motivate ourselves to do difficult things, to support and uplift ourselves so we can make a change:

- Make a back-and-forth fist pump while saying enthusiastically, "You can do it!" three times.

- See if you can sense the forward movement of this supportive energy. How does it make you feel? Positive, hopeful, inspired? With this form of fierce self-compassion, we express *encouraging, wise vision*.

These gestures aren't designed to be done repeatedly in everyday life; they're more of a demonstration to help you understand and experience the various forms of self-compassion. But if you found any of the gestures particularly helpful, you can always use them as a way to call forth the type of self-compassion you need in the moment.

BALANCING YIN AND YANG

In order to harness the full power of self-compassion, yin needs to accompany yang (and vice versa) so they're always in balance. If not, self-compassion is in danger of slipping into an unhealthy way of being. "Near enemy" is a useful Buddhist concept referring to a state of mind that appears similar to the desired state—hence it is "near"—but actually undermines it, which is why it's an enemy. Each of the forms of self-compassion can morph into a near enemy when yin and yang aren't in balance. For instance, when yin acceptance occurs without yang willingness to take action, it can turn into passivity and complacence. The Tibetan teacher Chögyam Trungpa termed this "idiot compassion." Although it's important to love and accept ourselves as we are in the moment, that doesn't mean we want to *stay* as we are in the moment. If a herd of cattle is stampeding toward you, it's not the time to just accept the situation. When we engage in harmful behaviors such as smoking or are in a bad situation like an emotionally abusive relationship, we don't want to only accept our pain, we also want to do something about it.

At the same time, when the force of protection arises without access to feelings of loving, connected presence, it can turn into hostility and aggression toward others. We may start to see a situation as us versus them, I'm right and you're wrong. Compassion must always be caring. Compassion can be fierce and brave, but it's not aggressive. It can be empowered, but it's not overpowering. It's clear when it comes to speaking the truth but isn't blindly self-righteous. Similarly, trying to meet our needs without sufficient yin energy can morph into self-ishness, or the motivation to improve can slide into perfectionism.

We'll be exploring these issues in greater detail later, but suffice it to say that when yin and yang are balanced and integrated, it's more constructive. We let go of patterns of behavior that aren't serving us and take action to make things better—not because we're unacceptable as we are, but because we care about ourselves and don't want to suffer. The more secure we feel in this unconditional self-acceptance, the more energy we'll have to protect ourselves, fulfill our needs, and achieve our goals.

A good friend who's been practicing fierce and tender self-compassion with me for about a year says she's a different person because of it. I met Jess shortly after I moved to Texas. Jess is about my age, practices meditation, and has a son named Billy with severe ADHD, so we have a lot in common. Tender self-compassion helped her cope with her son's neurological condition by giving herself the kindness and support she needed when Billy acted out. She could also accept her parenting mistakes more easily, reassuring herself that she was only human and doing her best. However, this wasn't enough to help her cope with someone whose behavior was even more challenging: her mother, Samantha.

Don't get me wrong, Jess loves her mother deeply, but she drives Jess absolutely batty. Samantha feels it's her right as the elder in the family to tell her (middle-aged) daughter when she's doing something wrong and how to fix it. She doesn't just overstep boundaries; she won't even acknowledge they exist. Although Jess knows her mother genuinely cares, she constantly feels violated by her unwanted advice. "Why can't she just let me make my own mistakes rather than always butting in?" she'd fume.

Jess's typical pattern with her mother would be to keep the peace for long periods, explaining that she heard her and appreciated her care, but that she would make her own decisions, thank you very much. Her years of meditation training usually paid off. Usually. The problem was that her resentment kept simmering, and at some point she would eventually blow up, often over something minor. For instance, once at Thanksgiving dinner, when Samantha subtly suggested that she not have that second helping of stuffing, Jess blurted out "F*** you!" and stormed away from the table. She felt horrible afterward and ashamed that she got so angry—on a day that's supposed to be about gratitude for family! She started to feel hopeless, that even after all her years of meditation, she still lost it over a side dish.

When we started talking about fierce self-compassion, I asked her what it would feel like if her anger wasn't something to manage, but to celebrate? What if she actually appreciated her inner Momma Bear rising up to protect her whenever her boundaries were being violated? "Sounds kind of scary," she said. "I might *really* lose it and say something that can't be taken back. I love my mother, and I know she's actually trying to help."

"I'm wondering if the reason you get reactive is that you are judging and devaluing this really important part of you," I said. "What would happen if you welcomed your inner warrior when it arose, while also remaining in touch with the part of you that is kind and loving?" Jess decided to give it a try.

At first things were pretty bumpy. When Samantha tried to tell her what to do at their weekly lunch, Jess would attempt to use caring force to draw a line in the sand, but she still got triggered and sometimes blasted her. After a while, it began to get easier to hold these two energies together. At one point she called me to say how proud she was of herself for handling another one of Samantha's boundary violations. "I was telling her how I dealt with an incident at school when Billy got in trouble, and she said I should have handled it differently. Out from this deep place within came a forceful 'NO! It's not okay for you to tell me how to discipline my son!' We were both surprised by the power of that no, but it was cleanly done and there was nothing more to talk about." About an hour after the lunch ended, Samantha called Jess to apologize. "You're right," she said. "It's not my place. You've done a great job with Billy. I'm sorry." Jess was glowing from being able to stand up to her mother with such strength without being mean in the process.

I believe that exercising both fierce and tender self-compassion is a life-changing way to approach the imbalances that underlie much of our suffering. Fortunately, self-compassion isn't just an idea, it's a practice. As we claim our power as women, we can learn to develop and integrate these two sides of self-compassion to tackle the challenges we face in the world today. Women are socialized to avoid upsetting people rather than getting angry or fierce. But we can no longer be passive in order to avoid rocking the boat. The boat needs to be rocked! Self-compassion is a superpower we can access at any time—hidden in our back pockets. We simply need to remember that we have this superpower, and then give ourselves permission to use it.

CHAPTER 2

WHAT'S GENDER GOT TO DO WITH IT?

Why do people say "grow some balls"? Balls are weak and sensitive. If you want to be tough, grow a vagina. Those things can take a pounding.

—*Betty White, actor and comedian*

One of the reasons it's essential for women to develop fierce self-compassion is because expressing power in a meaningful way is limited by gender-role stereotypes, which represent society's conventional view of what men and women are like. In most cultures, females are considered "communal" and males "agentic." These stereotypes map closely to the qualities of yin tenderness and yang fierceness. Women are seen as sensitive, warm, cooperative, and concerned with the welfare of others, whereas men are seen as strong, aggressive, goal-oriented, and independent. In other words, tenderness is seen as a chick thing and fierceness is seen as a dude thing (you can substitute another word that starts with "d" and rhymes with chick if you like).

Gender stereotypes often clash with the reality of how individuals feel and behave. Some people are more communal than agentic (feminine), others are more agentic than communal (masculine), some are neither agentic nor communal (undifferentiated), and some are both (androgynous). All these traits are distinct from gender identity, which refers to whether individuals feel their gender matches their sexual anatomy (cisgender), the opposite gender (transgender), both (gender fluid), or neither (nonbinary). Individuals with a particular gender identity also differ in the extent to which they are agentic or communal. Human beings are incredibly complex and varied. The problems pop up when society tries to stuff us into a narrow box.

Culture encourages women to develop their tender qualities but not their fierce ones. Men are taught to suppress their tender side and be fierce instead. Yin and yang must be balanced and integrated in order for us to be whole, but gender-role socialization means that men and women are only allowed to be half human. The fact that gender roles curtail the development of yin and yang also means that their expression becomes extreme. Yin becomes sugar and spice and everything nice while yang becomes Rambo and G.I. Joe. We need to move beyond these confines so that yin and yang can flow and integrate in healthy and harmonious ways—regardless of gender.

Highly gendered behavioral expectations are problematic in both directions. Men are harmed by a culture of toxic masculinity that shames them for being soft, sensitive, or vulnerable. Psychologists have argued these norms hinder male emotional intelligence by emphasizing aggressiveness at the expense of interpersonal connection. In other words, men would be well-served by developing their tender yin qualities. But the corresponding need for women to develop fierce yang traits is even more critical. Circumscribed gender roles may harm both sexes psychologically, but they benefit men disproportionately since they're rewarded with leadership roles and access to resources. Female gender norms that prioritize tenderness at the expense of fierce action limit women's power and ability to combat unfair treatment.

Yin qualities of cooperation and caring for the needs of others, though beautiful and essential, serve to maintain social inequality if they're not balanced with yang qualities of self-assertion and agency.

When women are expected to "be nice" and give to others but not speak up or ask for too much, it maintains a pattern in which women are denied what they need and men get what they want. The ideal of female self-sacrifice perpetuates an expectation that heterosexual women will meet men's needs—for sex, childbearing, homemaking, and childcare—with little consideration of what's due to us, from our partners, society, or ourselves.

If women are ever going to obtain parity with men, our ability to stand up and demand what we want and need is essential. Women can't change society unilaterally: men also need to do their part. But breaking free of restrictive stereotypes is one important way we can enact social change. We don't want to gain equality by virtue of becoming aggressive and self-serving, or by adopting a ferocity that lacks tenderness. Instead, we want our force to be caring so that we can lead our world out of the hell of White supremacy, extreme health and wealth inequality, and global warming. Our ability to balance and integrate fierce and tender self-compassion is paramount to this task.

THREE LITTLE (SEXIST) PIGS

Although one might assume that gender inequality stems from the prejudiced views of men toward women, the reality is more complex. Research indicates that there are at least three forms of sexism, which often work to support each other. Hostile sexism promotes the belief that men are superior to women; it's closely associated with bias and discrimination. Men with this worldview actively dislike women who display nontraditional gender roles, such as feminists and female CEOs. Consider the words of televangelist Pat Robertson: "The feminist agenda is not about equal rights for women. It is about a socialist, anti-family political movement that encourages women to leave their husbands, kill their children, practice witchcraft, destroy capitalism, and become lesbians." These views have been part of American history since the 1600s, when women who didn't conform to societal norms were actually hanged as witches. They're still rampant in certain segments of society.

A prime example is the Make Women Great Again conference that was scheduled to be held in October 2020, before the pandemic hit. The conference never actually happened and may have just been a publicity stunt, but it's a poster child for hostile sexism. This three-day mansplaining conference, which was led by male presenters for an all-female audience, was described by the *New York Post* as a MAGA hat for the uterus. Its lineup of far-right speakers aimed to teach women how to be more feminine (i.e., submissive), to please their husbands, and have "unlimited babies." Attendees were promised "No longer will you have to give in to toxic bullying feminist dogma and go against your ancient, biological nature as a woman, the men have arrived to help." The organizers of the event were leaders in the "manosphere"—a collection of anti-feminist blogs, websites, and online forums that promote misogyny and sexual violence against women. While not always radical, hostile sexists are more likely to endorse the myths about rape that continue to justify sexual assault (i.e., she could have stopped it if she didn't want it).

In contrast, benevolent sexism is a "positive" form of prejudice that seeks to protect women. This ideology holds highly favorable views of women (at least those who conform to gender stereotypes), seeing them as naturally kinder, warmer, and more caring than men. It also considers men to be obligated to protect, cherish, and provide for women. Benevolent sexism firmly cements a separate-spheres ideology in which women are seen as best suited for private domestic roles and men for public leadership. The idea is that men and women are separate but equal (a legal status that was rejected by the Supreme Court in 1954—at least as it applied to race). From this perspective, a man should lead and a woman should follow. He should achieve and she should help. He should protect and she should nurture. A man who describes his wife as his "better half" may truly admire her communal traits, but he sees them as outside of himself. A woman may be proud of her kind and tender disposition but feel she must rely on her husband's agentic qualities to protect her, provide for her, and achieve success on her behalf. This worldview recognizes the importance and complementarity of both yin and yang, but instead of placing this duality within individuals, it locates it at the level of heterosexual couples. The gendered separation of yin and yang is the glue that holds patriarchy (and heterosexism) in place.

Although hostile sexist views are more strongly endorsed by men than women, many women support benevolent sexism. The most famous of these was Phyllis Schlafly, who successfully fought against the Equal Rights Amendment. She felt that feminism not only threatened the family structure but also the benefits of protection and financial support given to women in a traditional value system. Of course, asymmetrical dependency and full equality are incompatible, because the price of being taken care of is lack of power, authenticity, or choice. In order to have a man's protection a woman isn't allowed to actively challenge him. She must constantly prop up his identity as the one in charge in order to keep her place in the social order. In this case equal doesn't actually equal equal.

The third type, modern sexism, simply denies that sexism exists. This is the most insidious form because it doesn't argue that men and women should be treated differently, but rather claims men and women are *already* treated the same. Modern sexism acknowledges that inequality exists (it's hard to deny the facts) but argues that this isn't due to any form of systematic disadvantage for women. Success is seen to primarily depend on one's own abilities and motivation. Male agency leads men to work hard and achieve their success, while female communion leads women to focus on mothering and relationships, disrupting their careers.

Modern sexism views feminists who rally for equal treatment as complainers trying to work the system by seeking special advantages rather than playing by the rules. This justifies claims by men that *they* are the victims of reverse discrimination by policies intended to help women obtain gender parity. From this perspective, a woman with strong agentic qualities could theoretically achieve just as much success as a man, given that the playing field is level.

Gender inequality isn't seen as the result of discrimination, but the result of essential differences in male agency and female communion. A good example of this view comes from University of Toronto professor and right-wing hero Jordan Peterson, who believes that gender differences in achievement stem from the fact that "Women are likely to prioritize their children over their work" and that "people who hold that our culture is an oppressive patriarchy . . . don't want to admit that the current hierarchy might be predicated on competence."

What these three forms of sexism all have in common is the rigid belief that men are agentic and women are communal, justifying the status quo of inequality.

SEXISM AND BIOLOGY

Individuals holding sexist worldviews typically argue that gender distinctions in agency and communion are natural. There's some research suggesting there may be small biological sex differences in the tendency toward each. Sex-related variability in hormones such as oxytocin and testosterone, for instance, may play a role in female communal and male agentic behavior, respectively. Oxytocin is a hormone that enhances care, affiliation, and social bonding, while testosterone is implicated in agentic qualities of competitiveness, motivation, and aggression. There's also neurological evidence that suggests female brains are better at empathy and cooperation, which makes evolutionary sense given that a mother's ability to understand a baby's needs is crucial for the survival of the species.

However, biology and social forces always interact. For example, the experience of power increases testosterone in both women and men. In one study, participants in a mock workplace setting were directed by researchers to act out firing a subordinate, and subsequent testing showed that testosterone significantly increased in women as a result. Similarly, the amount of time spent caring for infants predicts oxytocin levels in both men and women.

The way that biologically based genetic predispositions manifest as behavior depends on the environmental context in which they occur. For instance, there's a slight biological tendency for boys to be more physically active than girls, and for girls to be more focused. But this is greatly amplified by the behavior of parents, who tend to engage in rough-and-tumble play with boys, requiring movement, and pretend play with girls that requires concentration.

In general, research finds larger individual differences within, rather than between, sex groups, and sex differences tend to be quite small. This argues against biology as the main driver of gender differences. If there's a kernel of truth underlying gender stereotypes, it's a minimal one that is exaggerated by social factors. Therefore, any consideration of gender differences in agency and communion needs to take social-ization into account.

GENDER MAPS

From the time we're little, girls are dressed in pink and given dolls to play with and receive the message that a good woman is sweet, nurtur-ing, and caring. Boys are dressed in blue and given trucks and guns to play with and receive the message that a good man is strong and active. Our adult identity is centered on these gendered ideals, which affect almost every important area of life, shaping how we interpret our own behavior and that of others. Understanding how gender socialization occurs helps to provide insight into how we can be freed from its con-straints.

As children we internalize detailed—but mostly unspoken—instruction manuals for our gender-prescribed roles, characteristics, and activities known as gender schemas. Schemas are organized knowl-edge structures that act like internal maps. They operate unconsciously and filter our psychological perceptions to help us interpret the world.

For instance, in North America, when someone invites us to a birthday party, we know what to expect because we have a birthday-party schema. We know to bring a present, to anticipate cake and candles, and, if it's a surprise party, that we shouldn't say anything until we yell "Surprise!" as the birthday person walks through the door. In short, schemas help us make sense of things. We use gender schemas to categorize people so we can predict behavior, helping us form expectations of what to wear to the party, how others will act, what type of gift to buy, and so on.

We feel uncomfortable when things don't fit with our schemas—a phenomenon known as cognitive dissonance. I had a colleague who told me how she once used cognitive dissonance to good effect. She wanted to surprise her boyfriend for his birthday, so she arranged it so that when he walked through the door all his friends were naked. When they yelled "Surprise!" he was *really* surprised! (I wish I had been there to see his face.) Because we don't like to experience dissonance, our mind does what it can to help us feel the calm of schema congruence. If possible, we'll distort information to be consistent with our schemas—so we may remember a picture of a boy cooking as a girl cooking, for instance.

Ignoring information that doesn't fit our preconceived notions strengthens our schemas. Research indicates that female students are less self-confident about their math ability and are judged by male students to be less talented in science, even when they have higher grades than males. The grade information is ignored because it doesn't fit with the schema that males are better at math and science than females. This isn't a result of a general sense that females are less intelligent than males. Girls are just as confident as boys about their reading and writing ability, and boys concur, since there isn't a schema that males are better at literacy.

Our schemas are often held unconsciously, so we don't realize their pervasive influence. Even people who consider the sexes to be equal are influenced by this invisible filter of perception. We may consciously judge men and women to be similarly competent, but still tend to rely on our stereotypes of men as agentic and women as communal to make judgments, especially when there isn't a lot of clear-cut information on which to base our evaluations. We didn't choose to have these unconscious stereotypes and they don't stem from our rational mind. Instead, we absorbed them from a lifetime of books, movies, TV shows, and music that portray men as powerful and agentic and women as caring and nurturing. These biases are so pervasive it's hard to see them—they're the water we swim in.

The typical way researchers study unconscious gender bias is by having different participants read descriptions of people who are identical except for having a male or female name and then determining if there are differences in reactions to each. Researchers at the Duke University School of Business found that house designs were considered more innovative when the purported architect was given the name John rather than Katherine. Researchers from New York University found that business strategies were rated as more original when the manager in charge had a male name; those managers were also judged to be more worthy of a bonus, raise, or promotion. Similarly, when evaluating collaborative projects involving team members, credit for the team's success was more often attributed to male members unless information about a woman's contribution was clear and unambiguous. (The fallout from unconscious bias will be explored more fully in Chapter 9 when we consider how fierce self-compassion can help women in the workplace.)

Unfortunately, gender stereotypes are deeply entrenched in our psyches and resistant to change. Although there have been many gains for women in society over the last three decades, and people generally hold more egalitarian attitudes than they used to, one study found almost no change in the stereotype that men are agentic and women are communal from 1983 to 2014. These stereotypes are remarkably stable over time and also appear to become more ingrained with age.

Shortly after arriving at UT Austin, my research lab conducted a study looking at the development of gender stereotypes from early adolescence to early adulthood, with a particular focus on perceptions of traits associated with dominance ("has leadership ability," "independent") or submissiveness ("compliant," "sensitive to the needs of others"). We found that perceived gender differences became more extreme with age: young adults viewed men as dominant and women as submissive to a greater extent than early adolescents, perhaps as a result of more exposure to the media and greater knowledge of American culture. We also looked at underlying beliefs about *why* these distinctions existed. We found that young women were more likely to say they were due to how girls and boys are raised, whereas young men were more likely to say they were due to biological differences like genes or hormones. Young women also had more egalitarian attitudes— believing that women should be given more opportunities in business and government—in part because they saw gender differences as originating from the way women had been socialized. In other words, even though women were highly aware of the stereotype of female submissiveness, they judged power inequality to be fundamentally unfair. This offers hope for our ability to change oppressive gender roles.

WHO AM I?

One reason it's challenging to overcome internalized stereotypes is because they take root nearly from birth and our sense of self actually forms around our gendered identity as communal or agentic. Gender is one of the first categories infants learn—they begin perceptually distinguishing men and women between the ages of three and eight months. By the time they turn four or five years old, stereotypes equating men with agentic personality traits such as tough or brave and women with communal traits such as gentle or kind are deeply embedded.

These stereotypes are strengthened by observing social reactions to those who don't conform to their assigned gender role. Boys who show tender communal traits are called sissies. They're derided not only for their nonconformity, but also because acting like a girl is interpreted as less powerful. In early childhood, girls who show agentic traits aren't ridiculed and are typically accepted as tomboys, in part because their behavior is a step up rather than a step down in status. Still, the very fact that agentic girls are labeled tomboys calls attention to the fact that a girl acting in these ways isn't "normal." By adolescence there's more pressure on girls—especially heterosexual ones—to conform to gender-role stereotypes in order to be popular and succeed at the dating game. To be liked and accepted, they may start to use more tentative language, focus on sexual attractiveness, and downplay their competence.

In adulthood, regardless of sexual orientation, women who are forceful or dominant tend to experience social backlash. Assertive be-havior that would be perfectly acceptable in a man often results in a woman being disliked, insulted, and distrusted. If a man clearly and firmly rejects someone else's idea because he thinks it's inadequate, he is seen as decisive and confident. If a woman does so in the exact same manner, she's seen as a domineering bitch. Fear of backlash leads many women to suppress their fierce side in order to gain social approval (again, we'll be taking this up in more detail later).

However, it's actually agentic, not communal, traits that predict mental health among women. Women who can be firm and express themselves authentically are happier and more satisfied with their lives. Those who can't assert themselves are more anxious and depressed when facing challenges. Without the ability to draw boundaries, say no, or ask for what they want, women can easily become stressed and overwhelmed. Moreover, women who are highly communal but not agentic tend to be doubly distressed: not only are they overwhelmed by their own difficulties, they may identify so strongly with the role of caregiver that they also become distressed by the problems of loved ones.

Women who are androgynous and rate themselves as high in both agency and communion tend to have better mental health than those who are underdeveloped in one quality or the other. Research shows they're more able to deal with stress and bounce back from failure. This is because they have two ways of coping: taking proactive steps to improve their situation when possible and accepting things with equanimity when change is not an option. They're also more likely to be authentic and comfortable expressing their true selves.

Those who are "undifferentiated"—meaning they score low in both agency and communion—tend to struggle the most since they have trouble with both nurturing and self-assertion, leading to personal and interpersonal difficulties. Again, it's clear that the development and balanced integration of both fierceness and tenderness is what allows women to be whole and healthy.

TEST YOUR LEVEL OF AGENCY AND COMMUNION

The scale below is an adapted version of the Personal Attributes Questionnaire (PAQ), which was created by Janet Spence and Robert Helmreich at the University of Texas at Austin. It's one of the most common ways to measure masculinity and femininity in research.

Instructions

For each pair of traits, choose a number that describes where *you* fall on the scale. Choose 1 if the option on the left describes you and 5 if the option on the right describes you, or choose somewhere in between. For example, when deciding where you fall on a continuum between "Not at all artistic" and "Very artistic," if you think that you have no artistic ability, you should choose 1. If you think that you are pretty good, you might choose 4. If you are only medium, you might choose 3, and so forth.

1	Not at all independent	1 2 3 4 5	Very independent
2	Not at all emotional	1 2 3 4 5	Very emotional
3	Very passive	1 2 3 4 5	Very active
4	Not at all able to devote self completely to others	1 2 3 4 5	Able to devote self completely to others
5	Not at all competitive	1 2 3 4 5	Very competitive
6	Very rough	1 2 3 4 5	Very gentle
7	Has difficulty making decisions	1 2 3 4 5	Can make decisions easily
8	Not at all helpful to others	1 2 3 4 5	Very helpful to others
9	Gives up very easily	1 2 3 4 5	Never gives up
10	Not at all kind	1 2 3 4 5	Very kind
11	Not at all self-confident	1 2 3 4 5	Very self-confident
12	Not at all aware of feelings of others	1 2 3 4 5	Very aware of feelings of others
13	Feels very inferior	1 2 3 4 5	Feels very superior
14	Not at all understanding of others	1 2 3 4 5	Very understanding of others
15	Goes to pieces under pressure	1 2 3 4 5	Stands up well under pressure
16	Very cold in relations with others	1 2 3 4 5	Very warm in relations with others

Scoring Instructions:

Total Agency score (sum of 8 odd items) = _____

Mean Agency score (Total/8) = _____

Total Communion score (sum of 8 even items) _____

Mean Communion score (Total/8) = _____

As a rough guide, a mean agency or communion score below 3.0 indicates you are low in the trait, and above 3.0 indicates you are high in the trait. Those who score low in agency and high in communion are classified as feminine, high in agency and low in communion as masculine, low in both as undifferentiated, and high in both as androgynous.

GENDER AND SELF-COMPASSION

So what's the link between gender and self-compassion? This question has been of great interest to me and is a topic I continue to explore in my research. One might assume that because women are socialized to develop qualities of warmth and care that they're more self-compassionate than men. But research shows the opposite: women are less self-compassionate than men. In a meta-analysis of seventy-one studies, we found that women consistently had lower self-compassion scores, although the difference was a small one. The reason we're less self-compassionate is partly due to the fact that we tend to be more self-critical. As mentioned earlier, when the threat-defense response is triggered, it often manifests as self-judgment, feelings of isolation, and overidentification. Individuals in subordinate positions have to be more vigilant against danger, leading women to rely on self-criticism as a way to feel safe.

Although women are less self-compassionate than men, they are more compassionate to others. We gave almost 1,400 adults the SCS and an analogous compassion scale that assessed kindness, a sense of common humanity, and mindfulness toward the suffering of others. Women scored slightly lower on the SCS than men but a lot higher on the compassion scale. Although both women and men had the general tendency to be more compassionate to others than to themselves, this discrepancy was more extreme for women. We found that 67 percent of men were significantly more compassionate to others than to themselves, 12 percent were more compassionate to themselves than to others, and 21 percent were equally compassionate to self and others. Among women, 86 percent were significantly more compassionate to others, 5 percent were more compassionate to themselves, and only 9 percent were equally compassionate to self and others.

These findings reflect the ways that women are taught to prioritize others' needs over their own. Power determines who gets their needs met, and historically women have been required to subordinate their needs to those of men in order to keep the peace in relationships. Men, who feel more entitled to get their needs met, appear to have less of a problem being compassionate to themselves.

It's not biological sex that leads to differences in self-compassion, however. Gender-role socialization is the real culprit. In another study of approximately one thousand adults, we found that androgynous women who are both agentic and communal are just as self-compassionate as men. They feel confident and worthy, enabling them to turn their well-developed skills of nurturing inward in times of struggle. Women who are low in both traits have the lowest levels of self-compassion because they can draw on neither warmth nor strength to care for themselves. These findings mean that as women we don't need to renounce our communal qualities to fully embrace self-compassion. To unlock its full potential, we simply need to strengthen our sense of agency to bring our yang into balance with our yin.

Luckily, the fact that women are socialized to value compassion means they're less afraid of self-compassion than men and are more open to learning the skill. Although we don't keep data on this, I would estimate that about 85 to 90 percent of participants who attend MSC workshops are women. The idea of using compassion as a source of coping and resilience appears to make more sense to women than to men. They also arrive as compassion experts, having been trained from an early age to care for others. This means they're in a better position to give themselves compassion because they already know how to be warm, sensitive, and supportive.

And although female communal gender roles tend to be gentle, there's one context in which we're allowed to be fierce. We're encouraged to act like a powerful Momma Bear as long as we do so to protect our children. Agency in the service of communion—i.e., taking strong action to help our kids—is not only acceptable, but becomes the stuff of legend. Whether or not they have children, most women can sense the power of Momma Bear within. The trick is to make a conscious U-turn and turn this caring force inward.

MOVING BEYOND GENDER

We've all been harmed by the gendering of agency and communion, of yin and yang. Our development is stunted when we limit our capacity to express these two essential ways of being, and each energy may become distorted. Yin qualities of sensitivity, acceptance, and understanding can morph into powerlessness and dependence when separated from fierce yang energy. Yang qualities of bravery and action may become twisted into aggression, dominance, and emotional cluelessness when separated from tender yin energy.

What would happen if yin and yang were not linked to being male or female? If every individual could express their unique voice? Instead of prioritizing one quality over the other, we could harness and integrate both. When yin and yang are freed from the dynamics of dominance and submission, we can use caring force to transform ourselves, and also harness this power to transform a broken social system.

Over the last few years, I've deeply explored my own balance of yin and yang. Although culture generally suppresses the fierce side in women, everyone's journey is unique. For me, the journey has been to reclaim and integrate my tender side. For most of my life I've been more yang than yin. This was an intentional choice. I have a very clear memory of walking down the halls of my high school when I was around sixteen. Boys were starting to notice me, and I was feeling all the tension of having to be attractive and popular to gain a sense of self-worth. I said to myself, "Screw that! I'm not going to make my way through the world by being pretty. I'm going to make my way by being smart!" I understood the lack of power that came from relying on a man for support because my own father had abandoned our family when I was two. My mother's dream of being a stay-at-home housewife supported by a benevolent husband didn't work out so well, and she took a job as a secretary (which she didn't enjoy) to pay the bills. I wanted none of it.

So I focused on my studies, getting a full-ride scholarship to UCLA, then a Ph.D. at Berkeley, a postdoctoral position at Denver University, followed by a professor position at UT Austin. I basically never left school. Intelligence became my source of safety. I could argue with the best of them, and fierceness came naturally to me. And although my tender side was well developed in relation to teaching self-compassion or parenting my son, these two parts of me felt very separate. So much of my time was spent *doing*—conducting research, writing papers, developing training protocols, giving talks—that my yin and yang were thrown out of balance.

Since coming to this realization, I've intentionally focused on getting to know my softer, more intuitive yin side that sometimes feels overpowered by my intellect. I do very unscientific things like praying to my female ancestors for guidance. I practice letting go of the need to know, trusting life, learning to open to uncertainty. I honor both sides of my being and invite them to merge and integrate within me.

I've found that purposefully calling forth fierce and tender self-compassion simultaneously allows me to feel more complete and fulfilled. I can operate in the world with more equilibrium. And then I forget and get knocked off-center, and then I remember and try again.

It's not a linear progression where once we integrate yin and yang we're done. It's an iterative process that needs to be evoked continually. When we ask ourselves what we need, sometimes we need more fierceness, sometimes more tenderness, but we always need both.

BREATHING YIN AND YANG

This practice draws on classic breath meditation to work with the energies of yin and yang so we can bring them into balance. I developed it as a way to integrate both sides within myself, and I now teach it in workshops. Many people say that they can feel the effects of the practice immediately in their body, helping them to feel more whole and centered. (A guided audio version of this practice can be found at FierceSelf-Compassion.org.)

Instructions

- Sit comfortably but make sure your back is straight. Put both hands on your solar plexus or some other place that helps you feel strong and supported.

- Start to notice your breathing. Don't change it or control it, just breathe naturally.

- Your mind will wander. When it does, bring back your attention without judgment.

- Now start to focus on your in-breath specifically, feeling each inhalation.

- As you breathe in, imagine that you are breathing in fierce yang energy. Feel the power rising from the base of your spine.

- If you like, you can imagine the fierce energy as a bright white light flowing through your entire body.

- Do this for about two minutes, or longer if desired.

- Take a big breath in and hold it for about five seconds, then release.

- Now put your hands on your heart or some other soothing place.

- Begin to focus on your out-breath, feeling yourself relax with each exhalation.

- As you exhale, let go and let be.

- With each out-breath imagine that tender yin compassion is being released—loving, connected presence. Let it nurture you, heal you.

- If you like, you can imagine this tender energy as a soft golden light flowing through you.

- Do this for two minutes or more.

- Once again, take a big breath in and hold it for about five seconds, then release.

- Now bring yin and yang together, putting one hand on your heart and the other on your solar plexus or some other place that feels comfortable.

- As you breathe in, imagine that you are breathing in fierceness, and as you breathe out, imagine that you are breathing out tenderness.

- Allow these two energies to flow freely in your body, merging and integrating.

- Let the inward and outward flow be as natural as the movement of the ocean, waves going in, waves going out.

- If it feels right, you can focus more on the in-breath or out-breath, depending on what you need most in the moment.

- Do this for about five minutes, or longer if you like.

- When you're ready, gently open your eyes.

It should be noted that there's no right way to do this practice. Some people like to summon tenderness on the in-breath and send fierce energy out into the world on the out-breath, and you can also switch the order of the in-breath and the out-breath. Experiment with the practice and see what works best for you.

CHAPTER 3

ANGRY WOMEN

The truth will set you free, but first it will piss you off.

—*Gloria Steinem, author and activist*

After a narrow party-line vote confirmed Brett Kavanaugh to the US Supreme Court, many social commentators reflected on the role that anger played in his Senate Judiciary Committee hearing. Dr. Christine Blasey Ford, who'd come forward voluntarily to testify at the hearings, displayed incredible bravery in front of the Senate committee as she detailed her personal memories of Kavanaugh's sexual assault when she was a teenager. Equally striking was her demeanor during the hearing. While she testified with confidence in her area of expertise—the psychology of trauma—at other times she spoke like a young girl who needed to placate the powerful men around her. This doesn't undercut the courage she showed for being there. It was tremendous. But she clearly felt she had to be soft and sweet to have any hope of being heard.

Ford was probably right. If she had shown her anger at Kavanaugh, she likely would have experienced backlash for violating the stereotype of a "good" woman. Any outburst on her part would have discredited her testimony in the eyes of many. She was allowed to demonstrate her pain at feeling victimized, but no more than that.

Kavanaugh, by contrast, was celebrated by much of the public and many senators for being righteously enraged. His display of anger helped assure his confirmation to the Supreme Court.

NICE GIRLS DON'T GET ANGRY

Anger is a powerful expression of yang energy. It sounds an alarm and signals the presence of danger. It motivates us to act with urgency to reduce threats. Although boys and girls experience anger at the same rate early in development, the anger of girls is treated differently from that of boys. Almost as soon as they learn to walk and talk, girls are encouraged by parents and teachers to display tender qualities—to be pleasant, helpful, and cooperative—but are actively discouraged from showing the fierce quality of anger. Adults react to anger as natural and acceptable in boys but not in girls. Little girls are told to use a "nicer" voice three times more often than boys, hammering home the message that it's our role to keep the peace rather than upset the applecart.

The idea that anger is appropriate for boys but not girls is so entrenched that mothers tend to identify a distressed child as sad if she's a girl and mad if he's a boy. Not surprisingly, young children believe it's normal for boys to be angry but it's abnormal for girls. For little girls this is quite confusing. Having our emotions invalidated and misunderstood is the first step on the road to suppressing our ability to speak up and assert ourselves.

Sandra Thomas and her colleagues from the University of Tennessee conducted a pioneering examination of women's anger in the 1990s. The study included 535 women and asked open-ended questions about their experience of anger. They found that many participants weren't in touch with their anger or else felt deeply uncomfortable with it. As one woman said, "I believe that I have been socialized to not acknowledge anger as a valid human emotion. The result of this socialization is that I have not always known when I am angry nor do I have many effective ways of expressing anger. I often feel powerless when I am angry. I feel hopeless. I feel foolish. I feel afraid. Feeling angry can scare me." The researchers found that the most frequent causes of women's anger were feelings of helplessness, not being listened to, injustice, irresponsibility on the part of others, and the inability to make the changes they wanted.

They also found that when women suppressed their anger, holding it as physical tension in their body, they often felt powerless, small, and diminished. Moreover, bottling up anger eventually led to an explosion that also made them feel out of control—and therefore even more powerless. As one woman wrote, "My husband tells me I'm like Jekyll and Hyde. I can just be talking in a real sweet, normal tone of voice, and then I'll explode. . . . I'll get squealy, get this distorted look on my face of pure hate. . . . I don't know that I'm doing it. It's kind of like I've just gone into somebody else. I got so mad at him that I took his teacup and shoved it in his face. He could not believe that I had done that to him. And I cried because I couldn't either." It's ironic that anger, which is an inherently powerful emotion, causes women to feel powerless because we're not allowed to acknowledge anger as part of our true nature. Instead, we feel like an alien force has taken us over and say things like "I lost it" or "I wasn't myself." This is because women have been taught to reject their anger and to see it as foreign.

And the belief that anger isn't natural for women is supported by the reactions of others. Angry women are seen as crazy, irrational, and unhinged. People generally feel that a woman must be mentally disturbed if she's angry or "disruptive." She's emotionally unbalanced, hormonal—perhaps on her menstrual cycle. (As Trump famously said about news commentator Megyn Kelly after she aggressively questioned him in a debate, "You could see there was blood coming out of her eyes, blood coming out of her wherever.") The stereotype that women are communal nurturers is so ingrained that when they show any other behavior, it's interpreted as deviant. It's okay for women to be sad, however, since sadness is a tender, yielding emotion that accepts what is. We just can't be angry. Men, on the other hand, are seen as passionate, righteous, and committed when enraged. Their anger is in line with their stereotyped identity as agents of action and change. Men are celebrated when angry because it shows they have balls. Women, on the other hand, are reviled: it shows they're ball-breakers.

BLACK WOMEN AND ANGER

Although the majority of participants in Thomas's study of women's anger were White, she conducted in-depth interviews with some of the Black participants to see if their experiences differed. She found that while they also feared being taken over by the force of anger, they were more aware of the positive functions of this emotion than other groups were. Because of the double-barreled threat of sexism and racism, their mothers and grandmothers taught them that anger is sometimes needed for protection and survival in an unjust world. Still, researchers from Clayton State University found that Black women are actually no more angry than other women in terms of feelings of anger in the moment, having an angry temperament, verbal or physical expressions of anger, or controlling anger. In fact, Black women were found to report lower levels of reactive anger in situations in which they were criticized, disrespected, or negatively evaluated compared to others. These findings were interpreted to demonstrate the maturity that develops from having to deal with racism and sexism on a daily basis; Black women are able to recognize the protective function of anger but are also more able to regulate it.

Unfortunately, this hasn't prevented society from stereotyping Black women as angry and antagonistic. The Angry Black Woman trope is sometimes referred to as the Sapphire stereotype, based on the character Sapphire on the 1950s "Amos 'n' Andy" show who was depicted as hostile and constantly nagging her husband. Scholars argue this negative stereotype was developed to justify the mistreatment of Black women, and it continues to have destructive consequences. For instance, one study of almost three hundred White undergraduates examined perceptions of how culpable women were for provoking domestic violence between same-race spouses. Researchers found that after reading identical accounts of domestic violence involving a Black couple or a White couple, Black women were described as being more responsible than White women for the violence, presumably due to the stereotype that they are angrier and more aggressive. This finding was even more pronounced among those with traditional views on gender. These disturbing findings are in line with statistics showing that the police tend to take the accounts of Black victims of domestic abuse less seriously than those of White victims. Any woman who breaks the mold of ideal femininity by getting angry is shunned by society, but this damaging judgment hits Black women the hardest.

ANGER, GENDER, AND POWER

The suppression of women's anger helps maintain unequal power relationships. The same anger that tends to enhance a man's power in the eyes of others, supporting the archetype of male strength and confidence, diminishes a woman's. One study out of Arizona State University examined this perceptual bias by telling participants they were taking part in a mock jury deliberation about a murder case. The experiment took place on the internet, and was designed so that four jurors, via written comments, would agree with the participant's verdict on the case, but one juror would dissent and disagree. The other jurors didn't really exist; the setup was designed to examine participants' reactions to the online feedback. When the dissenter had a male name and expressed anger, the participants felt less confident about their own views and were more swayed by his dissenting opinion. When the dissenter had a female name and expressed anger, participants felt more confident and were less swayed by her opinion—even though she made the same arguments and expressed the same degree of anger as her male counterpart.

Expressions of anger instill respect and enhance perceived competence for men but invite scorn and imply lessened capability for women. The delegitimization of this basic emotion robs women of their ability to effectively impact others. It also harms our mental health.

WOMEN, ANGER, AND WELL-BEING

Because women aren't allowed to express anger outwardly the same way that men are, we tend to turn it inward in the form of self-criticism. When we feel threatened and can't confront the danger by taking action externally, the fight response is directed internally. We try to reassert control through self-criticism, hoping it will force us to change and thus restore safety. We are also more likely than men to negatively judge ourselves for getting angry, leading to even harsher self-criticism. Internalized anger in the form of self-criticism is a primary reason that women, especially those with a feminine gender-role identification, report lower levels of self-compassion than men.

It also helps explain why women are twice as likely as men to be depressed. We fold under the pressure of self-loathing and become shell-shocked from our own constant attacks. The increased cortisol and inflammation caused by constant sympathetic nervous system activation results in our bodies and minds shutting down. Self-criticism can also lead us to develop anxiety disorders such as panic attacks or eating disorders such as anorexia.

The inability to express anger can lead to rumination, which also contributes to depression. Remember that rumination represents a freeze response to danger and, like self-criticism, is a basic safety behavior. It's a form of resistance to what's happening rooted in the desire to make our pain go away. Instead of naturally rising and passing away, our anger is held in place by our resistance (women aren't supposed to be angry after all). This means that our minds get stuck to it like Velcro, with angry thoughts endlessly repeating themselves.

Robin Simon at Wake Forest University and Kathryn Lively at Dartmouth University conducted research on a large nationally representative sample of 1,125 Americans and found that women's anger is stronger and lasts longer than that of men—even after controlling for socio-demographic factors like education, income, and race. The researchers found that the higher incidence of depression observed among women in their sample could be partially explained by the increased intensity and duration of women's anger. By denying women the free expression of their justified anger, society is forcing us to swallow it, making us ill.

THE GIFTS OF ANGER

Not only do norms against female anger damage our mental health, they also deny us access to an important and powerful resource. Professor Raymond Novaco, an expert in the study of anger from the University of California, Irvine, has described at least five ways that anger can be a helpful emotion. First, anger energizes us. When we're angry, our back is tall and we can feel energy pulsing through our veins. This energy mobilizes us to act and overrides inertia or complacency. It gives us the blast of motivation needed to stop injury or injustice. Whether it's talking with authorities, going to the polls, or taking to the streets the way so many of us did after Donald Trump's election or George Floyd's death, we need to get angry to create change.

Second, anger provides incredible focus on what threatens to harm us. It acts like a laser beam pinpointing present danger. While it can be debilitating if it turns into rumination, the ability of anger to illuminate a problem that demands attention is a gift that shouldn't be taken for granted. It provides incredible clarity in the exact moment it's needed.

Third, anger helps us to defend and protect ourselves. It overrides the fear response and helps us to fight back against someone who is hurting us or treating us unfairly. Sometimes we need to be angry in order to have the courage to confront those threatening or disrespecting us. If we don't get angry, we'll be much less likely to stand up for ourselves. Because anger energizes us and focuses us on the threat at hand, it equips us to take self-protective action.

A fourth useful aspect to anger is that it has a clear communication function. It alerts us to the fact that something is wrong, at the same time that it lets others know we're unhappy about it. If we don't get angry at the subtle but snide comment a coworker just made about our job performance, we might not even realize the comment was inappropriate or hurtful. While screaming or shouting doesn't serve a useful communication purpose if it causes the listener to shut down, anger expressed as firm conviction ("I didn't find that last comment to be helpful") can often cause a listener to pay more attention to us, both in the moment and for the foreseeable future.

Even when anger is simply an expression of pain, like swearing after stubbing a toe, it serves an important cathartic function. In fact, one study found that when participants had to submerge their hands in freezing water, those who were instructed to swear had greater pain tolerance and could hold their hands under for longer than those who were instructed not to react. This effect was especially marked among women, who typically swear less than men. Because women were less familiar with the cathartic power of anger, they found it especially effective as a pain reliever.

Finally, anger provides a sense of personal control and empowerment. When we're angry and engaged in changing things for the better, we're no longer the helpless victim. Even if we can't change our situation, anger prevents us from collapsing into a heap of fear and shame. We take on the spirit of a survivor. Anger reminds us that we have a powerful voice in how we choose to live our lives.

CONSTRUCTIVE AND DESTRUCTIVE ANGER

Not all anger is beneficial, of course. In fact, there are two types of anger identified by researchers: constructive and destructive. Destructive anger rejects and blames people in a personal way: *they're evil villains!* It's a hostile and aggressive energy, often seeking to retaliate and destroy. Destructive anger is self-righteous and doesn't care about the potential fallout for its recipients, who deserve whatever's coming to them. It also acts in an ego-defensive manner, protecting our self-image as if it was a matter of life and death. It's reactive and mindless and leads to poor decision-making. It's the white heat of rage that blinds us from seeing things clearly, focused only on punishing the person threatening harm. This holds true even when that person is us, as we pummel ourselves with harsh criticism for getting things wrong. It can destroy relationships and lead to violence, including verbal and physical attacks. Because it activates the sympathetic nervous system, it can also lead to hypertension, immune system dysfunction, and major health issues in the form of increased blood pressure and coronary heart disease.

Destructive anger supports the truth of sayings such as "Anger corrodes the vessel that contains it" or "Anger is like picking up a hot coal to throw; you're the one who gets burned." When we're angry at ourselves or another person, we're cutting ourselves off from interconnectedness. We turn the person we're angry at into the enemy. In short, we're undermining compassion. This hurts ourselves (as well as others) by increasing feelings of isolation and hatred.

Constructive anger, on the other hand, is the process by which a person stands up for herself and defends her rights without hostility or aggression. It focuses on protection against harm and unfairness. It directs anger at the wrong being done, seeking to understand the conditions leading to harm, rather than attacking the person or people who are doing wrong. It considers the impact of its expression on others. Anger that is aimed at reducing suffering doesn't exacerbate problems but seeks to unravel them. Constructive anger is a wellspring for focused action aimed at preventing injustice and saying no.

Constructive anger has a positive effect on our mental and physical health. In one large study of almost two thousand adult men and women, researchers at the University of Alabama observed how participants expressed anger in videotaped interviews. They coded participants as displaying constructive anger when they met one of the following four criteria: were assertive and dealt directly with the person they were angry at; discussed why they felt upset; tried to understand the other person's point of view; or discussed their anger with others as a way to gain insight into possible alternative ways to view the situation.

Study results indicated that participants who displayed constructive anger were less cynical, aggressive, and hostile to others, and were less anxious and depressed than those whose anger was not constructive. They also had better physical health in terms of lower blood pressure.

Anger that seeks to understand rather than destroy can also be harnessed for effective conflict resolution. An important goal of anger is to correct violations of rights or fairness. When this emotion is constructive, it motivates individuals to resolve conflicts in a balanced manner. For instance, a group of researchers examined Israeli support for compromise over the status of Jerusalem and of Palestinian refugees and found that when anger was accompanied by hatred it lessened support for compromise. However, when anger occurred without hatred—when Palestinians were seen as human beings and not as the enemy—it resulted in increased support. Constructive anger can be a force for good, as long as it's aimed at preventing harm and isn't personal.

ANGER AND SOCIAL JUSTICE

Anger calls things like they are. It allows us to see when we're being discriminated against or treated unfairly—and to fight against it. If women don't get angry, it means our wants, needs, and desires don't count. It means we can't effectively change our situation. Prohibitions against women's anger as "unbecoming" and "unladylike" are a form of social control, a way of keeping us in our place. The willingness to get angry is therefore a political act as well as a personal assertion of our rights. As Soraya Chemaly, author of *Rage Becomes Her*, writes, "The truth is that anger isn't what gets in our way—it is our way. All we have to do is own it." Anger arises when we want to have a say over our circumstances. The fierce energy of anger motivates action and fuels self-assertion and a sense of agency. It allows us to speak up loudly and authentically about being treated fairly and helps us get our needs met. While wanton rage mindlessly directed at others isn't helpful, the energy of anger can be incredibly useful when properly harnessed and focused on unjust systems that cause suffering.

A woman who's afraid of getting angry may be less likely to speak up in the face of injustice. In a study by Diana Leonard and colleagues at the University of California, Santa Barbara, researchers examined how stereotypes about women's anger affected the desire to take action against injustice. Undergraduate women were told about a hypothetical situation: "In a kickboxing class with mostly male students, the instructor comments that he has decided to gear the sessions toward strength training. Afterward, he calls Jessica over to tell her that she should really consider transferring into an aerobics class." Participants who endorsed negative stereotypes about women's anger in general were less likely to be angry about this situation in particular. They were also less likely to see it as an act of discrimination or to want to join with other women to confront the kickboxing instructor. Blowing off sexist remarks such as these means that injustice will go unchallenged.

Women's anger is key to being able to protest gender inequality by motivating women to band together to take action. Collective action is defined as the steps taken by a group to fight against injustice and discrimination. This may entail protests, marches, boycotts, signing petitions, voting, or speaking up to denounce mistreatment. Historically, collective action has been one of the most effective ways for women to enact social change. Think of the protests of suffragettes that secured the vote for women in 1920, or Mothers Against Drunk Driving, which successfully petitioned Congress to increase the minimum drinking age to twenty-one and stiffen penalties for DUIs, cutting drunk-driving fatalities in half. The current American political landscape is shaped by the anger of "Rage Moms," a term that *New York Times* journalists Lisa Lerer and Jennifer Medina coined to describe anger-driven social action groups like MomsRising, a million-member political action group, or Moms Demand Action, a gun-control advocacy organization. The Black Lives Matter movement was founded by three women—Alicia Garza, Patrisse Cullors, and Opal Tometi—who were enraged by the violence being inflicted on their children, families, and community. Anger is the rechargeable battery powering the social justice movement.

SELF-COMPASSION AND ANGER

There's not a lot of research on self-compassion and anger, but the little there is suggests it can help lessen anger's negative effects. To this end, a study by Ashley Borders and Amanda Fresnics at The College of New Jersey examined the link between self-compassion and anger in over two hundred undergraduates. First, they found that individuals with higher levels of self-compassion were slightly less likely to report being angry—i.e., getting highly irritated with or wanting to yell at someone—but the difference was a small one. Self-compassion is not incompatible with anger. It does allow us to wield it more effectively, however, as evidenced by the fact that self-compassionate individuals were much less likely to ruminate or feel besieged by angry thoughts, memories, or revenge fantasies. Because self-compassion allows us to feel angry without self-judgment or suppression, we don't fixate on our anger in an unhealthy manner. Participants with greater self-compassion were also less likely to report being physically or verbally aggressive in the last six months, and this lack of aggression was explained by lessened rumination. It's primarily when we get swept away by our anger that we're at greatest risk of attacking others. When we're mindful of our angry feelings, on the other hand, remembering that they're a central part of living a human life, we can assert ourselves without causing harm.

I saw the transformative impact of self-compassion on anger in the life of a neighbor named Celeste, a White retired librarian in her late sixties with two grown children, three grandchildren, and a neurotic poodle named Tutu. Celeste grew up in Grand Rapids, Michigan, and had been raised with the idea that women should smile and be pleasant, sweet, and accommodating. Her husband, Frank, had recently retired from his job managing a car dealership and they were spending a lot of time together. Frank could be long-winded and tiresome. He constantly interrupted Celeste while she was talking or would explain a political situation in the news as if she were a child. But she never said anything; she didn't want to be the complaining shrew. She became more and more unhappy as time went on. Even though retirement was supposed to bring ease, Celeste was more agitated than ever. She criticized herself for not being more grateful, and her self-judgment just made things worse. Her agitation eventually turned into anxiety, and she began to feel uncomfortable in her own skin.

Celeste knew about my work on self-compassion, and we used to talk about it. She read one of my books and was interested in learning to be kinder to herself. I suspected she would benefit from therapy, so I gently tried to suggest this, telling her that I'd seen a local therapist named Laura who'd been very helpful to me. Laura used an approach called Internal Family Systems (IFS) therapy, developed by Richard Schwartz. IFS helps people to get in touch with different parts of themselves and have compassion for them all. Did she want her number? Luckily, Celeste was receptive.

Celeste told Laura that she was seeking therapy because she needed help with her agitation and anxiety. Not only was it uncomfortable, it was starting to have a negative impact on her marriage. When Laura asked why she'd become so perturbed, Celeste said she thought it must be hormonal changes and age. Laura asked her where she felt the distress. Celeste explained it was in her stomach. Laura then asked her, "If your stomach could talk, what would it say?"

At first Celeste thought Laura was crazy. "I'm hungry?" she ventured, trying not to roll her eyes. But she went along with it, and eventually said, "I'm irritated."

"Can you tell me more about the irritation?" Laura asked her. Was it possible that she was angry at her husband?

"No, of course not," Celeste replied. Then she felt her cheeks flush. When Laura pointed this out, Celeste realized there *was* a part of her that was angry, but she felt embarrassed about it. She had learned when she was young that anger was a bad thing, and had a clear memory of one of her aunts telling her that she was ugly when she was angry.

"How old were you when you got that message?" Laura asked.

Celeste figured out she'd been about seven.

Under Laura's guidance, Celeste spoke to that little girl, the part of her who'd been shamed for being angry, telling her, "It's okay. I'm an adult now and I can handle my anger. But thank you for your efforts to keep me safe." Afterward, the young part of Celeste relaxed. This allowed her to get in closer touch with the angry part of her, which she felt as a hot burning knot in her gut. When giving voice to this part of herself, Celeste was surprised at how much rage she'd bottled up over the years. She felt humiliated, devalued, and patronized by her husband. She realized that her anger was trying to protect her from being treated in a condescending manner, but it was repeatedly shut down by the little girl part of her that was afraid of being angry. As Laura helped Celeste get more familiar with her anger, she felt as if she'd found a piece of herself that had been lost for many years.

At first Celeste's anger was destructive. Like a genie let out of a bottle, she became furious at her husband whenever he interrupted or talked down to her. She shouted and called him all those names she'd heard in the movies but never dared to utter herself. His response was to become silent and withdraw, and their relationship became highly strained. Although Celeste was grateful to be more in touch with her emotions, she did love Frank and the tension was tearing her marriage apart. She knew they needed to work things out, but she also didn't want to shut her emotions down as she had for most of her life.

Over a few months of therapy, Laura taught Celeste to embrace her anger, to see it as a friend rather than the enemy. Celeste learned how to have conversations with the angry part of her, listening to what it had to say and appreciating the energy it gave her. She allowed her anger to flow freely in her body, and consciously tried to relax when she felt she was fighting or repressing it by tensing up. After a while, whenever she was triggered by Frank, rather than immediately shouting at him, she learned to internally thank her anger, then direct it at her husband's behavior rather than at Frank himself. She calmly but firmly asked her husband not to interrupt her and to stop explaining things unless she'd asked him for his opinion.

I'd be lying if I said their marriage radically improved or that Frank accepted her new way of being. He didn't. But he didn't completely shut down either. He dealt with his wife's anger more easily when she didn't swear at him, and he stopped interrupting her so often. Over time, they came to a truce. Celeste felt much more authentic and self-confident, and, as she started to focus less on her marriage as her primary source of happiness, her agitation and anxiety eventually passed completely.

UNDERSTANDING YOUR ANGER

This practice follows the basic principles taught in Internal Family Systems therapy, which are that we need to honor, validate, and understand emotions like anger and recognize how they're ultimately trying to help us stay safe or achieve a goal. Research shows that this therapeutic approach can decrease depression and self-criticism. I know from my personal experience that IFS works, and it's one of the best systems I've found to integrate disowned parts of ourselves. This is a writing exercise, so grab a pen or pencil.

Instructions

Think of a recent event that occurred in your personal life that made you angry at someone else. (Try not to focus on events in politics or the larger world stage for now, or on events where you felt anger at yourself.) If you choose something that makes you very angry, it could become overwhelming and it will be difficult to learn the practice, but if it's trivial, it won't challenge you. Please focus on something that is in between these extremes. What was the situation? (For example, your partner hid something from you, your daughter used a disrespectful tone of voice, an employee blew off an important work task, etc.)

- How did your anger express itself? (For example, did you yell, use a cold tone or sharp words, say nothing but simmered inside?)

- What was the result of your anger? Did anything destructive occur? Did anything constructive come out of it?

- How did you feel after getting angry? What were the impacts on you personally? (For example, did you feel empowered, ashamed, confused?)

- Can you be curious about what your anger may have been trying to do for you? Was it trying to point out a danger or protect you in some way, even if the end result of your anger wasn't beneficial? (For example, was it trying to prevent you from feeling hurt, or help you to stand up for the truth or draw clear boundaries?)

- Try writing some words of thanks to your anger for its efforts to help you. Even if the methods your anger used to express itself were not ideal or the consequences of your anger were not actually helpful, can you honor this energy inside of you that was trying to protect you? (For example, you could write something like "Thank you anger for standing up for me and trying to make sure that the truth was revealed. I recognize how much you want to keep me safe . . .")

- Now that your anger has been thanked and appreciated, are there any words of wisdom your anger has for you? What are they?

- At the end of this exercise, check in with yourself, and if you feel at all overwhelmed, you can use the Soles of the Feet practice on page 30 to ground yourself. If any feelings of judgment or shame arise around feeling angry (or maybe you found it hard to even contact your anger) try using some tender self-compassion to be kind and accepting toward yourself. Can you allow yourself to be just as you are in this moment?

THE CARING FORCE OF ANGER

Fierce self-compassion sometimes expresses itself as anger. The Hindu goddess Kali is a wonderful symbol of women's fierceness, and we can turn to her for inspiration. She's often depicted as blue or black, with her tongue sticking out, wearing a necklace of skulls and standing on a helpless, flailing man (her husband, Shiva). She's naked, her full breasts proudly exposed. Her multiple arms are usually holding a sword and a severed head. Kali represents destruction but is also considered to be the mother of the universe, the ultimate creator. What Kali destroys is illusion, especially the illusion of separation. Her ferocity is an instrument of love and justice. It sweeps away structures that separate and oppress, making space for equality and freedom.

As women, we have access to the power of Kali. This isn't a scientific fact, just something most women intuitively know. We need to stop being so afraid of her, or of other people's reactions to her. Instead, we need to honor our inner Kali, not judge or disown her. The more we repress this energy the more it will burst out in unhealthy ways, harming ourselves and others. But when encouraged to take shape as constructive rather than destructive anger, Kali's power can be utilized for good.

Kali is also wise (she's a goddess after all), and her ability to destroy the illusion of separation means she is deeply compassionate. Compassion recognizes the interdependence of people, causes, and conditions. It understands that the reasons we engage in harmful behaviors often stem from conditions beyond our control: genes, family history, social and cultural influences. This means we can have compassion for people who do wrong, understanding that they're part of the collective whole, while still being angry at their misdeeds. When we recognize interconnection, we see even more clearly that harming one person harms everyone, which is why we need to stand up to harm without adding to its effects by hating those who perpetrate it. Self-compassionate anger focuses on protection without becoming hostile to those who pose a threat.

The key to using anger compassionately is balancing yin and yang. When the force of yang isn't tempered by the gentleness of yin it becomes harsh and reactive. Our anger propels us into action without caring about the person we're angry at, leading to destructive behavior.

When we can be with ourselves and others with acceptance, keeping our hearts open, then anger can remain focused on the alleviation of suffering. The poet David Whyte writes in his book *Consolations:* "Anger is the deepest form of compassion, for another, for the world, for the self, for a life, for the body, for a family and for all our ideals, all vulnerable and all, possibly, about to be hurt. Stripped of physical imprisonment and violent reaction, anger is the purest form of care, the internal living flame of anger always illuminates what we belong to, what we wish to protect and what we are willing to hazard ourselves for."

The Chinese word for anger is *shēngqì* 生气. The direct, literal translation is "to generate qi." *Qi* is the Chinese word for "energy," and anger is a yang form of qi. As mentioned, Chinese medicine posits that when the yin and yang aspects of qi are in harmony with each other, there's health, well-being, and contentment. When yin and yang are in disharmony, there's illness, pain, and suffering. As long as the yang expression of anger is balanced with yin concern, it can be a healthy and constructive force. It's only when the fierce energy of anger isn't integrated with the tender energy of care that our anger becomes harmful and destructive. Our force needs to be caring to be sustainable and effective.

Anger without love is hate, but love without anger is hollow and sugarcoated. When love meets injustice, it's angry. As Zen Roshi Bernie Glassman writes, "Anger is considered a poison when it's self-motivated and self-centered. But take that attachment to the self out of anger and the same emotion becomes the fierce energy of determination, which is a very positive force." We're both tender goddesses and fierce warriors. One without the other is incomplete.

MY JOURNEY WITH ANGER

Before I started a regular practice of fierce self-compassion, I tended to swing between being kind to or angry at others and found integration difficult. I still find it challenging, to be perfectly honest. Especially in my work life—where I run on a lot of yang energy—I tend to be more

Bulldog than Momma Bear. This means my force isn't always caring. I'm not insulting or aggressive toward others, but I tell the truth as I see it without always considering the consequences of my words. I tend to be blunt and don't care if people like me or not, a dangerous combination. When someone makes an argument that doesn't make sense, overlooks an obvious fact, or conducts a study with major flaws, I become irritated. I've actually come to refer to this part of me as my "irritometer." When I'm bothered it means that something isn't working correctly, and my irritometer provides useful information. When Bulldog is running the show, however, and I forget to be mindful and compassionate in the moment, the results aren't so good. In such moments it feels like I don't have time to be nice; there are books to write and studies to run and workshops to conduct. The problem, of course, is that I don't pay enough attention to the impact of my reactions on other people.

For instance, a colleague recently sent me a paper on a self-compassion study he'd been working on for a few years. He'd just written it up and wanted my input before sending it off for peer review. I emailed him with the blunt words "Your methodology is hopelessly confounded," and pointed out all the problems in his research with no mention of the positive aspects of his paper. I know how to give constructive feedback, but when my irritometer is in the red zone and Bulldog shows up, all that knowledge tends to go out the window. My bluntness can be mean. Shortly afterward I realized what I'd done and sent a second email suggesting ways he might try to improve his analyses and commented on the study's positive features. He wrote back, "Oh, I see, you're trying to *help* me. I was shocked by your first email, I must admit." I apologized and asked for forgiveness.

People who get a full blast of my fierceness and don't know me well are often taken aback and unsure how to react, partly because much of the time I'm warm and kind. Also, because people expect fierocity to lead to physical or emotional violence, they tend to shrink in fear even when I'm not being threatening. Just being in the presence of this intense energy frightens people. In the past when this happened, I would realize that I was out of line and apologize, but also feel ashamed. I struggled with the issue for a long time; it was frustrating that after all those years of self-compassion practice I could still be so reactive. Although I tried to accept Bulldog and forgive myself for my imperfections, I tended to see this part of me as a weakness rather than a strength.

Fortunately, things started to change after making fierce self-compassion an explicit practice. I realized that Bulldog was really misdirected Kali. She was trying to cut through illusion and protect the truth as she saw it. The fierce energy that would sometimes propel me to blast others was actually the same energy that allowed me to be a good scientist and to succeed in the combative realm of academia. For example, there have been heated debates over the adequacy of the SCS as a measure of self-compassion (I refer to these as the "scale wars"), and my willingness to engage has spurred me to collect a ton of solid empirical data to validate the scale. After one scholar dismissed the data as a "scientific smokescreen" and used ad hominem attacks to make his arguments, I was so incensed that I wrote a comprehensive response in just three days that laid out how the empirical evidence confirmed my position and disconfirmed his in a novel and (to my mind) highly convincing manner. I was motivated! My anger has served a constructive purpose, helping me to sharpen my thinking and raise the quality of my contributions to the field.

I realize that my inner warrior is a part of me that I need to celebrate rather than judge or control. It's a powerful engine that provides focus in ways that are highly productive. But ferocity isn't useful unless it's balanced with tenderness. To symbolize my quest for integration, I bought a Japanese scroll with a picture of the Divine Feminine depicted as a pregnant mother with the earth as her belly and hung it on my bedroom wall. On the opposite wall right above my meditation cushion I hung a picture of Kali in all her destructive splendor. Now, when I'm angry, I sit underneath Kali and allow the energy of her anger to flow freely within my body. I thank her for giving me strength and courage and ask to harness her power to do the work needed in the world. I also thank the Mother for giving me a tender heart and ask her to fill me with peace and love so that my actions do no harm. Last, I imagine these two energies merging and integrating within my body, mind, and spirit, so that I am balanced and whole.

WORKING WITH ANGER

To work with anger skillfully, we need to fully own it. We must allow our fierce energy to flow, knowing it's there to protect us. We also need to be in touch with feelings of tender concern aimed both inward and outward so that our anger doesn't become destructive. Eventually we also need to be able to extend forgiveness to those who are hurting us—even if that person is ourself—but forgiveness is a later step and takes some time. (Practices designed to develop forgiveness for oneself and others can be found in *The Mindful Self-Compassion Workbook*.) The purpose of this exercise is to practice working with the fierce energy of anger itself and to integrate it with tenderness.

As you do this practice, please don't choose an anger-provoking situation that was very traumatizing or that might overwhelm you, unless you're doing it with the guidance of a therapist or mental health professional. You may want to start with something smaller, like an acquaintance who was rude to you, or a friend who acted irresponsibly, or a salesperson who was deceptive. Make sure that if you ever feel unsafe, you disengage from the exercise. You can always come back to it later if you'd like.

Instructions

- Think of a situation that is making you angry—it could be past or present. Please choose wisely, something that feels safe to work with right now.

- Review the details as vividly as possible, calling the situation to mind. What happened? Were your boundaries violated? Were you not given respect or due consideration? Did an injustice occur?

- Let the feelings of anger arise.

- Put both hands on your solar plexus or some other supportive place to help hold yourself steady as you feel your anger.

- Also feel your feet touching the floor. Ground yourself to the earth through the soles of your feet.

- Now see if you can let go of the story line of who or what is causing the anger and feel your anger as a physical sensation in your body. Where is it located? What are the sensations? Hot, cold, pulsating, throbbing, numb?

Owning Your Fierceness

- Know that it's completely natural for you to feel as you do. This is your fierce Momma Bear protecting you. It's a form of self-compassion. Perhaps say to yourself, "It's okay to feel angry! This is the natural desire to protect myself."

- *Fully validate* the experience of being angry, while trying not to get too caught up in what happened: stay with the anger itself.

- If at any time you get swept away by the anger, focus on the soles of your feet until you regain focus, and come back to feeling your anger as a physical sensation.

- See if you can allow the fierce energy to flow freely in your body. There is no need to stifle it, to contain it, to judge it. This too is an important aspect of the compassionate heart.

- While staying grounded through the soles of your feet and feeling the support of your hands, try to open to your anger (as much as feels safe). Perhaps you can even feel it flowing up and down your spine, giving you strength and determination. Maybe your anger wants to say something, has a message it wants to express. From a place of stability and centeredness, what does your anger have to say?

- Can you listen to this part of yourself and thank it for its efforts to protect you?

Bringing in Some Tenderness

- Continue to let the fierce energy of protection flow, while grounded to the earth through the soles of your feet.

- If you feel it's most helpful to simply stay with your anger, give yourself permission to do so.

- But if you would like to also bring in some tenderness, put one hand on your solar plexus and place the other on your heart or some other soothing place. Feel the space between your two hands.

- Stay in contact with the strength and determination of the fierceness that is arising to protect you, and from this place of strength, turn toward your heart.

- Recognize that your anger is an expression of love: a desire to keep yourself safe.

- See if you can also contact some of the more tender feelings of care and concern for yourself that are present, that are driving your desire to protect yourself.

- If any shame or judgment arises about your anger, can you hold that tenderly too?

- Invite loving, connected presence to merge and integrate with the anger.

- Allow yourself to be fierce and tender at the same time. Let the energies do whatever dance they need to do in this moment.

- Try to savor and embrace this feeling of wholeness.

- Feel your desire to alleviate suffering. From this place of compassion, is there any action you would like to take in order to address what occurred, even if it's just resolving to protect yourself in the future?

- When you are ready, let go of the exercise, and simply rest in your experience, letting this moment be exactly as it is, and yourself exactly as you are.

This practice can be pretty intense, so make sure you take care of yourself after completing it by taking a walk, having a cup of tea, or doing whatever feels calming.

After intentionally working with my own anger for some time, things are starting to get easier. I still get irritated and can be reactive, but the intensity and frequency has lessened (at least a little bit). I've made a commitment to try to consider the consequences of my anger on others, and to do as little harm as possible. I remind myself of this commitment throughout the day, so that it can support me in those moments when I'm triggered and am less likely to see clearly. Although the path toward integration is a long one and I'm still taking baby steps, I'm convinced it's the only way forward—not only for me, but also for women as a whole. We're at an important crossroads in history. After clearly recognizing and calling out the multiple ways that women, racial minorities, and so many other people are oppressed, exploited, and abused, we *have* to get angry. If we aren't angry, we're asleep. But what are we going to do with that anger? Hate White men with power, shout them down or become bitter, alienating those who might be potential allies? Are we going to turn away from our well-honed resources of kindness, nurturing, and love just because our communal roles have been used to suppress us?

As women, we can do things differently. We can be grateful for our anger, for the drive and determination it gives us, learning to own it fully as part of our true nature. We can become more comfortable in its presence, so that we're less frightened by it. Most of all, we can combine our anger with love so that this caring force can be used effectively to combat injustice. In our quest for the alleviation of suffering, fierce self-compassion is a potent resouce we can rely draw upon to help ourselves and all beings.

CHAPTER 4

#METOO

There is inherent strength in agency.
#MeToo, in a lot of ways, is about agency.

—*Tarana Burke, founder of the Me Too movement*

In October 2017, the high-profile director Harvey Weinstein was outed for sexually harassing and abusing dozens of women. In response, the actress Alyssa Milano tweeted a call for any women who'd been sexually harassed or assaulted to reply with the hashtag #MeToo. Within days almost half of all Facebook users had a friend who'd responded. In the short time since, hundreds of men in positions of power have been exposed for sexually harassing or abusing women. From politicians like Roy Moore, to actors like Louis C.K., to musicians like Ryan Adams, to news anchors like Charlie Rose, to CEOs like Les Moonves, to billionaires like Jeffrey Epstein, to self-help gurus like Tony Robbins. The list keeps growing every day. Many of these well-known men have faced consequences for their actions, although many—most notably Donald Trump—haven't yet. Of course, the sexual mistreatment of women has always been pervasive in society. The pre-Twitter Me Too movement was started by Tarana Burke in 2006 to call out the widespread sexual abuse of Black women. The main difference now is that we're talking about it more publicly. In many ways, the movement represents the collective uprising of women's fierce self-compassion as we say, "No more!"

A 2018 large-scale study called "The Facts behind the #MeToo Movement" attempted to quantify the scope of sexual harassment and abuse occurring in the United States. The results are sobering. The vast majority of women (81 percent) have reported experiencing inappropriate behavior in public or the workplace. The most common form of mistreatment women endure is degrading verbal comments (77 percent), but many have experienced unwanted touching (51 percent), cyber harassment such as being sent naked pictures (41 percent), being stalked or followed aggressively (34 percent), or genital flashing (30 percent).

Furthermore, one in three women has been subjected to harassment at work, causing stress and creating a hostile environment that undermines a woman's ability to do her job. And though one might think unwanted behavior is typically directed at working women in lower-level positions, research shows that those in leadership positions are at even greater risk. According to one study, 58 percent of female supervisors in male-dominated work environments report being harassed. Ironically, the power of these women threatens men's identities, so insecure men act out to humiliate and degrade them. After all, sexual harassment isn't about sex, it's about power.

In response, organizations like Time's Up have emerged to help women confront sexual mistreatment at work. Started by artists, producers, and executives in the entertainment industry, the movement spread like wildfire and soon expanded to include all fields, from farmworkers to academics. Additionally, the Time's Up Legal Defense Fund provides legal assistance to any woman who has experienced workplace sexual misconduct including assault, harassment, abuse, and related retaliation.

But this scourge extends well beyond the workplace. Over a quarter of women report having experienced coerced sexual contact at some point in their lives. Among those in marginalized communities such as lesbians/bisexuals, poor women, and those with intellectual disabilities, the number reporting assault is even higher. Approximately one out of five women has been raped (nonconsensual intercourse) or has experienced an attempted rape in her lifetime. Almost half of these are children under the age of seventeen. In four out of five cases, the victim knew the perpetrator, who could be a friend, family member, or romantic partner. And most rapes aren't reported to the police, especially those perpetrated by a non-stranger, due to shame or fear of being held partly to blame. Of those rapes reported, moreover, only a tiny fraction result in a conviction. This is the reality women live with.

YOUR PERSONAL EXPERIENCES OF SEXUAL HARASSMENT

This exercise is designed to help you identify incidences of sexual harassment. Sometimes events will be blatantly obvious, and other times more subtle. When we call attention to the particular ways in which we've been mistreated, we can become more aware of what's happening and therefore better able to protect ourselves.

If you've been sexually traumatized in the past, you may want to skip this exercise or complete it with the guidance of a therapist or counselor. Also, if you currently are experiencing or have recently experienced an incident of sexual harassment in the workplace, document and report the incident to a superior as soon as possible, making sure that you choose a superior who's likely to listen to you without retaliation. If no action is taken, you can get help from the US Equal Employment Opportunity Commission: https://www.eeoc.gov/harassment.

Here are some common types of sexual harassment (taken from RAINN.org):

- Verbal harassment of a sexual nature, including jokes referring to sexual acts or sexual orientation

- Unwanted touching or physical contact

- Unwelcome sexual advances

- Discussing sexual relations/stories/fantasies at work, school, or in other inappropriate places

- Unwanted sexually explicit photos, emails, or text messages

Instructions

- Think through your history at school, at home, or at work. Write down any incidents of sexual harassment you can remember.

- Now write down how you felt after the incident occurred. Angry? Confused? Offended? Frightened? Annoyed?

- What did you do, if anything, after the behavior occurred?

- Often when situations like this occur we're taken off guard and don't know how to react. Or sometimes we can't react as we would like to out of fear of retaliation.

- Now that you aren't in danger, write down how you would have ideally liked to have responded to the incident.

Sometimes women just blow off these behaviors as not important or as bad jokes, especially if the harassment wasn't highly egregious. It's important that we call attention to all behaviors that make us uncomfortable, so that we can start to speak up and let others know these acts are not acceptable. If one incident stands out in your mind as particularly troubling, you may want to write a compassionate letter to yourself about what happened (see the exercise on page 106).

THE SCARS LEFT BEHIND

What are the consequences of sexual mistreatment for women? Research shows it results in chronic stress, anxiety, depression, and difficulties with trust. In the workplace, it can lead to decreased job satisfaction, less commitment to the organization, lower levels of work engagement, and worsened mental and physical health. The consequences of sexual assault are even worse: PTSD, insomnia, disordered eating, substance use and abuse—even suicide. The #MeToo movement offers a chance for women to turn the tide, so we can finally start to reckon with the truth and heal.

Although men can also be victims of sexual harassment and assault, especially gay, bisexual, or transsexual men, the vast majority of victims are women. And the overwhelming majority of perpetrators are men. Some men feel entitled to use women for their sexual gratification because society and the media have given the message it's okay to do so. Women are often viewed as sexual objects—arm candy at a party, the seductive love interest in an action film, an advertising ornament that renders a product more enticing. Our worth is constantly evaluated relative to our ability to satisfy a man's sexual desire. Gender socialization cuts certain men off from the yin energy of care and compassion so deeply that they begin to dehumanize women as objects to be used. Hypermasculinity—defined as a macho attitude that glamorizes aggression and belittles tender emotions as weak and feminine—feeds directly into sexual harassment and abuse. A meta-analysis of thirty-nine studies found hypermasculinity to be one of the most powerful predictors of men's likelihood to commit sexual assault.

Although this points to the urgent need for greater integration of yin and yang among men, I'm primarily interested here in talking about the implications of integration for women. One of the reasons I'm so passionate about fierce self-compassion for women is because I believe its caring force can help us fight against this vile legacy of patriarchy. As women acknowledge, strengthen, and integrate fierce self-compassion more deeply into our way of being, it will empower us to rise up against sexual mistreatment and say, "No more!"

A CON MAN FROM TEXAS

The experience of having someone dear to me reveal she'd been the victim of sexual abuse was the primary inspiration for this book. The

revelation hit me particularly hard because the perpetrator was someone I'd trusted and supported for years. In those days, I would've even
said he was a close friend. And despite all my years of mindfulness
practice, the desire to see only the best in him blinded me to the horrible truth: he was a predator. Trying to cope with this situation made it
clear how desperately we need both fierce and tender self-compassion
to deal with the horror of sexual abuse. We need tenderness to hold
the hurt and shame that inevitably arises and fierceness to speak out
so that the harm won't continue. To protect the innocent, I've changed
the names and identifying details of the various people involved in my
tale.

George was a charming, handsome Southern gentleman in his
late forties with a musical drawl. He ran a nonprofit organization on
the outskirts of Austin that provided services for autistic children and
their families. The center was only a thirty-minute drive from Elgin,
where I lived, so I took Rowan there often when he was young. Rowan
responded well to the art, music, and play that was part of George's
nontraditional approach to working with kids on the spectrum. At the
time, I thought George was brilliant and inspiring, and we developed
a close connection. I was delighted to promote the organization: I held
self-compassion events as fundraisers for the center and was an annual
donor.

George staffed the center with a combination of volunteers and paid
employees—an altruistic group of bright-eyed, adventurous (and mainly
female) teens and young adults from the United States and abroad.
They were eager and committed to helping autistic children and their
families, wanting to make a difference in the world. Many of the staff
members lived at the center, which was a small compound with several buildings. Everyone worshipped George. He was the charismatic
figure running the show: a funny, intelligent, intense maverick who
defied conventional wisdom with his approach to autism.

Admittedly, George was also a bit of a lech. Sometimes he made
inappropriate comments about a woman's looks, and he was always
complaining of sore shoulders and asking for back rubs. "That's just

George," we'd say. "He's a big flirt, but a great guy who does so much for the kids." George was married to a pretty woman from Ireland almost twenty years his junior named Eileen, who helped run the center. They had two young children, both girls. I wasn't particularly friendly with Eileen, who seemed primarily focused on running the nonprofit and keeping it afloat. I suspected George was having affairs, but I told myself his honesty wasn't my concern. I assumed everything occurred outside the workplace and was among consenting adults.

Cassie, one of those bright-eyed teens at the center, was the daughter of a family friend who was a single mother working two jobs. Cassie had been helping me with Rowan for several years, and I really liked her—she was vibrant, playful, smart, and a pleasure to be around. She was great with Rowan, and given that I didn't have a daughter of my own, I got particularly attached to her. Cassie discovered that she liked working with autistic children and started volunteering at George's center when she was just fourteen. I sometimes gave her a ride and encouraged her new interest. I did worry a bit about George's flirtatiousness, but it was such an exciting atmosphere and Cassie was so happy there. I assumed George drew boundaries and would never hit on women who worked for him, especially the youngest ones. He had daughters of his own for God's sake.

Soon, Cassie started spending all her weekends at the center, growing closer to George and his staff, sometimes babysitting his children. This went on for a couple of years. George said he thought Cassie had natural talent and paid her a lot of attention. She was eventually employed by the center and became one of his protégés, learning his therapeutic method in hopes of a career working in autism. Sometimes George and Cassie would go on errands alone for hours at a time. A small voice in my head said, "Hmm, that's a bit strange," but then another voice would step in to say, "I'm sure it's fine. He's just giving her extra attention because he's such a good guy. It's good for her to have an older male presence in her life since her father isn't in the picture."

Nonetheless, because we were close, I checked in with Cassie from time to time just to make sure. "Has George ever been inappropriate with you?" I'd ask. And she'd say, "No, of course not! He's like a father to me and three times my age." She'd say it so quickly and dismissively that I felt guilty for being suspicious. After a while, I noticed that Cassie seemed changed; she'd become a bit withdrawn, but I assumed it was just adolescent moodiness.

At a party held in honor of George's birthday, he got drunk and began dancing with a young woman in an overtly sexual way. It was wildly inappropriate for many reasons, not the least because his wife and two young daughters were sitting just a few yards away. Eileen had her back to the dance floor, positioned in a way that shielded the two little ones from the display. I wasn't sure if she'd seen or not—she was just looking down and focusing on her children. I was very uncomfortable and left the party early.

Cassie had also attended, and the next day we talked about George's behavior. She agreed that he seemed out of control. I asked her again, this time more forcefully, if George had ever behaved inappropriately with her. "Well . . ." she wavered. And then it all came out. She told me that he'd begun to hit on her about two years after she started volunteering for the center.

At first, he primarily talked to her about sex. She felt uncomfortable but also flattered that he would discuss such grown-up topics with her. Then he exposed himself and masturbated in front of her. Afterward they started being physical, first just touching, but eventually more. She felt extremely confused and conflicted about the relationship, but he was the only fatherly source of love in her life and she didn't want to lose it. He took her virginity on her eighteenth birthday. "He stopped paying me as much attention after that. I guess it was all he wanted. I thought he cared about me, but it doesn't seem like it now. I feel so stupid."

As she told me her story, the fury of Kali took hold. His predatory behavior shook me to the core. I was enraged. But because I cared so much for Cassie, this fury was tempered by an intense feeling of tender concern. I felt the desire to protect her, a clear and purposeful force bent on preventing any further harm.

"You have nothing to be ashamed of," I reassured her. "He manipulated and took advantage of you."

"I guess so," she said uncertainly. "Whatever you do, please don't tell Mom, she'll be devastated."

I promised her I would let her make that choice for herself and tried to gently steer Cassie to the idea that she might want to tell some of the staff what had happened, to keep him from preying on others. But she was paralyzed by her desire to not cause trouble. She didn't want to harm George's family or damage the reputation of the center. It's so typical of females—even one as young as Cassie—to be conditioned to think first of not harming others, even to the point of letting themselves be harmed. The thing that struck me the most, however, was that she didn't seem angry, just strangely passive. It was hard to see the sparkling young girl I'd met years ago. The light in her eyes had gone, like no one was home.

We continued to talk, and as I listened—not saying much but primarily giving her support and unconditional acceptance—her deep disgust at having been involved with George started surfacing. She felt dirty and used, she told me, and guilty for letting it go on for so long. Her self-recrimination was terrible to watch. I tried to help her embrace the ugly feelings with compassion, the way she embraced the young autistic children she was committed to helping. George had been a father figure to her—*of course* she wanted his love, it was only human. The fact that she was his protégé and didn't want to jeopardize her job or career prospects also played a big role. The situation wasn't her fault. Once she could hold herself with some loving, connected presence, she started to soften.

I knew that for Cassie (as for many people) tender self-compassion was a necessary precondition for her self-love to take the form of anger. Over time she began to realize that while her behavior was understandable, his was wrong. He knew she was emotionally vulnerable, and he took advantage of her—not to mention he was her boss. The imbalance of power was so great she couldn't actually consent. At last, her own fierceness began to emerge. She started to acknowledge that she'd been abused. She shouldn't have been exploited in this way. It was not okay! Her back grew taller as she owned her anger. I could see the spark come back to her eyes as the yang energy started to flow in her veins. She was alive again, and she was pissed as hell. Then she got a pained but determined look on her face. "You're right," she said. "I'm probably not the only one. I bet he's been preying on other girls at the center! We have to stop him!"

We hatched a makeshift plan. I would first gather information to see if our suspicions were true and then we would figure out what to do. After a few phone calls to former volunteers and ex-employees, the truth turned out to be even worse than I feared. A number of women working closely with George had been sexually harassed, exploited, degraded, or worse. And it wasn't just the young ones. There was a sixty-year-old Peruvian nanny who'd left suddenly, and someone told me why: he'd forcibly groped her. Thank goodness she worked for an agency that found her another job—and blacklisted George.

Whenever someone at the center left abruptly, George usually made up some cover story portraying himself as a victim. This one stole money, that one lied, this one was incompetent. But my investigations revealed that many had left because they were sexually mistreated. One ex-volunteer admitted George had forced himself on her. She had told him no three times, but he didn't stop. Because the force he used to coerce her was psychological rather than physical, however, she felt ashamed and confused and doubted herself. She ended up having a consensual relationship with George afterward to try to make things seem okay in her troubled mind. This pattern is a common one: the reality of being violated is so awful that we do psychological backflips to make it feel acceptable.

George got wind of the fact that I was asking questions and started to tell everyone involved with the center that I'd gone crazy and was having some sort of mental breakdown. He warned people to stay away from me. Most of the volunteers and staff who were currently working for George believed him. He was incredibly persuasive and, as they say in Texas, slicker than a boiled onion.

George was brilliant at throwing up smoke to cover his tracks. The way he had managed to keep his sexual misconduct from being exposed for all those years was by confusing and disorienting his victims. He would manipulate people so they felt insecure ("Everyone has been complaining about you," he told one) or bully them ("You'll never work in the autism world again," he said to another); he made them feel needed ("The center would fall apart without you") and special ("You're the only one who understands me," he told more than one). He used these mind games to leverage their silence.

It was then that I realized that George was probably a malignant narcissist. Unlike grandiose narcissists who constantly brag and feel superior to others, malignant narcissists are people who use others in a self-centered way without remorse, lying and manipulating to get what they want. They use sex as a source of power, taking advantage of deeply rooted and unconscious feelings of unworthiness and insufficiency in the people they target. They feed on others like a vampire, using them to fill an inner void, often putting them down or manipulating them to buttress a sense of importance and to assert control. They also tend to pick victims who are kind, caring, and trusting, exploiting these noble qualities to their advantage. I realized that my close friend, a man I'd supported for years, was a better-looking Harvey Weinstein. The maverick I thought was the Wizard of Oz was really just a con man from Texas.

I was stunned that I hadn't seen what was happening. How did I allow myself to be fooled? How could I have put Cassie in such a dangerous situation? Not only that, I'd helped fund the center and gave it credibility with my university affiliation and reputation as a scientist. Unknowingly, I helped perpetuate the whole disaster! Now I had to do for myself what I had done for Cassie. First, I gave myself unconditional love and support. I tried to hold my own pain and shame with tender care and accept that I'd gotten it wrong. I had turned away from a monstrous truth because some part of me couldn't acknowledge it and made the easier choice. And that was very human.

Then I embraced my anger, which was like a volcano erupting. I had fantasies of telling George off, but decided not to confront him directly because I realized he was sick and it would be counterproductive. I also wanted to protect myself from what would surely be a traumatic encounter. Instead, I took action.

My house has an amazing gigantic ancient oak tree that has the spirit of a wise grandmother. I would habitually sit under her branches and ask for healing, for love, for self-forgiveness. This time when I sat with her, I asked for access to the full force of my rage. I allowed the fierce energy of the anger to flow freely within my body. I made a commitment that I wouldn't take the easy route and just move on. I would do whatever it took to stop the harm.

Cassie wanted to tell George's wife, Eileen, what had happened. She felt Eileen deserved to know the full extent of his predatory behavior, so that she could protect herself and her children. Cassie wrote Eileen a heartbreaking letter, apologizing for hurting her and telling her everything. She asked me to give it to her, an idea I felt extremely uncomfortable with, especially since Eileen and I weren't close. But since Eileen was cohead of the center, I worried that she was legally liable if anyone brought a lawsuit against George. I also felt it was my duty to inform her, woman to woman, so she could make informed choices. I thought it best to wait until George was out of town so that she could learn the truth while free from his immediate influence.

Along with Cassie's letter I printed out several statements written by other women who'd given me permission to share them. Since I knew George had probably convinced her that I was crazy, I wanted to give her tangible evidence of his behavior. Eileen's reaction was not at all what I expected. She was defensive. She didn't open the letters, and instead got angry at me. She even accused me of trying to blackmail them. I guess that was her way of coping. It was easier to see me as the villain instead of the man she loved.

Cassie finally found the courage to tell her mom what had happened, and I got an email from her mother asking to meet me for tea to discuss the situation. Her reaction was also not what I'd expected. I thought she would be enraged, but she wasn't. Instead, she was mainly worried. I told her that because the sexual behavior started before Cassie was seventeen (the age of consent in Texas), a case could be brought. But Cassie's mother didn't want to press charges; she was afraid of dragging her daughter into a public court battle. She also feared possible repercussions from George, who she now felt was dangerous. This is a common reason people don't report sexual abuse—the fear of making things worse. And given that the vast majority of perpetrators don't get convicted, it's a well-founded fear.

One of the current center staff members who was told I'd gone crazy sent me a text. "I heard you have written statements," she said. "Would you show them to me?" I agreed to meet her, and she read the statements for herself. She was horrified and told the other women on staff who lived at the center. They all decided to quit on the same day. They gathered their things and quietly slipped out before dawn one morning so that they didn't have to confront George, who they were now afraid of.

A few of the girls asked to stay with me for a couple days while they figured out their next steps. We had long, outraged conversations about what had happened. Each one admitted that they too had been having a sexual relationship with George. All were dismayed to find out that what they thought was a special and unique (though hidden) relationship wasn't unique at all. They realized that George was sleeping with almost any girl or woman who would have him and that they were part of what amounted to a harem. Or, perhaps more accurately, a cult, complete with a charismatic and unaccountable leader. Once again, they needed tender self-compassion to hold the shock and the grief of the truth, and fierce self-compassion to take action. They warned those who needed to know about what was happening, and news eventually started to spread through the autism world. George's charisma couldn't keep him afloat anymore. He closed down the center and moved his family out of state.

Eileen didn't leave George, probably because of her young children, or maybe because the emotional abuse had shattered her spirit. I don't know her well enough to say for sure, but it's very common for women to stay with partners who mistreat them. To this day George hasn't apologized to any of the people he harmed, and he blames Cassie and me for ruining his life.

As I talked with various women who felt victimized by George, we tried to figure out how things could have gone on for so long. Yes, it was difficult to see what was happening because of his skillful gaslighting—the lies and manipulation that narcissists use to keep people off balance. But there were clear signs that we should have paid attention to and didn't. I remembered when George took Cassie out to dinner for her birthday. It made me uncomfortable, but I ignored my doubts and assumed the best. I thought he wouldn't dare make a move on a teenage girl who was like a daughter to him. To be completely honest, I didn't think about it too much because it was easier not to. To take my suspicions seriously would've meant confronting something I didn't want to see. And it turned out that was the night he took her virginity.

After the center closed, the people I talked to about it were shocked, and yet few were surprised. The news made sense of telltale behaviors that many had noticed for years, even though some mental block had kept all of us from putting two and two together. One block appears to be the desire to see the best in others. Sure, everyone knew George's flirtatiousness was inappropriate and a bit gross, but he did so much good for the kids! Whenever we get information that doesn't fit with our schemas for how things are in the world—when we experience cognitive dissonance—we override reality so that things make more sense and fit into the world we want to see. There's an inability to believe that someone we think is good could be acting in a way that's bad—so we stuff down our doubts and confusion in order to carry on undisturbed. But as women we can't turn away any longer. We need to open our eyes to harmful behavior so that we can protect ourselves and each other.

A surprising number of women I've conversed with report similar experiences with ex-boyfriends, ex-husbands, ex-colleagues, or ex-bosses. The crazy thing is how little we talk about it. As I said, the behavior spurring the #MeToo movement isn't new. The only thing new is the fact that we're finally starting to discuss it openly. We need to look clearly at the ways we unwittingly enable predatory behavior with our silence, so that we recognize both the behavior and anything preventing us from sharing the information needed to stop it. Although the responsibility for this type of sexual abuse rests squarely on the perpetrators, we can't wait around for men to wake up and stop misbehaving of their own accord. As women we must act to protect ourselves now.

HOW TO STOP PREDATORY BEHAVIOR

How can we use fierce self-compassion to prevent sexual mistreatment from happening? It's hard to speak up if your abuser is your boss and you fear being fired. This is why we need to pass laws criminalizing sexual harassment and abuse everywhere. Believe it or not, in many states, like Texas, there are no laws against sexual harassment in businesses with fewer than fifteen employees, which is why the paid staff at George's autism center didn't take legal action in the end, even though they would have been willing to. This lack of legal protection for women needs to be rectified.

We can also call upon our inner Kali energy the moment mistreatment starts and say firmly and unmistakably, "No! That's not okay!" This type of fierceness has the potential to stop the predator in his tracks, since they prefer easy targets. I found out that some of the girls who worked at the center had rebuffed George's advances and that he left them alone afterward. I can't say for sure why he continued to pursue some and not others, but I noticed the girls he gave up on had a lot of yang energy. I suspect George felt it would be too much work to keep after them and set his sights elsewhere. Of course, saying no isn't always possible depending on many intersecting factors: power, privilege, financial circumstances, intoxicants, etc. Also, it's not a woman's responsibility to stop predators, the responsibility lies one hundred percent with perpetrators. Still, our inner fierceness can help to protect ourselves, and we mustn't be afraid to draw on it when needed.

When I talked to the staff who were able to successfully rebuff George, they all regretted staying silent about his advances. Although they gave subtle warnings to others working at the center (e.g., if he asks you for a shoulder rub when other people aren't around, be careful), no one outed George publicly. It was partly because they didn't realize the extent of George's depravity, but also because they just blew off George as a womanizer and didn't take his behavior seriously enough. Unfortunately, our long history of patriarchy often leads women to dismiss abusive behavior. "That's just the way George, Harvey, Charlie, Jeffrey, Donald (fill in the blank) are," we say, as if it's a given that men are predatory and we have no choice but to put up with it.

Women have fought long and hard for the freedom to be our authentic sexual selves. But sometimes we don't give enough thought to how power imbalances shape our ability to consent, or how harmful the actions of men who don't respect sexual boundaries really are. Hopefully with the #MeToo movement things are finally starting to change. I believe that women have come to a reckoning point in our history. Our silence enables predatory behavior. The only way things will improve is if we acknowledge what's happening, no matter how uncomfortable that makes us feel. Whether or not a woman chooses to speak up publicly is a personal decision and depends on many circumstances—whether it's safe, whether doing so causes more harm than good, and the various people involved. But we need to acknowledge the truth to ourselves at the very least, so we can try our best to protect ourselves, survive, and heal.

THE ROLE OF SELF-COMPASSION

Fortunately, studies show that self-compassion can facilitate recovery from sexual abuse. Much of the research on self-compassion for survivors has been done by conducting in-depth interviews to discover how self-compassion has helped women cope. One common theme in the testimony of survivors is that the experience of being abused filled them with shame and actually hindered their ability to be self-compassionate. As a participant in one study said, "You really can't give yourself love and nurturing if you have no sense of yourself. For me, sexual abuse, yes, it's hard, but it's actually all the embedded shame beliefs of not deserving. You think, 'I'm obviously a bad person or they wouldn't have done it.'" This is why women who've been abused benefit so much from self-compassion, because it helps undo the damage caused to their sense of self.

With time and professional help, women can realize abuse isn't their fault, and learn to develop compassion for their traumatic experiences. Research finds that self-compassion helps survivors work with difficult emotions like shame in a more productive manner, so that they're less overwhelmed by it. One study found the following themes when women discussed the role of self-compassion in recovering from abuse: it helped them affirm their self-worth; accept themselves as they were; absolve themselves of blame; honor their painful emotions; take time for self-care; connect with others who had similar experiences; appreciate the progress they had made; and, importantly, claim their power. As one woman named Dominique said, "I have realized that the sexual assault happened, but it doesn't define who I am. It's an empowerment of 'I'm fighting back. This isn't going to control me. This isn't going to control my life. I can have the power that was taken. I can have it back.'" These women also shared a commitment to stand up to gender inequality and to advocate for the rights of others.

Before getting to the point where we feel empowered after abuse, however, we need to give ourselves tender self-compassion. The first step is to hold the pain of our trauma in mindful awareness, so we can acknowledge and validate it without turning away. We need to be present with our suffering, as uncomfortable as it might be, just as we would stay with a crying child without abandoning her. I've heard from many women that they just wanted to forget and move on from their experience of abuse—but when our pain is forgotten rather than acknowledged, it inevitably prolongs the recovery process. It's important to clearly see and speak the truth of what happened, if even just to ourselves, or else to a therapist or friend. That being said, it's equally important that we don't retraumatize ourselves as we go about the work of healing. If the abuse came from a family member or a romantic partner, there will almost certainly be backdraft as we open up to the pain of what has transpired. We need to go at a pace that feels safe, and get professional help if possible. There's a saying we use in MSC—go slowly, walk farther. Patience with the speed of healing after abuse is one of the gifts self-compassion can offer.

It also helps to be as warm, understanding, and unconditionally accepting of ourselves as possible. If we feel broken, can we embrace our brokenness? We may feel tainted when we've suffered abuse (in the past we would've been called a "ruined" woman), but our souls are still pure and beautiful regardless of what has happened to us. When we fill our consciousness with loving, connected presence, our true self-worth is revealed.

Finally, we need to remember our common humanity. At least a quarter of the female population has been assaulted, and a large majority has been harassed. The reasons for this are not personal. We don't need to feel isolated or shamed by what has happened. We are not alone. We can feel connected to the millions of women around the globe and throughout history who've suffered as we have. Even if our trust has been shattered, we can form a new safety net by reaching out to other women who've had similar experiences. We can find strength in these bonds, joining in a shared commitment to end sexual abuse once and for all.

COMPASSIONATE LETTER WRITING

Compassionate letter writing is a practice taught in the Mindful Self-Compassion program. Research shows it's highly effective if done on a regular basis. If you've been a victim of sexual mistreatment, you can try writing a compassionate letter to yourself about the experience. It is safest to do this practice when considering an event that was disturbing (for example, having a man say something lewd to you) rather than traumatizing (such as rape). If you have suffered sexual abuse or assault, it could be too intense to do this practice on your own, and it may be better to complete it with the help of a therapist or other mental health professional. Also, everyone is different, and sometimes people are surprised by their reactions to an exercise, so if you start to feel overwhelmed, please give yourself permission to stop. That's also self-compassion.

If you have recently experienced sexual assault (coerced sexual contact), get help immediately. You can call 911, or else help can be obtained from RAINN (Rape, Abuse & Incest National Network), which is the nation's largest anti-sexual violence organization: www.rainn.org. They also provide a sexual assault hotline at 800-656-HOPE (4673) that can connect you with a trained staff member from a sexual assault service provider in your area.

Instructions

Think of a past situation of sexual harassment or mistreatment that feels right to work with right now. Something in the mild to moderate range. Make sure it is a *past* incident, one in which the event is over, you are now safe, and you would like to bring some healing to yourself. If thinking about this situation is too raw, please choose a less traumatic situation if possible. Decide what feels right for you.

- For the first step, just write about what happened. Include any details that feel relevant. If you start to feel very distressed, self-compassion might mean pausing to get a cup of tea, or feeling the soles of your feet touching the floor.

- After describing what happened, write a paragraph that brings mindful awareness to the pain caused by this experience. What emotions did you have at the time? What feelings do you have now? Can you describe how these feelings manifest as physical sensations (tightness in the throat, stabbing in the gut, hollowness in the chest, and so on)? Allow any emotions that arise to be just as they are, without judgment, no matter what. Shame, disgust, fear, anger, irritation, sadness, confusion, guilt, etc.—let them all surface in your awareness. Note how difficult it is to experience these feelings. Try to validate your pain—it's so natural to feel this way.

- Next, write a paragraph that remembers the common humanity of the experience. Sadly, situations like this occur every day. It's not just you. You are not alone. Most important, it's not your fault. The mistreatment of women stems from thousands of years of patriarchy and unequal power. But you can stand strong with your sisters knowing that we are no longer accepting this treatment. Feel the power of being part of something bigger than yourself.

- Now try writing a paragraph that expresses deep kindness toward yourself. Write some words of comfort and soothing for the pain and harm you've experienced. Make sure your words are tender and supportive, something you'd say to a close friend who had experienced something similar. If any feelings of shame or self-doubt arise, see if you can also hold those feelings in loving, connected presence. Can you be tender with yourself in the midst of your pain?

- Next, write a paragraph from your internal Kali or fierce Momma Bear. Let your words be strong, bold, and brave, as you commit to protecting yourself and your sisters. Clearly acknowledge the injustice of what was done to you. Allow the anger to rise up without resisting it. Let it flow through you, grounding yourself to the earth through the soles of your feet if you start to feel overwhelmed. Try not to get too lost in thinking about the perpetrator. Your brain cells have already used up enough glucose thinking about him and he doesn't need any more attention. Instead, aim the full force of your rage at the harm itself. This should not have happened!

- Finally, see if you can use your anger to energize you toward action. Is there anything you can do to prevent this from happening again to yourself or another woman? If so, can you commit to taking some small step in that direction?

- When you are finished with the letter, take a few deep breaths, and put the letter away somewhere safe. When it feels right, come back and read it, letting the words fully sink in. Some people like to actually mail the letter to themselves and read it when they receive it a few days later in the post.

If difficult feelings emerge during this exercise, please make sure you take care of yourself. Ask yourself what you need. A hug, a walk, talking with someone you trust, some quiet time alone? Try to give yourself whatever will be most helpful in the moment.

TAKING ACTION

Although it's important that we use self-compassion to help heal from sexual abuse, healing is not enough. It's also critical that we try to prevent harm to women in the future. A major cause of sexual mistreatment is societal: the structural inequality that gives men power over women. Banding together with other women helps to provide the courage needed to call out abusers. The #MeToo movement has shown that powerful men can be found guilty and brought to justice. If we stick together, we can start to dismantle the system that allows this outrageous behavior to occur.

But what's the best way to speak up about abuse, especially if we're in danger of repercussions? Some companies have ways to anonymously report predatory behavior, but most don't. Also, this behavior commonly occurs outside of the work context. In fact, sexual abuse often occurs within the family. What then? Unfortunately, I don't have the answer to these questions, and there are experts who know much more than I do about the topic (organizations such as RAINN have hotlines and can offer immediate advice). But I do know that the answer needs to be guided by the principles of self-compassion, and that we need to act with brave, empowered clarity to protect ourselves. If we work together with open hearts that are both fierce and tender, we'll figure out the best path forward.

Hopefully more and more men will join us and also start to use fierce compassion to call out other men they see engaging in predatory behavior—but we can't wait for them to come around. As women, we need to protect ourselves now. There is something happening, a shift in the feminine consciousness. Our anger is burning, a welling up of the yang to balance the yin. Women are finally waking up to their true nature, which is potently fierce as well as gently tender. Kali is rising.

PART II

THE TOOLS OF SELF-COMPASSION

CHAPTER 5

HOLDING OURSELVES TENDERLY

The way out of our cage begins with accepting absolutely
everything about ourselves and our lives, by embracing
with care our moment-to-moment experience.

—*Tara Brach, author and meditation teacher*

Self-compassion offers many ways to alleviate suffering depending on what's needed in the moment. Before we fully explore the tools of fierce self-compassion, we need to better understand tender self-compassion because yin must ultimately be balanced and integrated with yang for wholeness and well-being. I'll be covering the concepts briefly here, but for a deeper dive it may be helpful to consult my previous book, *Self-Compassion,* which focuses more closely on the development of yin self-acceptance.

Tender self-compassion is the capacity that allows us to *be with* ourselves just as we are—comforting and reassuring ourselves that we aren't alone, as well as validating our pain. It has the gentle, nurturing quality of a mother toward a newborn child. It doesn't matter if the infant is crying uncontrollably and just threw up on your new blouse. You love that child unconditionally. Tender self-compassion allows us to take this same attitude toward ourselves. Just as it's possible to hold the screaming baby, we can hold our intense and disturbing emotions with love so that we aren't overwhelmed. This nurturing quality allows us to be less concerned with *what* is happening in our experience—whether it's painful, difficult, challenging, or disappointing—and to be more focused on how we're *relating* to it. We learn to be with ourselves in a new way. Rather than being lost in and engulfed by our pain, we're compassionate to ourselves *because* we're in pain. The care and concern that we extend to ourselves allows us to feel safe and accepted. When we open our hearts to what is, it generates a level of warmth that helps heal our wounds.

While writing this book, COVID-19 hit. All my live workshops were canceled and Rowan had to attend school on Zoom. It was difficult to write as I tried to tutor and entertain him, making sure we had enough food (I actually bought fifty pounds of rice and beans just in case) and toilet paper (enough to cope with the potential aftermath of fifty pounds of rice and beans) and having to deal with all the other incredible life changes brought about by the pandemic. I was lonely and worried about the future. I've been incredibly lucky compared to many others who lost their job, a loved one, or their health, but that doesn't mean it's been stress-free. When feelings of fear, sadness, or uncertainty come up, I know what to do: I give myself tender compassion. I say things to myself like, "This is really hard. What do you need in this moment?" Sometimes I need to calm myself, so I'll go for a walk or take a hot shower. More often I'm needing emotional support. I might put one hand on my heart and one on my solar plexus and feel my own presence. I consciously bring in some warmth and love, reminding myself of the shared nature of this experience (in this case one shared with literally billions of others). Although the difficulty doesn't go away, taking a few minutes to check in with myself and give myself some kindness makes a huge difference.

When we're compassionate to ourselves when we struggle, our awareness is no longer completely consumed by suffering; it's also full of concern for that suffering. We are bigger than our pain; we are also the love holding the pain. This lifeline can be a source of great meaning and fulfillment, regardless of how hard things are in the moment.

The three components of self-compassion—kindness, common humanity, and mindfulness—each play a crucial role in tender self-compassion. Kindness is the emotional attitude that allows us to comfort and soothe ourselves. Common humanity provides the wisdom to understand that we're not alone, and to see that imperfection is part of the shared human experience. And mindfulness allows us to be present with our suffering, so that we can validate our difficult feelings without immediately trying to fix or change them. These three elements take a particular form when tender self-compassion is used to meet our needs: loving, connected presence.

LOVE

The element of kindness at the core of self-compassion takes on a loving quality when our need is to be with ourselves as we are. It's soft, warm, and nurturing. Women are typically very comfortable with the tender side of compassion because it's so ingrained in female gender roles. We're compassion specialists, raised from birth to care for others. But it can feel less familiar, even uncomfortable, when we turn that concern inward.

Most of us are much harsher to ourselves than to others. We often say cruel and unkind things that we'd never say to anyone else. Let's say you were really busy and forgot to call your mother on her birthday. If a close friend told you she did this, you'd probably say something like, "I know you're upset because you forgot to call your mom, but these things happen. It's not the end of the world. You were really stressed and busy and it just slipped your mind. You can call her now and tell her how much she means to you." But when we find ourselves in the same situation, we're more likely to say, "You're such a horrible daughter. I can't believe you'd be so self-centered. I'm sure Mom is crushed, and she'll probably never forgive you."

With our friends we typically focus on the behavior (you forgot to call your mother) rather than the person (you're such a horrible daughter). We attribute the behavior to the situation (you were busy) rather than core personality (you are so self-centered). We see the grav-ity of what happened objectively (it's not the end of the world) rather than catastrophizing (I'm sure Mom is crushed). And we remember the situation is temporary (you can call your mother now) rather than assuming things are permanent (she'll never forgive you).

So why do we treat ourselves so differently than we do our friends? One reason has to do with how we deal with threats. When we notice something about ourselves that we don't like or when we face a life challenge, we feel personally threatened. As discussed earlier, our in-stinctive reaction to threat is to fight, flee, or freeze, and when we turn this on ourselves, the instinct manifests as self-criticism, isolation, and overidentification. We feel that by reacting this way, we will be able to assume control and prevent missteps, thereby keeping us safe. Con-versely, we don't feel so directly threatened by the struggles of others (although I may feel bad for my friend who was fired from her job, it doesn't put me in immediate danger) and therefore we have more ac-cess to our tend-and-befriend response. By exercising self-compassion, we shift our instinctive source of safety from the threat-defense system to the care system, so that we can be more supportive to ourselves and cope more effectively with difficult situations.

One key element in creating this supportive atmosphere is the tone of voice we use when speaking to ourselves—either out loud or as an internal dialogue. We're all incredibly sensitive to tone of voice; for the first two years of life, before we understand language, tone is a primary means of parents and babies communicating. We can feel the emotional intent of words independent of their meaning. For ex-ample, if we use kind words but say them in a flat or cold manner, the overall message will be about as effective as a robo-call asking you to extend your car warranty. But when our tone of voice is infused with benevolence and goodwill, we feel it in our bones. We respond instinc-tively to our own warmth.

The amazing thing about shifting from harsh criticism to kindness is that moments of difficulty—including situations that elicit feelings of shame and inadequacy—become an opportunity to both give and receive love. We can be tender toward ourselves in the face of any experience that comes our way, no matter how challenging. As we learn to become more comfortable with the voice of self-kindness, our ability to love grows stronger. It doesn't have preconditions or require us to change because love can hold everything.

CONNECTION

The sense of common humanity inherent to tender self-compassion generates feelings of connectedness when we turn toward our pain. As we remember that hardship and feelings of inadequacy are something that we all share, we don't feel so isolated. But it's actually more typical for us to feel cut off from others when we struggle. Think about it. When you blurt out that completely inappropriate remark at a meeting, or can't pay your credit card bill, or get bad news from the doctor, it feels like something has gone wrong. Like this isn't *supposed* to be happening. As if what's supposed to be happening is perfection, and when things aren't going as we would like, something abnormal has occurred. The feeling of abnormality isn't a logical reaction, it's an emotional one. Yes, logically we know that no one is perfect and no one lives a perfect life, and that (as the song goes) you can't always get what you want. And yet when something challenging happens, our emotional reaction is to feel as if everyone else in the world is living a "normal" problem-free life, and it's just "me" having difficulties.

This self-focused view is exacerbated by Western culture, which raises us to believe that we're independent agents, that we control ourselves and our fate. When we buy into the narrative that we're running the show, we forget our essential interdependence—the truth that all our actions are carried out in a larger web of causes and conditions.

Let's say that I feel inadequate because I'm sometimes irritable and impatient with others and this has harmed my work relationships (completely hypothetical, of course). I might identify with this "character flaw," judging and blaming myself for it. But with the wisdom of common humanity, I can see that this behavior isn't fully under my control. If it was, I would've surely stopped it by now. My behavior is caused in part by my genetic makeup, hormones, early family history, life experiences, current life circumstances—financial, romantic, work, health—and so on. And all these factors interact with still other factors such as social conventions and the global economy, most of which are completely out of my control. Therefore, there's no reason to take any of it personally. My experience is intimately connected to what's happening in the greater whole. This doesn't mean I shouldn't take responsibility for my actions and do my best, which means trying to catch myself before I act out and often apologizing or making amends in some form if necessary. But I don't have to mercilessly blame myself.

When we remember that mistakes are an integral part of the human experience, we take our failings less personally. As we recognize that we're simply one stitch in a larger tapestry, our feelings of separation and isolation begin to lessen. We no longer feel abnormal, but see that all people have strengths and weaknesses tied to complex factors much bigger than any one individual. When we don't feel so alone, our pain becomes bearable. This feeling of connection fortifies the sense of safety needed to take on life's challenges.

PRESENCE

Mindfulness is central to self-compassion, and provides the awareness needed to be with ourselves as we are and to validate our pain. It's a balanced state that steers clear of two common reactions to suffering: avoidance and overidentification. Sometimes we turn away from our difficulties by closing our eyes and looking the other way. We ignore the problems in our marriage or our job or the environment, choosing the oblivion of denial over the discomfort of opening to what is. But in order to care for ourselves, we have to be present with our pain. We need to turn inward and make space for our difficult feelings of sadness, fear, anger, loneliness, disappointment, grief, or frustration. Only then can we respond to our pain with love, knowing that these feelings are part of the shared human experience.

At other times, we become fused with our negative feelings. We become so caught up in our suffering that we lose all perspective. We fixate on our problems, distorting and exaggerating them in the process. Think of how swept up you get when you see an action film, tensing up as if you were the one about to be hit by a skidding car. Suddenly the person next to you sneezes and you realize, "Oh, that's right, I'm watching a movie!" Mindfulness gives us the space and vantage point needed to clearly see what is happening, so we can give ourselves compassion for how hard it is in the moment.

When we open to the reality of what is, even if we don't like what is, it helps almost immediately. When something happens that we dislike, we typically try to fix it and make it go away. We fight what is, making things even harder than they need to be. We know from psychological research that the more we resist pain, the more we aggravate it. Think of what happens when you squeeze a balloon: it pops. Resistance can be defined as the desire to manipulate our experience of the present moment. When we resist discomfort, not only are we in pain, we also feel upset and frustrated by things not being how we want them to be. The meditation teacher Shinzen Young puts this into a mathematical formula: "Suffering = Pain × Resistance." In a meditation retreat that I once sat with him he joked, "Actually it's an exponential, not a multiplicative, relationship." Let's say your plane gets canceled and you fear you're going to miss a close friend's wedding. This stinks. It's disappointing. But if you rant and rave about how horrible it is, pulling your hair out, screaming, bashing your head against a metaphorical wall, it only amplifies the stress of the flight being canceled. And getting consumed by the thought "This should not be happening!"—in other words, resisting the reality that it *is* happening—just pours fuel on the fire. Mindfulness allows us to accept reality. We say to ourselves, "I'm crushed that the flight is canceled. I really don't want to miss my friend's wedding. I feel so upset and sad about it." This clear acknowledgment of the pain allows us to validate our feelings and take wise action to try to change things in the future (maybe you can rent a car, for instance).

Another benefit of being mindful rather than resisting our pain is that it allows difficulties to resolve more quickly. We know that resistance not only amplifies our suffering, it also helps lock it into place. What we resist, persists. If you feel anxiety and fight it, you may develop panic disorder. If you feel sad and fight it (especially if you judge yourself for feeling sad), you may become depressed. Typically, emotions have a limited lifespan. They spring up out of a difficult situation, then fade over time. When we fight our negative feelings, we actually feed and sustain them through the energy of our resistance. They're like stray cats sticking around because we leave them scraps at night. However, when we can simply be present with our difficult feelings, mindfully allowing our experience to be just as it is in the moment, they eventually move on.

That being said, it's natural to want to resist pain, which is why it's so hard to let go. Even an amoeba will move away from a toxin in a petri dish. It's our innate desire to be well that drives our resistance. I've tried to teach Rowan about mindfulness and self-compassion from an early age, knowing how well it would serve him in life. For years he completely rejected the idea. If he was upset about something and I would try to help him to accept the situation with warmth and kindness, he would sometimes snap, "Don't give me that self-compassion stuff, Mommy. I don't want to accept the pain." The honesty of his reaction was so heartbreaking. As his mother I wished that his resistance would work, that his pain would magically dissolve. But resistance is futile (the invading space aliens got that one right). It's only when we turn toward our pain with an open mind and open heart that it will begin to subside, in its own time and at its own pace.

The practice of mindfulness allows us to let go of resistance so that we can be with ourselves in a more compassionate way. By simply acknowledging that we're struggling and allowing it to be so, we take the first step toward healing. When we're present with ourselves and our pain, simultaneously remembering that we're not alone in our struggles and being kind to ourselves because it hurts, we embody a state of tender self-compassion. This loving, connected presence can be brought to bear on any experience, and it makes a dramatic difference in our ability to cope.

TENDER SELF-COMPASSION BREAK

The Self-Compassion Break is one of the most popular practices from the MSC program. It's designed to help you bring in the three components of self-compassion whenever you need acceptance or support in daily life. It's like hitting the reset button on a computer, taking a needed pause when we're struggling so that we can reorient and re-center. The basic format of the Self-Compassion Break involves intentionally calling on the three components of self-compassion—mindfulness, common humanity, and kindness—to help us relate to our experience in a more compassionate way. We'll first learn this practice for a situation in which tender self-compassion is called for. In later chapters, we're going to tailor the practice for the three forms of fierce self-compassion: protecting, providing, and motivating. (A guided audio version of this practice can be found at FierceSelf-Compassion.org.)

Instructions

Think of a situation in your life that's difficult, something causing you to suffer, that you want to approach in a more caring and accepting way. Maybe you're feeling inadequate, or you're really sad about something that's happening in your life, and you'd like some loving, connected presence to help you through. Please choose something in the mild to moderate range when you're first learning the practice, not something overwhelming. Allow yourself to feel your way into the problem, noting any uneasiness you experience in your body. Where do you feel it the most? Make contact with the discomfort in your body.

Make sure your posture is as relaxed as possible. You're going to be saying a series of phrases (aloud or silently to yourself) designed to bring in the three components of self-compassion in their yin form. Although words will be suggested, the goal is to find language that works for you personally.

- The first phrase is meant to help you be mindfully present with the pain you're experiencing. Try saying to yourself slowly and calmly, "This is a moment of suffering." If this language doesn't feel quite right, see if you can come up with some other way of expressing this message, such as "This is hard," "I feel so stressed," or "I'm really hurting."

- The second phrase is designed to remind you of how you are connected to humanity. Try saying to yourself, "Suffering is a part of life." Other options are "I'm not alone," "We all face challenges in our lives," or "This is how it feels when a person struggles."

- The third phrase calls in the power of love and kindness. First, put your hands over your heart, or any place on your body that feels soothing, feeling the warmth and gentle touch of your hands. Try saying with tenderness, "May I be kind to myself." Other options might be "May I accept myself as I am," "May I be understanding and patient with myself," or "I'm here for you." If it feels comfortable, you can even try saying, "I love you."

- If you're having difficulty finding the right words, imagine that a dear friend is having the same problem as you. What would you say to this person, heart-to-heart, to soothe and comfort them? Now, can you offer the same message to yourself?

After this practice you will probably be feeling one of three ways: positive, negative, or neutral. See if you can allow yourself to be just as you are in the moment, no need to fix anything. If you are experiencing a lot of backdraft, you might also want to do the Soles of the Feet practice on page 30.

SELF-COMPASSION VERSUS SELF-ESTEEM

One of the most important functions of tender self-compassion is radical self-acceptance. When we learn to be with our imperfect selves in a compassionate way, we stop judging and criticizing ourselves for not being good enough. We give up the continual striving to be other than we are, to be perfect, and instead embrace ourselves with all our flaws and foibles. This approach is radically different from boosting our self-esteem.

Self-esteem is an evaluation of self-worth. It's a judgment that we are good rather than bad. The way that most of us have learned to feel good about ourselves is by feeling special and above average. It's not okay to be average, which of course is a problem because it's logically impossible for us all to be special and above average at the same time. It also means that we're continually comparing ourselves to others. Does she have more Facebook friends than I do? Is she prettier than I am? Is Brené Brown really starring in her own Netflix special? This constant comparison makes us feel competitive with others—and therefore cut off from them. Not only does this reduce feelings of connection, it can also lead to downright nasty behavior, from physical bullying (if I pick on the weird kid, I'll look cool in comparison) to relational aggression (if I spread rumors about the new woman at work, maybe other people won't like her as much as they like me). Social comparison can also lead to prejudice. The roots of prejudice are complex and have much to do with maintaining power and resources. But a key factor driving prejudice is that when I tell myself my ethnic, religious, national, racial, (fill in the blank) group is superior to yours, I boost my relative status.

Another problem with self-esteem is that it requires judging our worth based on whether or not we meet the standards we set for ourselves. Did I lose the weight I wanted, did I make my sales target, did I use my free time productively? Our sense of value is predicated on achieving our goals. The three most common domains in which women invest their self-esteem are social approval, perceived attractiveness, and successful performance in those areas of life that matter to us (school, work, parenting, etc.). This is why we constantly ask ourselves, "Did I do a good job, do people like me, do I look nice?" We feel positive about ourselves when the answer is yes—but on those uncooperative hair days when the answer is no, we feel less valuable.

Because our self-worth changes according to whether we're meeting expectations (our own or those of others), it can vacillate wildly. Self-esteem is unstable, because it's only there for us in the good times. What happens when we get rejected from that job application, or dumped by our partner, or look in the mirror and don't like what we see? Our source of self-worth is stripped from us, and depression or anxiety often follow.

And the quest for high self-esteem is never-ending—a treadmill we can't seem to get off. There's always someone doing it better than we are—if not now, then soon. And the fact that we're imperfect creatures means that we'll repeatedly fail to meet our standards. We will *never* be good enough or successful enough.

Tender self-compassion avoids the self-esteem trap by accepting ourselves unconditionally. We don't have to earn the right to self-compassion. We are compassionate toward ourselves simply because we're flawed human beings intrinsically worthy of care. We don't need to succeed or be special and above average. We only need to warmly embrace the confused, struggling, works-in-progress that we are.

I know that self-compassion stepped in for me recently when my self-esteem threatened to desert me. Last summer, about a month before I was scheduled to give an important lecture on self-compassion in front of a large audience, I got what appeared to be a pimple on the tip of my nose. "That's strange," I thought to myself. "I haven't had a pimple in years. It must be the hormonal changes of menopause." But the pimple didn't go away. It got bigger and brighter—not quite Rudolph the Red-Nosed Reindeer but not far off either. I finally went to the dermatologist and sure enough it was a melanoma. Not serious, thank goodness, but it required immediate removal—the day before getting on the plane for my big presentation. So I had to give the talk with a large white bandage smack-dab in the middle of my face—not exactly my best look. Instead of worrying about how attractive I appeared, however, or fearing that people in the audience might judge me, I gave myself compassion for my embarrassment. This allowed me to take a more lighthearted approach to the situation and even make a joke of it: "You've probably noticed the bandage on my nose. Once you get past fifty, weird things start growing on your body and have to be cut off—what are you going to do?"

I did a research study with Roos Vonk at the University of Nijmegen in the Netherlands that directly compared the impact of self-esteem and self-compassion on feelings of self-worth. We examined data from 2,187 participants (74 percent women, ranging in age from eighteen to eighty-three) who'd been recruited through advertisements in newspapers and magazines. Over an eight-month period, the participants filled out a variety of items on a series of questionnaires. We found that compared to self-esteem, self-compassion was associated with less social comparison and was less contingent on social approval, perceived attractiveness, and successful performance. The sense of self-worth people got from self-compassion was therefore more steadfast over time. We measured individuals' feelings of self-worth a total of twelve different times over the eight-month period, and found that it was self-compassion, not self-esteem, that predicted stability of self-worth among participants.

The goals of self-esteem and self-compassion are polar opposites. One is about getting it right, the other is about opening our hearts. The second option allows us to be fully human. We give up trying to be perfect or lead an ideal life, and instead focus on caring for ourselves in every situation. I may have just missed my deadline or said something foolish or made a poor decision, and my self-esteem may have taken a big hit, but if I'm kind and understanding toward myself in those moments, I've succeeded. When we can accept ourselves as we are, giving ourselves support and love, then we've achieved our goal. It's a box that can always be checked, no matter what.

THE HEALING BALM OF SELF-COMPASSION

As mentioned earlier, there's a large and expanding body of research that shows self-compassion enhances well-being. It reduces depression, anxiety, and stress, increases happiness and life satisfaction, and improves physical health. One way it does so is by changing our physiology. When we practice self-compassion, we're deactivating the threat-defense system and activating the care system, helping us to feel safe. To illustrate, a study asked participants to imagine receiving compassion and feeling it in their bodies. Every minute they were told things like, "Allow yourself to feel that you are the recipient of great compassion; allow yourself to feel the loving-kindness that is there for you." Researchers found that the participants who gave themselves compassion had lower cortisol levels (a marker of sympathetic nervous system activity) compared to a control group, indicating they felt safer. They also had increased heart rate variability (a marker of parasympathetic activation), suggesting that they felt more relaxed and less defensive.

Self-compassion also enhances well-being by transforming negative states into positive ones. When we hold our pain in loving, connected presence the pain starts to subside, but it also feels good to open our hearts; it's a meaningful and rewarding experience. For example, researchers recruited participants on Facebook and asked them to write a compassionate letter to themselves once a day for seven days. Each day participants would consider something distressing that had left them feeling upset, and wrote a letter using the following instructions: "Think about what you would say to a friend in your position, or what a friend would say to you in this situation. Try to have understanding for your distress (e.g., I am sad you feel distressed) and realize your distress makes sense. Try to be good to yourself. We would like you to write whatever comes to you, but make sure this letter provides you with what you think you need to hear in order to feel nurtured and soothed about your stressful situation or event." The researchers included a control group of participants who were just told to write about their early memories each day for a week. They then tracked the well-being of participants over time, and found that compared to the control group, those who wrote with self-compassion were less depressed for three months afterward. Even more remarkable, they reported feeling happier for six months, demonstrating the lasting positive feelings that stem from loving, connected presence.

Another important way self-compassion helps is by counteracting shame. Shame occurs when we confuse our bad behaviors with who we are. Rather than simply recognizing that we've made a mistake, we believe "I am a mistake." Instead of acknowledging that we failed, we think "I am a failure." It's a self-absorbed state in which we feel hollow, worthless, and disconnected from others. The three components of self-compassion act as a direct antidote to shame: mindfulness prevents us from overidentifying with our missteps, common humanity counteracts feelings of isolation from others, and kindness allows us to feel worthy despite our imperfections. This allows us to clearly see and acknowledge our areas of weakness without defining ourselves by them.

The other day, Rowan quite spontaneously reminded me of the need to do this. We were driving in the car and I was singing along to the radio. Let's just say that my singing voice is not my best quality. In fact, it's something that I sometimes feel ashamed about. I said out loud, "I'm such a terrible singer." Without missing a beat he replied, "You aren't a terrible singer, Mom, you just sing terribly."

Shame is a uniquely problematic emotion because it tends to shut us down and can actually prevent us from trying to repair any harm we've caused. The intense feelings of disgust and isolation evoked by shame combined with the desire to hide from what we've done make it much more difficult to deal with our actions head-on. Shame is distinct from guilt, which isn't as debilitating. When we feel badly about our behavior without identifying ourselves as bad, it facilitates taking responsibility for our actions.

Edward Johnson and Karen O'Brien from the University of Manitoba examined the association between self-compassion, shame, guilt, and depression. They asked participants to think of an episode from their past in which they regretted their behavior, and told one group to write about the incident using the three components of self-compassion—mindfulness, common humanity, and kindness. Compared to a control group, those in the self-compassion condition reported significant decreases in shame and negative emotions. Interestingly, their levels of guilt were unchanged (self-compassion didn't make people feel more guilty, but it didn't make them feel less guilty either). Guilt can be helpful as a frank acknowledgment of wrongdoing, in contrast to shame, which doesn't help anyone. They also found that two weeks later, those in the self-compassion group were less depressed, and that this was partly explained by their lessened shame. The ability to feel unashamed while seeing ourselves clearly is one of the most powerful gifts of self-compassion.

COPING WITH PAIN

Self-compassion provides emotional resilience by helping us to get through painful times without being knocked flat. For instance, self-compassion helps us to cope in trying situations such as getting a divorce. Researchers asked divorcing adults to complete a four-minute stream-of-consciousness recording about their separation experience, then independent judges rated how self-compassionate their monologues were. Those who displayed greater self-compassion when talking about their breakups evidenced better psychological adjustment not only in the immediate crisis, but also nine months later.

Self-compassion also helps people deal with health issues such as diabetes, spina bifida, or multiple sclerosis—enabling them to stay emotionally balanced and get through the day more easily. In a qualitative study of how self-compassion helped women cope with chronic physical pain, one participant wrote, "As I eat my breakfast, I keep thinking that maybe my pain is not something I should try to separate from myself. Maybe my pain is part of my normal and maybe that's okay. If I . . . am kind [to myself] and then move on, everything is easier." Similarly, individuals facing life-threatening conditions such as cancer or HIV tend to feel less stress, depression, anxiety, and shame about their diseases when approached with compassion.

I conducted a study with a graduate student on the ballast that self-compassion provides to parents of autistic children. I'd learned from firsthand experience how important it is to have compassion for yourself when caring for a special-needs child, but wanted to explore the experience of other parents of autistic children. We recruited volunteers through our local autism society and asked parents to fill out the Self-Compassion Scale. We also had them fill out survey items that assessed how severe their child's autism was, and how stressed, overwhelmed, or depressed they felt due to their situation. Finally, we asked how hopeful they felt about the future and how satisfied they were with their lives. Findings indicated that parents with more self-compassion perceived less stress when dealing with their children. They were less likely to be depressed, and more likely to be hopeful and satisfied with their lives. In fact, self-compassion was actually a stronger predictor of how they were doing than the severity of their children's autism. This suggests that what's more important than the intensity of the challenge you face in life is how you relate to yourself in the midst of it.

When we don't have the emotional resources necessary to deal with problematic aspects of ourselves or our lives, we sometimes use negative coping strategies to avoid our pain. We may drown our distress in alcohol, drugs, or sex in a compulsive manner, desperately trying to feel good if only for a short time. But when the high wears off or the thrill of the experience fades, we come back to the same reality and try to escape it all over again. This is how the addictive cycle is born. Research shows that people who are self-compassionate, who can hold their pain with love and don't have to stomp it out with mind-altering experiences, are less likely to become addicted to alcohol, drugs, food, or sex. There's even one study that found self-compassionate people were less likely to be addicted to chocolate, a favorite feel-better remedy. Self-compassion also helps people recover from addiction, and is

actually one of the benefits of recovery programs such as Alcoholics
Anonymous.

Self-compassion can reduce other problematic ways of coping with
distress. For instance, one study tracked Chinese adolescents who were
bullied over the course of a year, and found that teens with greater
self-compassion were less likely to engage in self-harm such as cutting.
People who cut themselves often use physical pain to distract themselves from emotional pain or as a way to feel *something* if they've become emotionally numb. Self-compassion provides a healthier way to
feel and process pain. When things are really bad, people may even try
to end their lives as a way to escape. One study taught self-compassion
to low-income African-Americans who had attempted suicide within
the last year. Even though participants were dealing with major challenges such as poverty and systemic racism, they were able to learn
how to be kinder to themselves and reported a significant decrease
in depression and suicidal thoughts. In this case self-compassion was
literally a lifesaver.

THE PARADOX OF SELF-COMPASSION

While tender self-compassion helps us lessen our suffering and heal,
it's essential to not use it in a manipulative way to change our present
moment experience. A central paradox of self-compassion is: "We give
ourselves compassion not to feel better, but *because* we feel bad." This
may make you scratch your head a bit (that's what paradoxes do), but
it's a key point. Self-compassion does help us to feel better, but if in a
moment of suffering we put our hand on our heart or say kind things
to ourselves with the intention to get rid of our pain, it becomes a hidden form of resistance that will just make things worse. What we resist
persists and grows stronger. Instead, we must fully accept that things
are painful and simply be kind to ourselves *because* they're painful. This
has the effect of reducing our suffering by softening our resistance to
it. The benefit of self-compassion comes not through control or force,
but as a welcome side effect.

Here's an example of how it might work. Let's say I had trouble sleeping, and I found that giving myself compassion for the difficulty of chronic sleeplessness helped me fall asleep. However, I can't game the system. If I start to use self-compassion to try to end my insomnia, I'll become agitated when I don't fall asleep immediately, and that will make me less likely to sleep. Self-compassion used in the service of resistance will fail, because trying to control things inevitably amplifies our suffering. It's only when I can accept that I'm sleepless and am kind to myself just because insomnia is so awful that I'll feel cared for and calm down enough to fall asleep. Self-compassion used in the service of acceptance allows for healing to occur naturally, on its own.

A LESSON LEARNED

I gained insight into the paradox of self-compassion the hard way. When I was in my early twenties, my brother Parker developed cirrhosis of the liver. The doctors assumed he must have been an alcoholic. Parker admittted he liked to have the occasional beer, but he swore he didn't have a problem. An astute doctor remembered an extremely rare genetic disorder he'd read about in medical school called Wilson's disease. People with this condition can't excrete copper, which tends to build up in their bodies and lodge in places like the liver. A key sign of the disease is copper-colored rings around the iris called Kayser-Fleischer rings, named for the German ophthalmologists who first discovered them. My brother's doctor recognized them, and sure enough, Parker had Wilson's. It's a double recessive genetic disorder, so it requires the gene from both parents. This meant I had a one in four chance of also having it, and the dice didn't roll in my favor.

I tested positive, but my liver was fine. I started to take a mild chelator, which helped me excrete copper, and dutifully got my liver tested regularly. Whenever I had a medical appointment and put down Wilson's disease on the intake form, doctors would excitedly ask if they could call their colleagues into the room to observe my Kayser-Fleischer rings ("You'll never see this again in your lifetime!"). But other than these few moments of minor celebrity, not much seemed to come of it: I had no observable symptoms. This went on for some years.

Then, in my thirties, I started having strange episodes that I referred to as "dream déjà vu." I would be going about my day, shopping for a new comforter, taking a walk, petting my cat, when out of the blue, with no apparent trigger, I would get an intense feeling that whatever I was doing in the moment I had dreamed about before. The feeling was extremely seductive, like I was being pulled into some netherworld, but the experience left me with a sickening sensation of dread. Because of my self-compassion practice, I would try to simply meet the déjà vu feeling with warmth and acceptance, putting my hand on my heart and saying a few supportive words to myself. Typically, it would pass in a few minutes. The episodes were odd and a bit disconcerting, but déjà vu is common, and I didn't think too much about it.

In 2009, I was at the movies when another dream déjà vu hit me. I put my hand on my heart and tried to be self-compassionate, but this time I was unconsciously doing so because I wanted the episode to end. I was trying to watch a film for God's sake—I didn't have time for this! Instead of giving myself compassion because I felt bad, I did it to feel better. The déjà vu episode lasted for about forty-five minutes. When I came out of the theater, I had major memory loss. I couldn't even remember the countries I'd visited on my trip to Europe the summer before. My resistance to the episode—masked as self-compassion— made it last much longer than it probably would have otherwise.

I went to a neurologist as soon as possible. It turns out that unlike my brother, the copper wasn't gathering in my liver (which was fine) but was instead lodging in my brain. The deposits had caused me to develop temporal lobe epilepsy: small localized epileptic seizures near the temporal lobe that often manifest as a strong feeling of déjà vu. I got on medication, which helped tremendously, though I still have occasional episodes. Now, when I get the "didn't I dream this before?" feeling, I put all my awareness in my right big toe (don't ask me why, but it feels like it's as far away from my brain as I can get) and try to distract myself. I don't fight the déjà vu episodes, but I'm not complacent either; instead I do what I can to reduce their impact.

Having this condition has certainly increased my appreciation of tender self-compassion, which has been essential for dealing with its most problematic symptom—my Swiss-cheese memory. To give you an idea of how bad it can be, once when I was out to dinner with a gathering of college friends, the name of someone in our old inner circle came up. "How is he doing?" I asked. "I haven't heard anything from him in years."

"Kristin, don't you remember?" a friend asked. "He committed suicide twenty years ago."

My face turned beet red and I was filled with shame. My first thought was how cold and uncaring I must seem to not remember something so important and tragic. Fortunately, I had my self-compassion practice to fall back on. I closed my eyes for a moment and allowed myself to feel the shame, as uncomfortable as it was. Then I spoke warmly to myself. "It's not that you don't care. It's just that this particular memory was erased. These things happen. It's okay." Self-compassion goes with me everywhere, a constant support. Although things haven't gotten easier or less complicated, my capacity to hold it all with loving, connected presence has definitely increased—which is good news since life gives me so many opportunities to practice!

BEING WITH DIFFICULT EMOTIONS

There are a number of techniques to help us "be with" difficult emotions in a tender manner without resisting or being overtaken by them. These practices aren't strategies to get rid of difficult emotions; they just allow us to establish a new *relationship* to them. In MSC we combine these various techniques into a single practice that is specifically designed to work with painful emotions. The techniques are:

Labeling Emotions. Naming or labeling difficult emotions helps us to disentangle, or "unstick," from them. If we can say, "This is sadness" or

"Fear is arising," we get perspective on the emotion rather than being engulfed by it. This gives us some emotional freedom. Name it and you tame it.

Mindfulness of Emotion in the Body. Thoughts arise and take hold so quickly that it is difficult to work with them. The body, in contrast, is relatively slow moving. When we find the physical expression of an emotion and hold it in mindful awareness, we are in a better position to change our relationship to the emotion. Feel it and you can heal it.

Soften-Soothe-Allow. There are three ways to bring tender self-compassion to difficult emotions. Softening our body around the tension we feel is a form of physical self-compassion, soothing ourselves for how much it hurts is a form of emotional self-compassion, and allowing is a type of mental self-compassion that reduces suffering by lessening resistance.

This practice is best used for softer emotions like sadness, loneliness, or grief that need to be held tenderly, as opposed to fierce emotions like anger. As always, if you start to feel overwhelmed while doing this practice, give yourself compassion by disengaging and finding some other way of caring for yourself such as grounding the soles of your feet to the earth or practicing some other form of self-care. (A guided audio version of this practice can be found at FierceSelf-Compassion.org.)

Instructions

- Find a comfortable position, sitting or lying down, and take three relaxing breaths.

- Place your hand over your heart, or another soothing place, to remind yourself that you are in the room, and that you too are worthy of kindness.

- Let yourself recall a *mild to moderately difficult situation* that you are in right now, perhaps a health problem, stress in a relation-

ship, or a work issue. Do not choose a very difficult problem as you
are first learning this practice but do not choose a trivial problem
either—choose a situation that can generate a little stress in your
body when you think of it.

- Clearly visualize the problem. Who was there? What was said?
  What happened? Or what *might* happen?

Labeling Emotions

- As you review this situation, notice if any emotions arise within you.
  And if so, see if a *label* for an emotion comes up—a *name*. For
  example:

  - Sadness?

  - Grief?

  - Confusion?

  - Fear?

- If you are having many emotions, see if you can name the
  strongest emotion associated with the situation.

- Now, repeat the name of the emotion to yourself in a tender, understanding voice, as if you were validating for a friend what they
  were feeling: "That's longing." "That's grief."

Mindfulness of Emotion in the Body

- Now expand your awareness to your body as a whole.

- Recall the difficult situation again, if it has begun to slip out of your
  mind, naming the strongest emotion you feel, and scanning your
  body for where you feel it most easily. In your mind's eye, sweep
  your body from head to toe, stopping where you can sense a little
  tension or discomfort.

- If you can, *choose a single location in your body* where the feeling expresses itself most strongly, perhaps as a point of muscle tension in your neck, a painful feeling in your stomach, or an ache in your heart.

- In your mind, incline gently toward that spot.

- See if you can experience the sensation directly, as if from the inside. If that's too specific, see if you can just feel your general sense of discomfort.

Soften-Soothe-Allow

- Now begin to *soften* into that location in your body, letting the muscles relax, as if in warm water. Softening . . . softening . . . softening . . . Remember that you're not trying to *change* the feeling—you're just *holding* it in a gentler way. If you want, you can try softening just a little around the edges.

- Now, *soothe* yourself *because* of this difficult experience. Try placing a hand over the part of your body that feels uncomfortable and feel the warmth and gentle touch of your hand. Perhaps imagining love and kindness flowing through your hand into your body. Maybe even thinking of your body as if it were the body of a beloved child. Soothing . . . soothing . . . soothing.

- Are there some comforting words that you might need to hear? For instance, you might imagine that you had a friend who was struggling in the same way. What would you say to your friend? ("I'm so sorry you feel this way." "I care deeply about you.")

- Can you offer *yourself* a similar message? ("Oh, it's so hard to feel this." "May I be kind and supportive to myself.")

- Finally, *allow* the discomfort to be there. Make room for it, releasing any need to make it go away.

- Allow yourself to be just as you are, just like this, if only for this moment.

- Soften . . . soothe . . . allow. Soften . . . soothe . . . allow. Take some time and go through the three steps on your own.

- You may notice the feeling starts to shift or even change location—that's okay. Just stay with it. Soften . . . soothe . . . allow.

- When you're ready, let go of the practice and focus on your body as a whole, allowing yourself to feel whatever you feel, to be exactly as you are in this moment.

ACCEPTANCE OR COMPLACENCY?

When yin and yang are out of balance, tender self-compassion can morph into unhealthy complacency. It's not a good idea to sit around "being with yourself" if you haven't showered or changed your clothes in five days. To be truly self-compassionate, we must also take action to protect ourselves and provide for our needs, making any changes required. We do this in addition to—not instead of—accepting ourselves as we are.

The dance between acceptance and action can be tricky, especially in light of the already challenging concept that we give ourselves compassion not to feel better but because we feel bad. However, when yin and yang are integrated, our actions aren't aimed at resisting our pain or manipulating our present moment experience. Rather, they're the spontaneous outpouring of an open heart that does what it can to help without falling into the illusion that by doing so we can control the outcome. Paradoxically (once again), it's by radically accepting ourselves that we have the sense of safety and stability needed to make changes in our lives.

The difference lies in the motive underlying our actions. Rather than acting because we feel we're unacceptable as we are, or because we can't accept our experience, we act out of kindness and goodwill. If my job is highly stressful, I can hold this stress in loving, connected presence. I can acknowledge the difficulty, remember that there are many others in similar situations, and support myself with warmth. Tender self-compassion will prevent me from getting agitated and reactive to the point that life becomes even harder than it already is. But acceptance is not enough. The truth is also that the job isn't good for me and change is needed. Fierce self-compassion is what will give me the courage and motivation to do something different—talk to the boss and negotiate fewer hours, or else try to find a new job with better working conditions.

One common worry about self-compassion is that accepting ourselves will cause us to avoid taking responsibility for our misdeeds. "Oh gosh, I robbed a bank. Maybe I shouldn't have. Oh well, everyone's imperfect." As long as yin and yang are in balance, this won't happen. Research suggests that self-compassion increases rather than undermines the motivation to take personal responsibility for our behavior. In fact, a study by Juliana Breines and Serena Chen at the University of California, Berkeley asked undergraduate students to recall something they'd recently done and felt guilty about—such as cheating on an exam, lying to a romantic partner, or saying something mean. Students were then randomly assigned to one of three conditions: a self-compassion condition in which they wrote a paragraph expressing kindness and understanding about their behavior; a self-esteem condition in which they wrote about their positive qualities; or a control condition in which they wrote about a hobby they enjoyed. They found that participants who were encouraged to be self-compassionate about their misdeed felt more motivated to apologize for the harm they'd done and were more committed to not repeating the behavior again. Boosting self-esteem didn't help, as this often feeds an ego-defensive denial of responsibility. In fact, a study by researchers at the University of Pittsburgh found that one of the reasons self-compassionate individuals are more likely to admit when they're wrong and apologize for their behavior is because they're less debilitated by shame: they feel safe enough to own up to what they've done. Self-compassion, far from being a way to evade personal accountability, actually *strengthens* it.

Some have criticized the mindfulness movement because of its emphasis on acceptance and finding peace within oneself as a response to difficulty. Ronald Purser, in his provocative book *McMindfulness: How Mindfulness Became the New Capitalist Spirituality*, makes the argument that mindfulness places the blame on individuals for being so stressed. He claims the mindfulness movement is selling the ideology that stress is an individual pathology—as if learning to take a few deep breaths will solve all your problems. He also argues that this message distracts from the difficult work of changing capitalist systems so that they're less exploitive and more equitable.

The same could probably be said of the self-compassion movement— but only if you ignore fierce self-compassion. For instance, health-care institutions and schools are increasingly interested in self-compassion as a way to prevent burnout. When nurses or teachers give themselves compassion for the difficulty of their jobs, it helps them feel less overwhelmed, which allows them to cope more effectively (more on this later). But does this mean that institutions can keep overworking and underpaying teachers and nurses by just throwing a bit of self-compassion at them so they keep functioning efficiently? If this is the hidden goal, then hospitals and schools wouldn't be promoting true self-compassion but instead its evil twin complacency, in a bid to distract from poor working conditions.

Tender acceptance doesn't keep you from trying to improve your lot in life; in fact, it's the necessary first step in taking action. When combined with the fierce desire to protect ourselves, provide for our needs, and motivate change, it gives us the stable emotional platform needed to take on broken social systems. Acceptance means we give up the illusion that we can control things, or that life should be perfect, but we still do everything in our power to make things better. We do so not to resist the truth of pain, but because we care. The dance of acceptance and change lies at the heart of self-compassion.

CHAPTER 6

STANDING STRONG

A woman is like a tea bag—you never know how
strong she is until she gets in hot water.

—*Irish proverb*

As women, we've unconsciously internalized the message from our culture that we are the weaker sex, helpless maidens who need a big, strong man to save us. For too long we've been taught to value dependence over independence, to be attractive and sexy—not as a way of expressing ourselves, but as a means to attract a man who can protect us. We don't need men to protect us, we need to protect ourselves. Women are strong. We handle the pain of bearing children. We hold families together and skillfully navigate interpersonal conflict and adversity. But until we learn how to stand up for ourselves with the same fierce energy we use to care for others, our ability to take on the world's big challenges will remain limited.

Some people worry that self-compassion will make them soft, but it actually gives us incredible power. The belief that self-compassion is weak is a one-dimensional view. If we think only of the tender, nurturing side of things, it suggests a gentle, yielding stance toward life. And since nurturing is part of communal female gender roles, and women are accorded less power than men, self-compassion is sometimes associated with a *lack* of power. This is why it's so important for women to champion and model fierce self-compassion, so we can free ourselves from this misconception and embody the strong warrior within.

It can take incredible courage to alleviate suffering; think of first responders rushing in to help those in disasters like fires or floods. They don't just sit there "being with" the suffering of victims—they take swift and effective action to rescue people stranded on rooftops. And let's face it, in many ways each of our lives is a disaster, maybe not on the same scale as Hurricane Katrina or 9/11, although some days it can feel that way. Our suffering may be created by nature, by other people, or by ourselves—sometimes all three! We need to do whatever is necessary to stand strong in these crises in order to be fully self-compassionate. This power is already within us as women, but it's cloaked by stereotypes that say it's not part of our true nature.

Olivia Stevenson from University of Northern Colorado and Ashley Batts Allen from the University of Northern Carolina examined the link between self-compassion and inner strength in over two hundred women. They found that participants with higher scores on the SCS felt more empowered: they felt stronger and more competent, asserted themselves more, felt more comfortable expressing anger, and were more aware of cultural discrimination and committed to social activism. These findings are echoed in other research showing that self-compassionate women are more likely to confront others when needed and are less afraid of conflict.

The three elements of self-compassion—self-kindness, common humanity, and mindfulness—each have an important role to play when compassion is aimed at protecting ourselves. When we're fighting to keep ourselves safe, the three elements manifest as brave, empowered clarity.

BRAVERY

Kindness, when it's designed to protect us from harm, is strong and courageous. Facing danger requires audacity and determination—like when we climb out a window to escape a burning building or undergo chemotherapy to combat cancer. Bravery is equally required when we're in psychological danger: when someone disrespects us or invades our privacy and we need to draw boundaries. Kindness compels us to demand fair treatment when we're being treated unjustly. This may take the form of conducting voting drives, writing opinion pieces, demonstrating and protesting at a rally, going on strike, or staging sit-ins. Active and engaged kindness is the polar opposite of soft and fluffy.

One gateway to this type of strength that's familiar to women is the maternal protective instinct. If a bully calls our children names or a stranger threatens their safety, we know how strong Momma Bear can be. The force of love aimed at protection can be explosive. In fact, oxytocin, the hormone normally associated with tender maternal bonding, also promotes defensive aggression when a mother is protecting her young. Psychologists call this the "tend and *defend*" response.

I'll never forget the time I had to act on this instinct. I was visiting Romania with Rowan and his father, Rupert, on a wildlife expedition. In an irony that would soon become clear, we'd come to look for brown bears. Rowan was about nine. We stopped at an inn in the countryside to stay the night and moved into one of the small rooms. Our local guide had been talking with the innkeeper, a middle-aged Romanian woman, and then asked to talk with Rupert privately. Rupert came back to the room upset.

"The guide said we can't stay here. The innkeeper is worried about Rowan because he's autistic," he told me. "She's afraid he'll write on the walls or jump off the balcony or disturb the other guests."

I was gobsmacked. Although Rowan was clearly autistic, he wasn't being disruptive in any way. "I'll try to calm her down," Rupert said as he left the room. Something started to rumble inside me. It started at my core, rose up, and filled my entire body, a primal energy that was much bigger than me. It felt like I was tapping into a volcanic force. I remembered that this was Romania, the country that put "mental defectives" into orphanages where they were abandoned and left to rot. The children could spend years on cots without ever being taken to walk or play, so neglected that just moving could break their bones.

I made sure Rowan was safe and then went down to confront the innkeeper. I didn't know what I was going to do, but the force was overpowering. She was startled as I burst into the kitchen where she was standing with Rupert and the guide. I held my arm out and pointed my finger straight at her. "You bigoted monster! We wouldn't stay here if you paid us!!!" She didn't speak English, but she got the point. She cowered in the corner, terrified by my fury. "We're leaving," I said, as I slammed the kitchen door.

This is one of my most vivid recollections of being completely taken over by Momma Bear, and the power was awe-inspiring. I wish I would've integrated fierceness and tenderness more skillfully, so that I focused on the injustice of her reaction to Rowan rather than making it personal, but I wasn't there yet. I hadn't yet learned to own my power so that when I expressed my fierceness it was also caring. Still, it gave me insight into the atomic force of a mother protecting her child. It helped me see how this fierceness could be put to use to make the difficult changes needed in the world. It's important to remember that this force isn't generated from our small selves. When aimed at the alleviation of suffering, out of compassion for self and others, this is a force that comes from love itself.

EMPOWERMENT

Putting our sense of common humanity to work in the service of protection is a key source of empowerment. Malala Yousafzai, the Pakistani activist for female education and the youngest Nobel Prize laureate, said, "I raise up my voice—not so I can shout, but so that those without a voice can be heard . . . we cannot all succeed when half of us are held back." The truth is that whenever we protect ourselves, we're also protecting everyone else. We stand together with our sisters and brothers knowing that we're not alone. There's strength in numbers.

When we forget this and feel isolated by fear or shame, we think we're helpless. We may believe we can't change anything because the problem is so much bigger than us as individuals. It's hard to protect ourselves when we feel alone. From an evolutionary standpoint, we could never survive as individuals. Human beings evolved to live in cooperative social groups, and a core feature of humanity is that we owe our proliferation to our ability to work together. Remembering this fact—and acting on it—gives us power.

When we identify with others who suffer as we do—women, people of color, the LGBTQ+ community, the differently abled, service workers, immigrants, the list grows quickly—we feel our shared humanity. And when we take steps to protect the group that we identify with, that's fierce self-compassion in action. Although traditional notions of power have to do with controlling resources such as money, land, and food, or dominating others by distorting information or coercing behavior through military force, some modern social psychologists argue that it's actually group identity that underlies power. As John Turner from the University of Australia writes, "Group identity and influence give people the power of collective action and cooperative endeavor, a power to affect the world and pursue shared goals much greater than any member wields in isolation." When I identify with a larger whole so that "we" are protecting "ourselves," I—as a member of the group—become stronger.

The wisdom of common humanity not only helps us feel empowered, it also helps us understand the complexity of intersectionality— the fact that we can identify with many groups based on gender, race, ethnicity, class, religion, sexual orientation, disability status, body type, and so on—and that these identities all coexist. Honoring our connection with others through our shared identities—while also honoring our uniqueness through the particular intersection of identities that we express—allows us to position ourselves in an authentic way within the larger web. A Latina, transgender, atheist, able-bodied woman will have a different life experience from a Latina, cisgender, Catholic, disabled woman. By owning our uniqueness while being connected to something larger than ourselves, we truly come into our power.

Understanding common humanity spurs us to stand up to injustice. Researchers in Italy found that this aspect of self-compassion enhances our ability to take the perspective of others and promotes positive outgroup attitudes (measured by responses to such statements as "Our society should do more to protect the welfare of homeless people"). Understanding interdependence makes it easier to see the uncomfortable realities of discrimination and unfair privilege. It also helps us stay strong when subject to discrimination. If someone insults me and I take it personally, I might feel weakened or afraid. When I forget that my identity is part of a larger whole, and feel cut off from others when threatened, the danger will feel that much more over-whelming. But if I can remember that I have the same right to respect that all human beings do, I will be more able to defend our common rights as a matter of principle.

When Rosa Parks refused to give up her seat on the bus to a White passenger, she said, "I felt I had a right to stay where I was. That was why I told the driver I was not going to stand. I believed that he would arrest me. I did it because I wanted this particular driver to know that we were being treated unfairly as individuals and as a people." Her ability to connect with her community in that moment, rather than feeling isolated and alone, was critical to her ability to make a stand. Needless to say, this incredibly courageous act of fierce self-compassion helped ignite the civil rights movement in the United States.

CLARITY

Mindfulness in the service of protection allows us to see clearly with-out turning away from the truth. Sometimes we don't want to ac-knowledge when harm is being done to us. When our boss asks, "Can you get us some coffee, sweetie?" at a meeting composed primarily of male colleagues, it can be easier to laugh it off than call it out. Part of us knows it wasn't okay, but we may fool ourselves into thinking it's not a big deal so that we don't have to confront the knowledge that we were not so subtly put down in a room full of peers. It also means we don't have to deal with possible repercussions.

This tendency to avoid facing problems because it's easier not to is pervasive. Exhibit A: thanks to global warming, the world is speeding toward a crisis that threatens not just our survival as a species but also the equilibrium of the entire planet. However, many people simply ignore the threat or don't pay attention because, as Al Gore put it, it's an inconvenient truth. Similarly, one of the reasons many White people don't acknowledge the harsh reality of racial inequality is because it's too disturbing. Acknowledging the suffering of people of color—and our complicity in the system that sustains this suffering—would be too painful. We turn away to maintain our peace of mind, which conveniently also means we don't have to question the privilege we gain from systemic racism. We carry on as if there were no cost or consequence.

Mindfulness aimed at protection doesn't provide peace of mind; just the opposite. Mindfulness shines a light on harm being done and exposes what needs to change. It compels us to see and speak the truth to protect ourselves and others. It does so with balance and perspective, without minimizing the problem or blowing it out of proportion. When aimed at suffering, mindfulness is clear and vast enough to hold the whole truth, no matter how painful or unpleasant. It doesn't resist unpleasant facts by ignoring them, neither does it melodramatically exaggerate them. It sees things as they are.

Say your blind date shows up forty-five minutes late without a good excuse. There are three ways to react. One is to ignore it and brush it off because you really want the date to go well. But if you do this, you miss a potentially important red flag. Maybe it's a warning you should pay attention to: this person may be unreliable. Another possible reaction would be to get highly frustrated, creating a whole story line about this cold, uncaring narcissist. This is also not seeing clearly; there may be valid reasons for their tardiness that have nothing to do with self-centeredness. A mindful approach to the behavior would involve acknowledging what happened, asking about it calmly and directly, and keeping an open mind about what their explanation implies. This clarity provides the equanimity and stability needed to make wise choices about next steps.

Whether it's speaking out or simply keeping a dignified silence, we can use fierce self-compassion to protect ourselves from harm while still coming from a place of openness. The Zen meditation teacher Joan Halifax refers to this fierce stance as having a "strong back and soft front." When we hold our backs tall without being shut down, defensive, or rigid, we can take action in a way that's most effective.

PROTECTIVE SELF-COMPASSION BREAK

This is a version of the Self-Compassion Break that is aimed at engendering fierce self-compassion in the service of self-protection: brave, empowered clarity. (A guided audio version of this practice can be found at FierceSelf-Compassion.org.)

Instructions

Think of a situation in your life in which you feel the need to protect yourself, draw boundaries, or stand up to someone. Maybe you're being taken advantage of by a coworker, or your neighbor blasts music late at night, or a relative constantly tries to push their political views onto you. Again, please choose a situation where you feel mildly to moderately threatened, but not in real danger, so that you can learn the skill without overwhelming yourself. Call up the situation in your mind's eye. Try not to focus too much on the particular person or group of people causing the situation, but rather, *focus on the harm itself*. What's happening? What's going on? What is the boundary violation or threat or injustice? Allow yourself to feel whatever emotions come up. Fear, anger, frustration? See if you can drop the story of what's happening and make contact with the discomfort as a physical sensation. Just allow these bodily sensations to be there.

Now sit or stand up tall and roll your shoulders back, so that your posture embodies strength and determination. You're going to say a series of phrases (aloud or silently to yourself) designed to bring in the three components of self-compassion in active protective form. Although words will be suggested, the goal is to find language that works for you personally.

- The first phrase is meant to help you be mindful of what is happening. While focusing on the harm, rather than the person or persons causing the harm, say to yourself slowly and with conviction, "I clearly see the truth of what's happening." That's mindfulness: we see things as they are. Other options are "This is not okay," "I should not be treated this way," or "This is unfair." Find the words that seem right for you.

- The purpose of the second phrase is to help you remember common humanity, especially the power of connection, so you can draw strength from others while protecting yourself. Try saying, "I am not alone, other people have experienced this as well." Other options are "By standing up for myself, I stand up for everyone," or "All human beings deserve just treatment," or simply "Me too."

- Now put a fist over your heart, as a gesture of strength and bravery. Commit to being kind to yourself by keeping yourself safe. For the third phrase, try asserting confidently, "I will protect myself." Other options might be "I will not yield" or "I am strong enough to take this on."

- If you're having difficulty finding the right words, imagine that someone you really cared about was being mistreated or threatened in the same way you are. What would you say to this person to help them be strong, to stand tall, to have courage? Now, can you offer the same message to yourself?

- Finally, put your other hand over your fist and hold it tenderly. The invitation is to combine the fierce energy of brave, empowered clarity with the tender energy of loving, connected presence. Give yourself full permission to feel the force of your anger, your resolve, your truth, but also let this force be caring. Remember, we're aiming the fierce compassion at the harm or injustice itself, not at the person causing the harm. They are human and you are human—can you call on your fierceness to commit to taking action, while still keeping love alive?

After this practice you may be feeling very activated. Do what you need to in order to take care of yourself. Perhaps take some deep breaths, stretch, or you can always do the Soles of the Feet practice on page 30.

DRAWING BOUNDARIES

Fierce protective energy empowers us to draw clear boundaries and say no. Women are socialized to be giving and accommodating, and many of us believe that this is what gives us value, that people won't like us if we say no. We're expected to smile, be nice, and say yes. This training started early. Our parents gave us love and affection when we complied with their wishes. So did our teachers and bosses and our partners. By the time we're adults, it can be hard to disentangle our sense of worth as women from the perception that we are agreeable. Our self-concept forms around these nurturing, yielding qualities. But this training can keep us from standing up for ourselves. It's true that certain individuals may like us less for not giving them what they want, but when we have self-compassion, we aren't totally dependent on others' positive opinions. This allows us to choose integrity over pleasing others, giving ourselves support and care when there are negative consequences for doing so.

Sometimes we have difficulty drawing boundaries because we don't want to be rude or impolite. While civility and mutual respect is necessary for maintaining relationships, we don't want to be doormats. We want to be doors that we can either open or shut depending on what we want and need in the moment. In her book *The Assertiveness Guide for Women*, Julie de Azevedo Hanks provides some helpful standbys that can be used to say no to others without being disrespectful. Some of the responses she suggests are: "That's just not going to work for me," "I really appreciate you asking me, but I can't do it," "I'm not able to commit to that right now," or "I'm going to say no for now. I'll let you know if something changes." When we clearly and unequivocally say no (not hedging with responses like, "Umm uhh, let me see . . ."), we can take a stand in a way that allows our voice to be heard. Another option is to say, "I would really like to help, but I need to take care of myself by saying no." When framed as an act of self-care, it models and reinforces the message that we're all ultimately responsible for our own well-being, and that self-kindness means sometimes saying no. It also gives other people permission to do the same.

Self-compassion helps us to draw clear lines between behavior that we agree to and behavior that's unwanted. If a colleague makes an offensive joke, a friend isn't totally truthful with us, or our mother-in-law pokes her head in where it's unwanted, we need to be able to inform these people that their behavior isn't acceptable to us. If we're too focused on pleasing and not upsetting them, we may fall into the trap of acquiescing or simply shrugging things off. We have to be vigilant that our silence isn't interpreted as validation, otherwise it will tacitly encourage bad behavior in the future. Fierce self-compassion in the service of protection gives us the strength and determination to say no to what we don't like or know to be wrong. It's the force propelling us to stay true to ourselves.

PROTECTING OURSELVES FROM HARM

Sometimes we need to do more than draw boundaries; we need to actively protect ourselves from someone who's emotionally or physically abusing us. Although it's beyond the scope of this book to discuss how to confront such situations in detail (those in immediate danger of violence should call 911 or the National Domestic Violence hotline at 800-799-SAFE [7233]), I'll briefly outline the basic principles of how brave, empowered clarity can help us stay safe. First, we can acknowledge the truth of what's happening. When the person harming us is someone we love, this can be incredibly difficult, but minimizing the situation will just make things worse. If we're going to protect ourselves, we need to have absolute clarity about what is happening. It's not okay. It's wrong. It needs to stop now.

We can also connect with others who share our experience. This may occur online or in a support group. It also happens in our own minds when we acknowledge our common humanity. We aren't alone: sadly, countless others have suffered as we have. We don't need to blame ourselves or take things personally. Our situation stems from complex factors, many of which are beyond our control. We can draw strength from our sisters who have endured as we have, knowing that by protecting ourselves we're standing up for all women.

In order to find the courage to try to stop the harm, we can tap into our inner Mama Bear, channeling our ferocity to take protective action (see the Working with Anger practice on page 83, the Protective Self-Compassion Break exercise offered on page 148, or the Fierce Friend Meditation on page 156). This may involve confronting the person hurting us, ending a relationship, or, if the behavior is criminal, going to the authorities. The crucial step is making the commitment to protect ourselves. The time that we leave an abusive relationship is often the most dangerous, however, so we also need to be smart and plan carefully. Once our inner wisdom is no longer blocked by fear or uncertainty, we'll be able to decide the best course of action.

Finally, once we're safe, we can bring in tender self-compassion to do the work of healing, hopefully with the help of a mental health professional. (The Compassionate Letter Writing exercise offered on page 106 may also be beneficial.) When yin and yang are integrated, we will not let our guard down with others who pose danger, even as we open the door of our hearts toward ourselves.

SURVIVING TRAUMA

Fortunately, self-compassion provides the resilience needed to survive physical or emotional harm. As in the case of sexual mistreatment, research indicates that training in self-compassion helps women recover from interpersonal violence. One study by Ashley Batts Allen and colleagues followed the progress of women in a domestic violence shelter who met together in a six-week self-compassion support group. Group facilitators taught participants how to implement self-compassion in their daily lives through discussion, interpersonal sharing, exploring what self-compassion might look like in emotionally difficult situations, journaling, and other exercises. After the training, the women felt more empowered (in particular, more comfortable confronting others), more positive and confident, and more emotionally and physically safe.

Self-compassion provides tremendous fortitude to anyone who has experienced trauma—whether the trauma stems from interpersonal violence, sexual assault, discrimination, natural disasters, a serious accident, or war. The aftermath of trauma can continue long after the traumatic event itself has passed. A common outcome is posttraumatic stress disorder, or PTSD. This is a type of severe psychological shock, involving disturbance of sleep and constant vivid recall of the traumatic experience, with dulled responses to other people and to the outside world. When people are compassionate toward themselves after experiencing a trauma, they're less likely to develop PTSD, enabling them to remain on stable footing.

Studies focused on combat veterans illustrate this point well. I've taken part in research showing that American vets returning from Iraq or Afghanistan with higher levels of self-compassion have fewer symptoms of PTSD, function better in daily life, are less likely to abuse alcohol, and are less likely to contemplate suicide. This is partly because self-compassion reduces their feelings of shame and disconnection from others. A study by the Department of Veterans Affairs found that the amount of compassion soldiers displayed toward themselves after returning from their tour of duty—treating themselves with warmth and support rather than harshly criticizing themselves—was actually a stronger predictor of whether or not they eventually developed PTSD than their level of combat exposure. In other words, more important than how much action these soldiers had seen was how compassionately they related to themselves in the aftermath of combat. Were they an inner ally, supporting and encouraging themselves? Or were they an inner enemy, cutting themselves down mercilessly? Clearly when you go into battle—and when you come home—being your own ally makes you stronger.

Self-compassion also helps people cope with the trauma of prejudice and discrimination. A recent study of 370 cisgender women examined the traumatic impact of sexist microaggressions such as overhearing men refer to women as body parts (piece of ass, etc.), joking about rape, or making insensitive comments. They found that self-compassionate women were more resilient when enountering these sexist behaviors and experienced fewer negative emotional consequences as a result.

Self-compassion is also a powerful resource for LGBTQ+ youth, who are often stigmatized for being different. They're explicitly told they're sinful and wrong by certain religious groups, and when they're left out of media portrayals of life as a teenager, they get the implicit message that they're somehow abnormal. Physical and verbal abuse is directed their way at far greater rates than at their heterosexual or cisgender peers. This constant harassment contributes to higher rates of anxiety, depression, and suicidal ideation in LGBTQ+ youths.

Abra Vigna and her colleagues at the University of Wisconsin examined whether self-compassion helped LGBTQ+ teens at a Midwestern high school to persevere when faced with bullying. They found that teens who were more self-compassionate were better able to cope with being bullied, threatened, or harassed, and were less likely to become anxious or depressed as a result of being picked on. In a second study, these researchers found that self-compassion reduced anxiety, depression, and suicidal ideation among LGBTQ+ youth of color who were bullied due to their race as well as sexual orientation, underscoring the strength of self-compassion as a source of self-protection.

In fact, self-compassion has been found to lead to "post-traumatic growth" —which involves learning and growing from traumatic experiences. People who are more self-compassionate are better able to see the positives they've gained from past crises, including a sense of closeness with others, greater appreciation for the value of their own life, and confidence in their personal abilities. Rather than decimating us, self-compassion transforms setbacks into opportunities for learning. By tapping into the power of brave, empowered clarity, we're able to take charge of our lives and tackle challenges with more courage and determination. When we come through situations that seem impossible to bear at the time—and do so not with cold stoicism but with warmth and compassion—we discover strengths we never knew we had.

SURVIVING OUR CHILDHOOD

Fierce self-compassion also gives us the fortitude to survive early childhood trauma and function as healthy adults. When we're abused by parents or caregivers, the wounds are particularly deep. It can make it harder to have self-compassion as adults because feelings of love and care become fused with feelings of fear and pain early on. With the help of mental health professionals, we can learn to be compassionate toward our early trauma, giving us more ability to cope with the enormity of our pain. In many ways what's occurring is that we are re-parenting ourselves, giving ourselves the unconditional love, care, and safety that we didn't receive as kids. Although it takes time, through the consistent practice of self-compassion we can eventually develop secure attachment as adults. We can learn to rely on our own warmth and support as a source of safety, providing the stable platform needed to take on life's challenges. One study examined women who'd been sexually or physically abused in childhood. Those who learned to be self-compassionate about their experience as adults were more resilient, allowing them to bounce back more easily from setbacks, stay focused under pressure, and avoid growing discouraged.

Compassion Focused Therapy (CFT) is specifically aimed at

helping people with a history of childhood trauma use self-compassion to cope with the distress and intense shame they often feel. Paul Gilbert, creator of CFT, has long recognized the importance of fierce as well as tender self-compassion for recovery. He writes, "Compassion involves developing the courage to be open to our anger and rage, not some kind of 'soothing it away.' Indeed . . . soothing is useful [as] a safe haven but also in preparation to courageously engage with what we need to." CFT teaches clients to find safety in the ability to comfort themselves when experiencing painful emotions or traumatic memories, but also in discovering the backbone to stand up for themselves. Research shows this approach helps people to be more assertive and less submissive with anyone trying to harm them. As one British woman said after participating in a CFT group, "It's made me feel like I've put on like a compassionate armour where y'know I'm able to handle each day better and I feel like I've got a security armour on and I'm able to just be compassionate with all aspects of my life . . . it makes me feel stronger and feel more empowered." Multiple studies show that this approach is highly effective at giving people the resources they need to heal from the past and step boldly into the future.

FIERCE FRIEND MEDITATION

This practice is adapted from a meditation called the Compassionate Friend, a guided visualization that was originally developed in CFT and is also used in MSC. I have altered it to help you create an image of a fierce friend who embodies caring force, whom you can call upon whenever you need to protect yourself. (A guided audio version of this practice can be found at FierceSelf-Compassion.org.)

Instructions

- Please find a comfortable position, either sitting or lying down. Gently close your eyes. Take a few deep breaths to settle into your body.

Safe Place

- Imagine yourself in a place that is safe and comfortable—it might be a cozy room with the fireplace burning, or a peaceful beach with warm sun and a cool breeze, or a forest glade. It could also be an imaginary place, like floating on clouds . . . anywhere you might feel peaceful and safe. Let yourself linger with and enjoy the feeling of comfort in this place.

A Visitor

- Soon you'll receive a visitor, a strong, powerful, but also tender and loving presence—a fierce friend—who embodies the quality of caring force.

- What image arises? This friend may remind you of someone you have known in the past, like a courageous and protective teacher or grandparent. They may be a figure completely from your imagination like a warrior goddess or an animal like a jaguar. This being may not have any particular form, perhaps just a presence or glowing light.

- Please allow an image to come to mind.

Arrival

- You have a choice to go out from your safe place and meet your fierce friend or to invite them in. Please take that opportunity now, if you like.

- Imagine yourself with your visitor, in just the right position—whatever feels right. Then allow yourself to experience what it's like to be in the company of this being: their bravery and determination, how loved and protected you feel. There is nothing you need to do except to experience the moment.

- This friend is wise and sees clearly, and understands exactly what's going on in your life right now. They see the areas where you need to be firm, to stand up for yourself or draw boundaries. Your friend may want to tell you something, something that is *just what you need to hear right now so you can protect yourself.* Please take a moment and listen carefully to what this wise being might have to say.

- Your friend may also want to give you a gift, some symbolic object that symbolizes caring force. Perhaps it materializes in your hand.

- If no words or gift come, that's okay, too—just continue to experience the strength, love, and protection. That's a blessing in itself.

- Take a few more moments to soak in this being's presence.

- Allow yourself to realize that this fierce friend is actually a *part of yourself.* All the feelings, images, and words that you are experiencing flow from your own fierce and tender heart.

Return

- Finally, when you're ready, allow the image to gradually dissolve in your mind's eye, remembering that this caring force is always within you, especially when you need it the most. You can call on your fierce friend anytime you wish.

STANDING UP TO INNER BULLIES

Compassionate self-protection is not only essential for preventing external harm, but also internal harm. Many people who were traumatized as children internalized the harsh critical messages of their abusive caregivers as a way to feel safe. Children need to trust what the adults in their lives tell them. A kid can't say to her father, as he's tearing into her for some perceived wrong, "I'm sorry, Dad, but you're way off base!" Not only would it make him even angrier, but it would be frightening to think he didn't know what he was talking about given her reliance on him for shelter, guidance, and protection. However, as adults, we can stand up to this inner bully. Self-criticism is no longer keeping us safe, it's harming us by undermining our ability to give ourselves the support we need. Self-compassion offers the brave, empowered clarity necessary to confront our inner critic and ask it to back off.

It's important to realize that it's not just people with early childhood trauma who have a harsh inner critic, and it isn't always a voice from the past. As discussed earlier, attacking ourselves seems to be a natural reaction to threat. You might think my son, Rowan, is never harshly self-critical. I wish that were true. Although I've talked to him about self-compassion his whole life, he can still be extremely hard on himself. Autistic people, like all of us, become frightened when recognizing their own imperfections because it reminds them that they aren't in complete control. Rowan gets extremely upset whenever he makes a mistake (like losing his phone charger or missing an important school assignment). I've often overheard him hurl insults at himself out loud: "You stupid moron," he'll say. I can't tell you how much it hurts to hear him utter these cruel words, and he certainly hasn't had anyone say such things to him in real life. But he likes to watch cartoons, and cartoon bullies often use this type of language. Bullying is a way to try to control things, and part of Rowan feels that he'll be able to control himself and prevent mistakes in the future if he's harsh enough.

He's also afraid that others will get angry and shout at him for messing up, so he does it first. Even though he's never actually had anyone yell at him for making a mistake, he projects this possibility, and it scares him. Self-criticism isn't just a learned behavior, it's also a human one that arises out of fear and the desire to stay safe. But we don't have to be a victim to our early childhood, cultural, or biological programming. There's another choice.

We can bravely stand up to our inner bully. We can draw strength from knowing how many of us suffer from voices inside our heads telling us that we're bad or disgusting. We aren't alone. When we stand up to the abusive voice of this inner critic, we're also standing up for millions of people around the globe who are shamed every day by their internal tyrant. We can say clearly and firmly to this part of ourselves, "It's not okay for you to talk to me that way," just as I tell Rowan, "It's not okay for you to talk to my beloved son that way." Without blaming or shaming our inner critic, we can reject its bullying tactics and draw a line in the sand. (The exercise Motivating Change with Compassion on page 204 shows how to relate to your inner critic in a way that is highly effective at subduing its voice.)

HEALING FROM MISTREATMENT

Tender self-compassion has an important role in self-protection as well. After doing as much as we can to defend ourselves, we need to turn inward to hold our wounds with compassion, balancing yin and yang. When people mistreat us—whether it's a teenage daughter who calls us names, a boss who pays us an unfair salary, a partner who cheats on us, or a parent who abused us—it hurts. Deeply. Tender self-compassion can provide us with the respect, consideration, and safety that we didn't receive from others. It's important that we don't skip the step of soothing and comforting ourselves when we've been mistreated. Sometimes when we get angry at others or take action (grounding a child, filing lawsuits, ending a relationship), we don't face our underlying feelings of hurt or sadness. While fierce action is fully necessary, we don't want to use it as a way of shielding ourselves from our pain. It can be easier to focus our anger on the person who's caused the harm than to deal with the more vulnerable feelings, like grief or rejection, that lie below that anger.

And lying even deeper down are usually needs that aren't being met: for fairness, love, connection, respect, or safety. We can't rely on those who have harmed us to meet them; wishing that they would change is often unrealistic. However, with tender self-compassion we can directly bring healing to ourselves and meet many of the needs that were disregarded by others. When we're being harmed, we need both protection and healing. One without the other is incomplete.

RESPONDING TO HARM

This practice is adapted from an exercise in MSC called Meeting Unmet Needs, and it can help you integrate both fierce and tender self-compassion when you've been mistreated in some way. Protective emotions such as anger or indignation are "hard" because they act like a shield and serve to protect us from experiencing softer, more vulnerable emotions such as hurt or sadness. We need to honor and attend to both our hard and soft feelings after being harmed, but they require different energies to hold them. Ideally this practice should be done after the danger or harm has passed and you're ready for some healing. If the mistreatment is ongoing, you may want to focus all your energy on stopping the behavior before bringing in the healing power of tender self-compassion. The Protective Self-Compassion Break exercise offered on page 148 or the practice of Working with Anger offered on page 83 may be more fitting in this case. If you start to feel overwhelmed at any point in this exercise, remember that you can always disengage and practice self-compassion in some other way.

Instructions

Think of a *past situation* in which you were mistreated in some way. Please choose a situation that was mildly to moderately disturbing but not traumatizing. It will be difficult to learn the practice if you are overwhelmed. Try to remember the details of the situation as vividly as possible.

Feeling your fierceness

- See if you can identify any hard emotions generated by the situation that feel protective, such as anger or bitterness.

- Now focus on your body. How do these feelings manifest? Is it a burning in your gut, a pounding in your head? See if you can get in touch with the physical sensation of the emotions.

- Recognize that these emotions stem from self-compassion, and that they are trying to keep you safe.

- Clearly acknowledge that it was not okay to be treated this way. Try saying to yourself some simple words acknowledging that harm was done, such as "It was wrong" or "I wasn't treated fairly."

- Now call upon common humanity, remembering that many people have experienced similar situations. Say some words that recognize your connection with others, such as "I am not alone" or "A lot of people have felt this way."

- Next, allow your emotions to flow freely as an energy in your body, without trying to control or suppress them. As you do so, also feel the soles of your feet firmly planted on the floor, helping to ground and stabilize you.

- *Fully validate* the experience of these protective emotions. Try not to get too caught up in who said or did what to whom, and instead focus on the hard feelings themselves. You might also say some words like "I need my anger for protection" or "I care about myself and that's why I'm so frustrated."

- It's not necessary to move on from here, if validating your emotions is what you need the most right now. Maybe you have suppressed your anger in the past, for instance, and need to fully feel it right now. If that's the case, just allow the emotions to flow through your body while grounding through the soles of your feet, without judgment.

- Try offering yourself a supportive gesture, such as placing a fist over your heart (a sign of strength) and covering it with the other hand (a sign of warmth).

Finding soft feelings

- If you are ready to bring in some healing, you need to see what's underneath the protective feelings. Are there any soft or vulnerable emotions, such as hurt, fear, rejection, sadness, shame?

- If you can identify a soft feeling, try naming it for yourself in a gentle, understanding voice, as if you were supporting a dear friend: "Oh, that's hurt" or "That's sadness."

- Allow yourself to be present with these feelings with warmth and acceptance.

Discovering unmet needs

- If you feel ready to move on, see if you can release the story line of what caused this hurt, if only for a while. Try to set aside thoughts of the transgression for a moment, asking yourself, "What *basic emotional need* do I have, or did I have at the time, that was not met?" Perhaps the need to be seen, heard, safe, connected, valued, special, respected, or loved?

- Again, if you can identify an unmet need, try naming it in a gentle, understanding voice.

Responding with tender self-compassion

- Feel the warmth and support of your hands on your body.

- Even though you wished to receive kindness or fair treatment from another, that person was unable to do so for a variety of reasons. But you have another resource—your own compassion—and you can start to meet your needs more directly.

- For example, if you needed to be seen, the compassionate part of you can say to the hurt part, "I see you!" If you needed to feel supported or connected, your compassionate part can say, "I'm here for you" or "You belong." If you needed to be respected, you can say, "I know my own value." If you needed to feel loved, perhaps you can say, "I love you" or "You matter to me."

- In other words, try to say to yourself, right now, what you wanted to hear from the person who mistreated you.

- If you're having trouble directly meeting your unmet needs, or if you feel confused, can you give yourself compassion for *that* difficulty?

- Finally, see if you can commit to treating yourself as you deserve to be treated, and vow to try to protect yourself from harm as much as possible in the future.

- Now let go of the exercise, and simply rest in your experience, letting this moment be exactly as it is, and yourself exactly as you are.

PROTECTION OR HOSTILITY?

When we're protecting ourselves, and yin and yang are out of balance, self-compassion can take an unhealthy form. Instead of focusing on preventing harm, we may focus on attacking the person or group causing the harm. As a result, our fierceness can become aggressive, which causes suffering and therefore undermines compassion.

What determines whether brave, empowered clarity is an expression of love or aggression? The difference lies in the intent underlying our actions. Are they done in the service of alleviating suffering or in the service of retaliation? Do they come from your heart or your ego? If fierceness comes from a place of protecting one's sense of self-worth, it can become emotionally violent. We may think we're standing up for ourselves when we snap back with a cutting comment at the person who just blew us off ("Keep rolling your eyes, you might eventually find a brain") or when we call the politician on TV a douchebag, but in fact we're just adding to the ill will in the room. However, when love is present in our response, and our intention is rooted in the desire to help, it becomes a strong and targeted force for the greater good. We can denounce harmful behavior and take action to prevent it without making it personal.

Compassion is rooted in connection, but when we forget this and recast those posing a threat as the "other," it creates a destructive us-against-them mentality. Sadly, this is what's happening with the incredible political polarization in the United States, making it almost impossible for our government to function. For our fierceness to be compassionate, we need to recognize that while physical, social, and emotional violence must be stopped, those causing harm are still human.

Of course, recognition of common humanity shouldn't be used as a way to deny differences either. Some people use the slogan "All Lives Matter" as a rebuttal to "Black Lives Matter." But this doesn't really honor common humanity, it just ignores the history of racial oppression, police brutality, and the dehumanization of Black people in particular. Fierce self-compassion acknowledges distinctions, including crucial differences in the source and amount of suffering individuals and groups experience, at the same time that it recognizes the powerful thread of humanity connecting us all.

Sometimes brave, empowered clarity can slip into self-righteousness. If we lose the open-minded acceptance of tender self-compassion, we can become too sure of ourselves and our ability to know the truth. When we become fixated on determining right versus wrong, it can actually work against our ability to see clearly. If we retain an open mind, however, we can more easily identify harmful behavior and speak the truth, even as we acknowledge the possibility that we might be mistaken in our view or that someone may have a different perspective.

When fierce and tender compassion are integrated as we protect against harm, the caring force that emerges is powerful beyond measure. As Martin Luther King Jr. wrote, "Power without love is reckless and abusive, and love without power is sentimental and anemic. Power at its best is love implementing the demands of justice, and justice at its best is power correcting everything that stands against love."

SELF-COMPASSION AND SOCIAL JUSTICE

Martin Luther King Jr. was inspired by Mahatma Gandhi, one of the most effective agents for social change in the twentieth century. Both fierce and tender compassion infused Gandhi's approach to fighting for justice: he advocated a form of nonviolent resistance called *satyagraha* (literally, "truth-force" or "love-force" in Hindi) to free India from British rule. Gandhi distinguished *satyagraha* from passive resistance, which he argued may come from fear. Satyagraha was a weapon of the strong that required incredible bravery and courage.

Although it might be easier to hate and attack one's oppressors, it's self-defeating to harm others as a means of ending personal suffering. It's also contradictory to use unjust methods to obtain justice or violence to obtain peace. This is why caring force must be directly aimed at preventing the harm being done rather than attacking the person or people causing it. As Gandhi said, "'Hate the sin and not the sinner' is a precept which, though easy enough to understand, is rarely practiced, and that is why the poison of hatred spreads in the world . . . It is quite proper to resist and attack a system, but to resist and attack its author is tantamount to resisting and attacking oneself, for we are all . . . children of one and the same Creator."

Lately, the phrase "Hate the sin and not the sinner" has been co-opted by certain fundamentalists who believe the quote comes from the Bible (it doesn't) and use it to justify their discrimination against the LBGTQ+ community. Fundamentalists argue that they can hate homosexuality without hating homosexuals. But their idea of sin, in this case, is behavior that doesn't conform to narrowly defined norms of gender and sexuality, and not behavior that's harming anyone. Compassion rejects harm, not nonconformity. Nonconformity to dominant patterns of gendered heterosexual behavior doesn't cause harm—just the opposite. It's a brave expression of love and authenticity. Twisting Gandhi's ideas to justify discrimination in this way only dishonors his intention. This is why clarity is so essential to fierce self-compassion. We need to be able to distinguish real harm from social norms designed to keep oppression in place.

When we protect ourselves from a place of compassion, we may be firm and unyielding, but there's love rather than hate in our hearts. This sense of fierce self-compassion formed the foundation for the Women's March on Washington on January 21, 2017, the day after Donald Trump was inaugurated as president. People around the world were furious at Trump's bragging about sexual assault in the infamous *Access Hollywood* tapes. ("You know I'm automatically attracted to beautiful—I just start kissing them. It's like a magnet. Just kiss. I don't even wait. And when you're a star, they let you do it. You can do anything. Grab 'em by the pussy. You can do anything.") However, the goal of the organizers wasn't to bash Trump, but to demonstrate support for the fair treatment and rights of women by holding a nonviolent protest in the tradition of past movements. It was also intended to show support for other groups being discriminated against based on race, ethnicity, sexual orientation, gender identity, immigration status, or religion. The Women's March set records for the largest single-day protest in US history, with approximately five million people participating in cities across the country. By combining care with the fierce determination to stand up against injustice, the movement was incredibly peaceful, with no arrests reported anywhere in the United States.

FIERCE SELF-COMPASSION AND ANTI-RACISM

Sexism and racism are intertwined because both are the result of oppression. They aren't the same—women can be racists and people of color can be sexists—but they are intertwined. Developing self-compassion won't dismantle entrenched structures of racial inequality on its own, but I believe it has a role to play. Just as unconscious gender bias leads us to collude with gender oppression, unconscious racial bias leads us to collude with racism. If White women hope to wake up and fight against racism, we need tender self-compassion to hold the pain of our collusion and see it for what it is, as well as fierce self-compassion to take action to stop it.

The feminist movement has been rightly criticized for, at best, not taking a strong enough stand against racism and, at worst, perpetuating it. Early suffragettes like Elizabeth Cady Stanton fully supported White supremacy. Southern feminists often supported Jim Crow— after all, lynching was purportedly intended to protect White women. The recent cliché of "Karen"—the tone-deaf White woman asserting her privilege—is still very real, as exemplified by Amy Cooper's 911 call to the police saying that "an African-American man is threatening me" in New York's Central Park just because a Black bird-watcher had dared to ask her to follow the rules and put her dog on a leash.

Often racism is displayed in more subtle ways, like assuming your experience as a White woman is universal, and ignoring the distinctly different experiences of women of color. Many feminist works focus exclusively on White women without even mentioning race. Racism explains how this has gone largely unnoticed and unremarked for decades. Because White women have more power than women of color, their narratives are considered the standard. The prototypical person is a man and the prototypical woman is White. As intersectional invisibility theory proposes, this means that women of color often don't even come into the picture in surveys of the human experience.

We need to call out power inequality and oppression wherever it's hiding in order to create sustainable change in society, because our fight against patriarchy will be meaningless unless it takes race into account. Oppression is oppression, and compassion is rooted in the motivation to alleviate the suffering caused by *all* injustice. Self-compassion will be crucial as White women do the hard work of recognizing our privilege and our own role in perpetuating a racist system. Tender self-compassion will help us to acknowledge how we've benefitted from being White, without averting our gaze in shame. Fierce self-compassion will enable us to take responsibility and commit to doing things differently.

As a White, cisgender, heterosexual woman, self-compassion has helped me begin to see my own role in a racist system. Like many, I consider myself a moral person and feel resistance when I'm asked to examine my own privilege. "But I'm not a racist!" my ego cries. The shame that wells up at the insinuation that we're racists interferes with our ability to acknowledge that we're indeed part of the problem. This can happen when committing microaggressions, like the time I was unhappy with my room assignment at a hotel and asked the Hispanic woman helping me if I could speak to her manager (she was the manager). If we're at all ego-defensive in such situations, we end up invalidating the experience of the person we've offended, silencing their voice. Being kind and understanding toward myself has facilitated my ability to see that, like most of us, I don't consciously oppress, but racism unconsciously influences my interactions with others simply by virtue of growing up in a racist society. I didn't create the unjust system of White supremacy I live in. The legacy of slavery and segregation existed long before I was born. Self-compassion counteracts the shame that arises when I recognize my passive participation in this system, allowing me to acknowledge how I benefit from it (I assume I'll be protected by the police; I never receive suspicious looks when hanging out in a coffee shop, etc.).

When I was a child, we didn't have a lot of money—my mother was a secretary who raised two kids on her own without any financial help from my absent father. But when I was eleven, my mother moved us to an inexpensive apartment on the far edge of a wealthy neighborhood with an amazing school district so that my brother and I could get a good education. I earned straight As, allowing me to go to UCLA on scholarship and eventually complete my Ph.D. at UC Berkeley. I was fully accepted in middle school and high school and fit right in. If I'd been Black, one of the lone Black faces in a sea of White ones, would my mother have felt comfortable putting me in that situation? Would I have had the same network of friends? Would teachers have supported me the same way? It's hard to know, but I certainly never had to waste a moment thinking about the color of my skin, a luxury that came from being White.

We need to have tender self-compassion to clearly see the role we play in racism, holding this uncomfortable truth with love and acceptance, so we can take the brave and difficult steps needed to do things differently. Many of the changes must come at the societal level, and the complexity of the restructuring that's needed is daunting. But each of us has a part to play, whether it's voting, protesting, speaking up whenever we hear racist comments, checking in to see if our interactions are being distorted by racial stereotypes, or apologizing sincerely if we unintentionally offend someone. To be honest, it's hard to know exactly what to do to make change happen, so we also need to be humble and listen and learn from others.

The bottom line is that sexism harms us all. Racism harms us all. Discrimination against any group—those with a different gender identity, sexual orientation, religion, ability level, body shape—harms us all. We're not separate individuals. Our ability to alleviate our own suffering is intricately interwoven with the commitment to end the suffering of all, because the peace of our neighborhoods, our societies, and ultimately the planet depends on it. Our power to change the world is stronger than we might think, so long as we always remember to develop and integrate fierce and tender self-compassion—the two faces of love.

CHAPTER 7

MEETING OUR NEEDS

I am my own muse, the subject I know best.
The subject I want to know better.

—*Frida Kahlo, artist and activist*

The essential self-compassion question is: What do I need? If we're going to care for ourselves, this means taking charge of our own well-being. In order to alleviate our own suffering, we have to take our needs seriously and value ourselves enough to meet them. Once we acknowledge that our needs matter—one of the first principles of self-compassion—we can stand our ground when we're asked to sacrifice what's important to us. We don't have to rank our needs below those of others, the way women have been socialized to do. If women only feel valued and worthy when we're helping children, partners, friends, family, coworkers—basically anyone other than ourselves—then we're supporting a system that's rigged against us. Sure, it's good to be kind and giving to others, but kindness must also be balanced so that it includes ourselves. If it doesn't, this generosity only serves a patriarchal system where women aren't considered valuable in their own right, as full and equal participants. It reduces women to the role of helpmate and prevents us from being authentically fulfilled.

The dictate that women should give rather than receive is a source of significant hardship. Women do the majority of household work, childcare, and eldercare even in marriages where both partners work full-time. This extra burden leads to stress and tension. Research shows that women are more likely than men to be strained by continually sacrificing our own needs to the demands of family, friends, and partners. One consequence of this pattern is that women wind up with less free time. A University of Maryland study carefully recorded the time men and women spent on various activities during the course of a typical day. Women not only had less time for themselves, but they also benefited less from the little they did have. The researchers attributed this to the fact that during their free time, women were still worrying about family issues, so that the leisure time available to them wasn't as refreshing or fulfilling. Ideally, free time provides escape from some of the tedious aspects of life and offers opportunities for personal growth and reflection. It helps increase creative thinking and enjoyment of life. Without it, life can lose much of its meaning and value.

When we include ourselves in the circle of compassion, our priorities start to change. We don't put our own needs first or last, but instead take a balanced approach. We say yes to others when we have the energy, but we're not afraid to say no. We judge our own needs to have equal weight in decisions about how to spend our time, money, and focus, giving ourselves full permission to care for ourselves. We decide what we value in life, then align our activities with these priorities.

When our goal is to alleviate suffering by meeting our own needs, the three elements of self-compassion—self-kindness, common humanity, and mindfulness—manifest as fulfilling, balanced authenticity.

FULFILLMENT

If we're kind to ourselves, we'll do what it takes to be happy. We'll ask what meaningfully contributes to our well-being and then take proactive steps to make it happen. If we value time in nature, we take that time. If it's sensuality that feeds us, we slow down and savor our partner's caress rather than just doing the deed. If it's artistic expression that makes us come alive, we nurture the flame of creativity. If spirituality is our deepest calling, we don't let the busyness of everyday life stand in the way of turning inward. We *must* do so if we care, because we suffer when we're not fulfilled. Being stuck in an unsatisfying life weighs on our happiness like a concrete block.

The search for fulfillment is closely related to finding meaning in life—understanding ourselves, making sense of the world, and knowing our place within it. Studies have demonstrated that people who are self-compassionate report experiencing greater meaning, and are more likely to agree with statements like "My life has a clear sense of purpose." They also experience more "harmonious passion": they engage in activities that they truly enjoy and find satisfying.

Most of us weren't raised to think much about emotional or psychological fulfillment, or the kind of life we truly want to live. We were directed toward passing set milestones—graduating high school, receiving a college degree (if that was the expectation), getting a job, finding a life partner, having children and raising them, advancing in our career. It's often not until retirement that we even pause to seriously consider what makes us fulfilled or satisfied.

But when we truly care for ourselves, the question "What do I need?" becomes woven into the fabric of our lives. Instead of leaving that question for later, neglecting something we know to be important but don't have the time to answer, we orient our lives to be satisfied while living it, right now, in the present moment. The type of work we do and how we spend our free time is integrated with what we care about: the environment, music, learning, diversity, spirituality, health. It becomes part of our approach to daily life, rather than a goal to be achieved sometime in the distant future.

Finding fulfillment involves spending time to become competent at those activities we enjoy, so we feel a sense of mastery. This allows us to effectively participate in and influence our world. Whether it's learning to meditate, running a marathon, organizing a national conference, or creating interesting after-school activities for our kids, developing our potential gives our days meaning and purpose. Personal growth takes energy and effort and sometimes courage. It can be frightening to try something new, especially if we feel comfortable with the way things are. We might also be afraid of failing. The beauty of self-compassion is that unconditional self-acceptance makes it safe for us to take this brave leap forward. When we know it's okay to fail, we can challenge ourselves in novel ways that have the potential to make us happier. Self-kindness pushes us out of complacency, into the unknown terrain of growth and discovery.

BALANCE

When we meet our needs as an act of self-compassion, it's not selfish or one-sided. The recognition of common humanity at the core of self-compassion requires that we're neither self-focused nor other-focused. Instead, we use wisdom to see the larger whole and figure out what's fair, balanced, and sustainable. Connection is a core human need, so if we take actions that damage our relationships with others, we're actually harming ourselves. A healthy balance between doing what we want and helping others is essential in self-compassion.

I've been interested in how people balance their own and others' needs for some time. Early in my research career I conducted a study with one of my graduate students on how college undergraduates resolve conflicts when their personal needs came into conflict with those of someone important in their life. For instance, maybe a student wants to spend a year studying abroad but it would mean leaving her boyfriend behind. Or maybe she wants to stay on campus during Thanksgiving break to spend time with friends, but Mom wants her to come home for the holidays. Our goal was to determine the impact of self-compassion on young people's ability to balance their own needs with those of friends and intimates when they clashed, and how this affected their emotional well-being. First, we determined how they resolved the conflict. Did they give in and subordinate their needs to those of someone else? Did they prioritize their own needs at the expense of another? Or were they able to compromise and come up with a creative solution that met everyone's needs? We then asked participants to tell us how distressed they were when figuring out what to do about the conflict, and how authentic they felt their resolution was. Finally, we assessed their psychological well-being in their specific relationships with their mother, father, best friend, or romantic partner. Did they feel good about themselves in the relationship or did they feel depressed and unhappy?

We found that young people who had more self-compassion were significantly more likely to report compromising in a way that took into account the needs of each party. They didn't give up what was personally important, but they didn't put their own needs first either. We also found that participants with more self-compassion reported less emotional turmoil when resolving relationship conflicts and felt more valued and less depressed in their relationships. In fact, findings indicated that the tendency of self-compassionate people to compromise in conflict situations helped explain *why* they were happier, suggesting that having balance is key to well-being. And an important finding was that self-compassionate individuals were more likely to report feeling authentic when resolving relationship conflicts, suggesting that a central benefit of self-compassion is the permission it gives us to be our true selves.

AUTHENTICITY

Mindfulness helps us to be authentic by clarifying our inner beliefs, values, and emotions. It allows us to turn inward, facilitating the introspection necessary for authenticity. When we lead an unexamined life, we can get lost in an endless quest for more money, more stuff, more praise, none of it ever bringing real happiness. Many a midlife crisis has been fueled by the realization that we were in the wrong place doing the wrong things with the wrong people, or as the Talking Heads put it: "And you may tell yourself, this is not my beautiful house! This is not my beautiful wife!" If we just go along with the program, we may wake up one day to find that we're frustrated and bored. We might leave our relationship or get a new car or plastic surgery in a quest for happiness. But none of it will help until we look inside ourselves and ask, "What's truly right for me?"

Mindfulness gives us the perspective needed to reflect on our actions, so that we don't heedlessly drift into a shallow life. It allows us to pay attention not only to what we're doing but *why* we're doing it, so that we can act with integrity. Jia Wei Zhang at the University of California, Berkeley spearheaded a series of studies examining the experience of authenticity cultivated by self-compassion. In one study, participants completed a short survey every day for a week and were asked to rate how self-compassionate they felt that day and also how authentic they felt in their interactions with others. Researchers found that daily variations in levels of self-compassion mapped closely to variations in feelings of authenticity.

A second study found that the authenticity of self-compassion allows us to acknowledge our weaknesses. Authenticity isn't a cherry-picking process that views our strengths as true and shortcomings as false; it's about embracing our whole self—the good, the bad, and the ugly. Researchers asked participants to consider a personal weakness that made them feel bad about themselves. They were then randomized either to a self-compassion condition: "Imagine that you are talking to yourself about this weakness from a compassionate and understanding perspective"; a self-esteem condition: "Imagine that you are talking to yourself about this weakness from a perspective of validating your positive (rather than negative) qualities"; or a neutral condition where they were given no instructions at all (meaning they probably beat themselves up about their weakness). Immediately afterward, participants were asked to indicate how authentic they felt acknowledging their shortcoming. Participants who were instructed to be self-compassionate reported significantly stronger feelings of authenticity compared to participants in the other two conditions. Self-compassion gives us the freedom to be true to ourselves without having to meet unrealistic standards of perfection, something that self-esteem doesn't offer.

When we take action to fulfill ourselves, we find a type of contentment that eludes many women, who are told from birth that happiness lies primarily in caring for others. That's why it's so important that we intentionally reflect on what we truly need and value in life, then commit to meeting those needs.

PROVIDING SELF-COMPASSION BREAK

This version of the Self-Compassion Break cultivates fierce self-compassion so we can provide for our needs with fulfilling, balanced authenticity. (A guided audio version of this practice can be found at FierceSelf-Compassion.org.)

Instructions

Think of a situation in your life where you feel your needs aren't being met. Maybe you aren't taking enough time for yourself, or maybe you're in a job you really dislike, or maybe you are spending your free time doing things that don't make you happy. Call up the situation in your mind's eye. What's happening? Allow yourself to feel whatever emotions are coming up. For example, are there feelings of exhaustion, boredom, resentment, hopelessness? Make contact with the discomfort as a physical sensation. Now focus on the need that isn't being met. For example, the need for rest, for peace, for learning, for fun, for excitement, whatever you've identified. Let go of the particulars of your situation and just focus on your unmet need.

Now sit up so that your body is alert. You're going to say a series of phrases (aloud or silently to yourself) designed to bring in the three components of self-compassion to help you take action to meet your needs and provide for yourself. Although words will be suggested, the goal is to find language that makes sense to you and feels natural.

- The first phrase evokes mindfulness so you can become aware of and validate your deepest needs. Say to yourself with meaning, "This is what I need to be authentic and whole." Other options are "This is really important to me," "My needs matter," or "My true self needs this to be happy."

- The second phrase is meant to help you remember common humanity, so that you can balance your needs with those of others. Recognizing the needs of all helps to maintain equilibrium. Try saying to yourself, "I will honor my needs as well as the needs of others." Other options are "All humans have important needs," "My needs count and so do those of others," or "Life involves receiving as well as giving."

- Now put both hands over your solar plexus, feeling your center. As an act of self-kindness, we can take concrete steps to give ourselves what we need. Try saying to yourself, "I will commit to fulfilling my needs as best I can." Other options might be "I deserve to be happy," "I will provide for myself joyfully," or "I will do what's necessary to be healthy and well."

- If you're having difficulty finding the right words, imagine that someone you really cared about was feeling unfulfilled. What would you say to this person to help them respect their own needs, to put in the time and effort needed to be happy? Now, can you offer the same message to yourself?

- Finally, put one hand over your heart and leave the other hand on your solar plexus. The invitation is to combine the fierce energy of pursuing your needs with the tender energy of loving, connected presence. Can you take action to be more fulfilled, while also realizing that you are already whole and complete exactly as you are? The desire to meet your needs doesn't come from a place of deficiency, but from an abundant heart.

DEVELOPING OUR POTENTIAL

The importance of meeting our needs was emphasized by the Human Potential Movement, which eschewed psychology's traditional focus on pathology and proposed that people have untapped capacity to develop extraordinary lives filled with creativity, meaning, and joy. Abraham Maslow, the founder of the movement, described this as a process of self-actualization. When we foster our natural talents and inclinations so they're allowed to unfold without hindrance, we can fulfill our potential. We can also accept ourselves and our human imperfections, having actively explored our inner and outer worlds so that we know what we're capable of. Maslow argued that if we don't take meeting our needs for growth seriously, we'll stagnate.

Psychologists Ed Deci and Rich Ryan, creators of Self-Determination Theory, propose that competence, relatedness, and autonomy are core human needs, and that healthy development can be defined in terms of how well we meet these needs. Competence is a function of acting effectively in a way that's satisfying and rewarding. Relatedness means we're in reciprocal and balanced relationships with others. Autonomy involves acting in harmony with our inner values and desires. There are thousands of research studies supporting the idea that meeting these core needs leads to optimal well-being. There's also research showing that self-compassion helps us do so. For instance, one study examined a group of undergraduates during their first year at college and found that students who were more self-compassionate also experienced greater autonomy, competence, and relatedness, and that increased fulfillment of these needs led to enhanced mental health, a sense of aliveness, and greater vitality over the course of the year.

I saw this play out for a student who took my undergraduate course on self-compassion at UT Austin. Tania (pronounced Ta-NI-a) was a funny and wise African-American woman in her sixties. She sometimes stopped by my office hours to talk about material we covered in class, and she told me how she came to be a proud sixty-five-year-old Longhorn junior. Tania had grown up in Houston and got a job right out of high school to help support her family. She found stable employment at a dry cleaners and worked there for years, eventually becoming manager of the business. She raised three girls with little help from her husband, whom she'd divorced long ago. Tania's children eventually got married and had babies of their own—six in total. They all lived close by and relied on her to babysit the little ones on weekends and after school. But Tania had a terrible secret. She didn't like babies or toddlers. They cried too much and had very few interesting things to say. And she especially hated changing diapers—hadn't she finished with that a long time ago? Regardless, her children depended on her help, "So I did my doodie duty," she joked. "My life was crap, literally." It eventually started to get to her, despite her good humor, and she became mildly dispirited.

Apparently, an old friend who'd noticed the change asked Tania what she needed to be happy. The question, she told me, stopped her in her tracks. She'd never seriously considered it before—she was too busy working and caring for everyone else. After mulling it over, Tania realized that she wanted to go to college to study English. She'd always found solace and refuge in books growing up, and she knew the flames of her intelligence had never really been fanned. She dreamed about going to community college in the evenings and weekends to get an associate's degree, perhaps even transferring to a university to earn a bachelor's. But this would mean she wouldn't have time to babysit her grandchildren. Would it be selfish to put her own needs first?

Still, this was an opportunity to learn and grow in a way she'd never fully experienced before, and the possibility tantalized her. She decided to go for it. When she told her daughters they would have to find other childcare, at first they were upset, but they quickly changed their minds and threw their full support behind their mother. They loved her deeply and were grateful for all she'd given them.

Tania took to her community college classes like a duck to water. She got straight As even while managing the dry cleaners and applied as a transfer student to UT. She got in. Tania was about to turn sixty-five, so she decided to retire and draw on her social security to rent a small apartment in Austin—and became a full-time student. Although Tania said she enjoyed my class, it was clear she'd already learned about the importance of meeting her own needs. She was able to dive into the experience of self-compassion with a depth of appreciation that was beautiful to behold. I asked her about her plans after graduation—what did she want to do? She just gave me a big smile and said, "I'm not thinking about tomorrow. I'm living for today."

WOMEN'S NEEDS IN A PATRIARCHAL WORLD

One reason that cultivating self-compassion is so essential for women is because the norms and expectations of patriarchy work so strongly against us acting to meet our own needs. People who adhere to an ideology of benevolent sexism see women as born nurturers who are happy to sacrifice our own interests for others. From this viewpoint, giving is our calling in life. Of course, if that were true, we'd always find self-sacrifice to be a source of authentic fulfillment. But that isn't the case—especially when giving isn't spontaneous but merely what's socially expected.

I conducted my dissertation research in Mysore, India, because I was curious about how culture shaped people's views of gender and meeting personal needs. Scholars sometimes describe non-Western societies like India as having a duty-based morality, where emphasis is placed on meeting the needs of others rather than on rights or personal autonomy, which are presumed to be Western concerns. This broad distinction between East and West closely parallels the proposition that women have a care-based morality and that men are more concerned with rights and justice. My dissertation advisor Elliot Turiel argued against both of these simplistic characterizations and believed that concerns with autonomy, justice, and caring for others were universal. However, their expression partly depends on power relations.

Cultures that emphasize duties are often hierarchical. This means that while caring for others is emphasized for subordinates, rights and personal prerogatives are plentiful for those in power. In India, for example, Hindu women are trained from an early age in self-sacrifice (termed *sewa*) to men through practices such as serving food to males first, with females eating the remains only after they're finished. Traditionally, a dowry had to be paid to the family of a bride's husband, reinforcing the perception that women are a burden and not as valuable as men. As married adults, women are expected to care for their husbands and children, but tend to receive significantly less food, clothing, health care, and education than males. I hypothesized that when thinking about conflicts between wives and husbands in India, males would judge that wives should do their duty and that husbands should have the right to do what they want. I thought females might see things a bit differently.

I had two amazing graduate students from the local university who conducted the interviews for my research—Susmitha Devaraj and Manimala Dwarkaprasad. They were strong young women who helped me understand the amazing complexity of gender roles in India and showed by example that women were not content to be suppressed. They talked about the weight of tradition in India, how hard it was to swim against the tide, pointing out how often women simply accepted their roles as a part of life because it seemed there were no other options. However, that didn't mean they thought things were fair. Not to mention, India had produced great female leaders like Indira Gandhi, the world's longest-serving prime minister, who ruled with an iron fist from 1966 to 1988. Would these varied and seemingly contradictory views of female gender roles show up in people's moral reasoning?

I recruited seventy-two Hindu youths for my study (children, adolescents, and young adults), and included equal numbers of males and females. Participants were given a series of vignettes about married couples in which the needs and desires of spouses conflicted. The research was designed so that the actor in each situation was either a husband or a wife. For instance, one question focused on a husband named Vijay who wants to take music lessons on the veena (an Indian string instrument), but his wife wants him to do odd jobs around the home instead. A parallel story focused on a wife named Suma who wants to take classical dance classes, but her husband wants her to stay home to do housework. Participants were asked to decide what the actor should do and why.

Unsurprisingly, I found that responses tended to emphasize meeting personal needs more for husbands than for wives. However, Indian females often believed that the wife *should* be able to meet her own needs, even if the culture didn't allow it. In response to the dance story, for example, they typically said Suma should do what she wants. As one adolescent girl put it, "Suma should go to the dance class, as that is the only way she can fulfill her interests. She also must do what she is interested in, or else it will leave her very unhappy and disinterested in life. . . . Whatever the tradition demands is not right always. Many a time tradition seems very absurd. I will not respect a tradition which comes in the way of one's own self-interest. How will an individual grow if the tradition becomes a barrier for dynamism? I will surely want Suma to go to the dance class." My experience taught me that girls and women deeply value self-fulfillment, even in traditional, highly patriarchal societies. When the larger social structure imposes restrictions on our ability to meet our own needs, we still want an equal shot at happiness.

Although the barriers to self-fulfillment are more subtle for women in the West, they're still there. While prioritizing others is no longer described as our *duty*, it's an unspoken expectation of being a good woman. We're told that in order to be "nice" we must agree to others' requests: "Would you mind covering my shift?" or "Could you walk my dogs while I'm on vacation?" or "Can you make the travel arrangements?" If we don't mind doing these things, it can feel good to say yes, but if we do mind it doesn't feel so good. Every time we unthinkingly say yes to our friend or partner or child or colleague because we think we *should*—without checking in with ourselves to see whether this is what we really want—we're reinforcing gendered norms of self-sacrifice. This isn't to say that we should never choose to meet others' needs instead of our own, but we should do it as a conscious choice, after considering all our options, not because we think we must in order to be a good person. And when we recognize that a choice isn't right for us, self-compassion demands that we honor our needs and try to do something else if possible.

DISCOVERING WHAT MAKES US HAPPY

When I first got a faculty position at UT Austin, my then-husband Rupert and I bought a house in the countryside on seven acres. The property was in the small town of Elgin, forty-five minutes outside of downtown Austin and the UT campus. We moved there because Rupert, a riding enthusiast, wanted to keep horses. Later, our son, Rowan, was homeschooled at the New Trails Learning Center, an equine therapy center his father created on our land.

I continued to live in Elgin for years after Rupert and I split up (we remained friends) because Rowan seemed happy there. But the honest truth is that I don't like horses. I'm a city not a country gal. There's no coffee shop to hang out at in Elgin and the food choices are extremely limited. The town is mainly known for its sausage; not exactly a culinary haven for a gluten- and dairy-intolerant pescatarian like me. It's also extremely conservative Trump country, the cultural opposite of liberal Austin. To give you a sense of it, during the pandemic, a bar in Elgin made national news by forbidding patrons to wear masks. But I lived in this alien place—well out of my comfort zone—for almost twenty years in order to meet others' needs.

I finally moved to the heart of Austin a couple years ago, in part so that Rowan could get a better education, but also because I was sick and tired of Elgin. It's only now that I realize how much I gave up by living in a cultural milieu that wasn't authentic for me. I love being close to things now, a five-minute drive from a coconut milk matcha latte and ten minutes from campus. It makes me happy. I don't necessarily regret the decision I made to stay in Elgin for longer than I wanted to, but I have a much greater appreciation for how important it is to lead a life that authentically meets our needs. I won't compromise and wind up living somewhere that isn't right for me again.

When we really care about ourselves, our needs matter. They *must* matter. Our ideals of being loving, caring, giving women must include ourselves or else it's not really loving. By denying our own authenticity and fulfillment, we are, on a spiritual and psychological level, limiting the natural expression of a unique and beautiful individual whose story cannot be told by any other. And on a political level, we're unwittingly maintaining patriarchy. Fortunately, we have a chance to upset this status quo if we take an active role in questioning these norms and find the courage to do things differently. Self-compassion provides a way for women to value ourselves, which is the first step toward changing a biased system. It will happen in rallies and the voting booth, but it also needs to happen in our own hearts as we ask ourselves, "What do I need in this moment?"

It's helpful to distinguish between wants and needs, as well as goals and values. Wants are longings for something pleasant or desirable, such as financial success, a nice house or car, physical attractiveness, or a fancy meal. Needs are what's essential to our emotional or physical survival, such as being safe, healthy, and connected to others, or having meaning in our lives. Needs also tend to be general rather than specific (i.e., needing a peaceful household versus wanting my argumentative roommate to move out).

Goals, on the other hand, are particular objectives we want to achieve, such as earning a master's degree, getting married, losing twenty pounds, or traveling to Africa. Values are beliefs about what's important that orient us toward our goals, then keep us going after they're achieved. Values provide meaning and purpose in our life. Examples of values are generosity, honesty, learning, friendship, loyalty, hard work, peace, curiosity, adventure, health, and harmony with nature. In short, goals are something we do, values are something we live. As Thomas Merton wrote, "If you want to identify me, ask me not where I live, or what I like to eat, or how I comb my hair, but ask me what I am living for, in detail, and ask me what I think is keeping me from living fully for the things I want to live for."

So how do we know if our actions are congruent with our authentic needs and values and that we aren't merely acting to please others or to meet some societal ideal? One way is by becoming aware of the emotional consequences of our actions. For instance, let's say you were raised to value service to others, and every Sunday after church you make sandwiches to give to the homeless people in your community. If this is a fulfilling and authentic action, you'll feel joyous and energized after a day spent making ham-and-cheese sandwiches and handing them out on the street. If it's inauthentic and you're doing it because you think, "That's what a good person is supposed to do," you'll feel drained and annoyed at the end of the day. Figuring out what we really need and value in life, and taking the actions necessary to live in harmony with what's important, is central to personal fulfillment.

LIVING A FULFILLING LIFE

This exercise is adapted from a practice we teach in the MSC program called Discovering Our Core Values. It draws on Acceptance and Commitment Therapy developed by Steven Hayes and colleagues, which emphasizes committed action to our most important values as the cornerstone of living a fulfilling and authentic life. This is a written reflection exercise, so take out a pen and paper.

Instructions

Looking back

- Imagine that you are some years in the future. You're sitting in a lovely garden as you contemplate your life. Looking back at the time between now and then, you feel a deep sense of satisfaction, fulfillment, and contentment. Even though life hasn't always been easy, you managed to stay true to yourself and spent as much time as possible doing what gave you joy.

- What were the deep needs you fulfilled or values you honored that were so satisfying? For example, adventure, creativity, learning, spirituality, family, community, spending time in nature? Please write down what fulfilled you.

Looking at the present

- To what extent are you currently meeting your needs for happiness? Is your life out of balance in any way? Are you spending too much time meeting others' needs, or are you too busy to tend to yourself? Please write down any way in which you are unfulfilled.

Obstacles

- We all have obstacles that prevent us from meeting our needs. Some of these may be *external obstacles*, like not having enough money or time. Often the obstacle is that we have other obligations; for instance, we may have to support a family or take care of someone who is ill. Please reflect on this for a moment and then write down any external obstacles.

- There may also be some *internal obstacles* getting in the way of your ability to meet your needs. For instance, are you too cautious, do you want to please others, are you afraid of being selfish, or maybe you feel you don't deserve to be happy? Please drop inside and reflect, and then write down any internal obstacles.

- Notice the deep yearning and desire within you to be happy, and whether there are any feelings of sadness or frustration if your needs are not being fulfilled.

Calling up fierce self-compassion

- Now write down any ways you think fierce self-compassion could help you overcome some of the obstacles that are getting in the way of meeting your needs. Could it give you the courage to say no? Help you feel safe and confident enough to take new actions, risk disapproval, or let go of things that aren't serving you? What can you do to help yourself be happier and more fulfilled?

- If you feel some hesitancy, remember that the more you meet your own needs the more energy you will have to give to others. Can you commit to taking action to care for yourself?

Calling up tender self-compassion

- Of course, sometimes there are insurmountable obstacles to being truly fulfilled. Part of being human is the fact that we can't have everything exactly the way we want it.

- So close your eyes for a moment and put your hands on your heart or some other soothing place. Can you make space for the reality that we can't always be fulfilled, that we can't always meet our needs the way we want to?

- Write down some words of kindness and acceptance about these human limitations.

Balancing yin and yang

- Finally, try to integrate the energy of fierce and tender self-compassion. At the same time that we accept our present moment experience as it is, we can also make a good-willed effort to change our circumstances. Is there any creative way you can fulfill your needs that you haven't considered before, even if this expression is incomplete? For instance, if you love nature and you work in an office all day, can you walk instead of drive to the office or bring in plants to make your environment more natural? Are there small things you can do to fulfill yourself? If so, please write this down too.

SELF-COMPASSION OR SELF-INDULGENCE?

Some people are afraid that using self-compassion to meet our needs can act as a cover for self-indulgence. If I call in late to work one morning because I need to catch up on sleep that may be self-compassionate. But if I do it several times per week? Can one be *too* self-compassionate? If we truly care about ourselves, we won't engage in feel-good behaviors that are bad for us. Self-indulgence involves choosing short-term pleasure at the expense of long-term harm, and self-compassion always has its eye on the prize: alleviating suffering.

First, mindfulness allows us to look clearly at what we authentically need, not just what we want. Do I really need to turn the alarm off, or am I just wanting the temporary pleasure of slipping off into slumber once more? Second, we can draw on kindness to ensure that our behavior is truly in our best interest. Is getting to work late really helping, especially given that it will surely have negative repercussions? Or would it be better to go to bed earlier to ensure that I get sufficient rest? Finally, the wisdom of common humanity—the ability to see the larger picture and how everything is interconnected—ensures that our behavior is balanced and sustainable. How will my behavior affect my job or the ability of my coworkers to function effectively? Self-compassion helps us to answer these questions in a way that reduces self-indulgent behavior.

Studies have shown that self-compassionate people engage in self-care behaviors that are healthy rather than indulgent. For instance, they're more likely to read the nutrition labels on packaged foods to make healthier choices, engage in regular physical exercise, and get enough sleep. Among those grappling with illnesses such as fibromyalgia, chronic fatigue syndrome, or cancer, self-compassion leads to greater adherence to medical advice and treatment plans, whether that means taking medication as prescribed, changing one's diet, or exercising more often. Elderly people who are self-compassionate visit the doctor more regularly and are more willing to use assistive devices such as walkers. A large multinational study of individuals living with HIV/AIDS found that those with greater self-compassion were more likely to protect themselves and others by using condoms during sex.

When researchers explored why self-compassionate people were more willing to engage in self-care behavior, they found it stemmed directly from what they called "benevolent self-talk." They speak to themselves in encouraging and supportive ways that emphasize the importance of being good to oneself.

PROVIDING FOR OURSELVES OR SELFISHNESS?

Another common misconception is the idea that being self-compassionate is selfish. This creates an especially strong barrier for women, who've been raised practically since birth to care for and meet others' needs. Of course, if we don't make sure that the elements of fierce and tender self-compassion are all in place, meeting our own needs can run the risk of becoming a cover for self-centeredness. Without a clear understanding of connectedness and interdependence, we might turn things into a zero-sum game: I meet my needs at the expense of yours. When we do this, happiness eludes us. If I have a friend who requires time and attention because she's going through a bad breakup and I ignore her because I'm busy with my own pursuits, I'll also suffer. I'll feel bad when she gets upset with me, the quality of our friendship will deteriorate, and I won't be able to count on my friend's support if I ever find myself in her position in the future. But when yin and yang are balanced, it doesn't work this way. When we remember that love is our deepest need, then giving to ourselves automatically includes giving to others. In fact, fulfilling, balanced authenticity is what allows us to sustain our generosity of heart. We don't deplete ourselves so that we wind up with nothing left to give. Instead, we nourish ourselves by feeding our connections.

There's ample research to support the idea that self-compassion isn't selfish. For instance, self-compassionate people tend to have more compassionate goals in their close relationships, meaning they tend to provide a lot of emotional support to others they are close to. They are also described by their romantic partners as being more caring and giving in their relationships. They're more accepting of the flaws and shortcomings of others, and better at perspective-taking or considering outside viewpoints.

It may surprise you to learn that the link between self-compassion and compassion for others is generally small. In other words, people with a lot of self-compassion tend to have slightly more compassion for others than those low in self-compassion, but not a lot more. That's because the vast majority of people are significantly more compassionate to others than they are to themselves. There are many people, women especially, who are compassionate, generous, and kind souls to others but treat themselves poorly. If there were a strong association between self-compassion and compassion for others, it would mean that people who lack self-compassion would also lack compassion for others. But that just isn't true.

Nonetheless, learning to be self-compassionate does increase our ability to be compassionate to others. In one study, we found that participation in MSC increased participants' compassion to others by 10 percent. Most people were high in compassion to others to begin with (they started with an average of 4.17 on a five-point scale and ended with a 4.46), so there wasn't a lot of room for improvement. Self-compassion increased by 43 percent—partly because participants started with an average of 2.65 and ended with a 3.78 on a similar five-point scale. This demonstrates that growing in self-compassion doesn't mean you become *less* caring toward others—quite the opposite. More important, self-compassion allows us to *sustain* caring for others over time without draining ourselves or burning out (we'll discuss this more in Chapter 10).

There's another reason why self-compassion isn't selfish: because it spurs other people to treat themselves compassionately as well. In their paper titled "Is Self-Compassion Contagious?" researchers at the University of Waterloo examined how displays of self-compassion influence others. Students were asked to recall a personal academic failure and were then randomly assigned to listen to an audio clip of another student talking to themselves about a failure in a self-compassionate way ("I understand that you are disappointed—that's so natural after an experience like this . . .") or in a neutral manner ("I ended up barely scraping by, passing, but not by much . . ."). Participants who listened to the clip of someone being self-compassionate subsequently wrote about their own academic failure with greater compassion. The researchers attributed their findings to a process of social modeling, in which we learn behavior by observing others. So, by being compassionate to ourselves—especially when we do so obviously—we're helping others to do the same.

Because we're so interconnected, it's nonsensical to draw an arbitrary dividing line between ourselves and others when dealing with the pain of life. Albert Einstein famously said, "Our task must be to free ourselves by widening our circle of compassion to embrace all living creatures and the whole of nature and its beauty." We're the center of that circle. We don't want to limit the scope of concern to ourselves, but we don't want to cut ourselves out of that circle either. To do so would be to betray our own humanity.

When Maslow described self-actualization, he emphasized that letting go of egoic concerns was central to the process. He argued that to realize our true nature, we have to discover a calling or purpose that's larger than our small selves. In fact, the "self" in terms like self-compassion and self-actualization is misleading, because these states actually lessen the focus on a separate self.

The beautiful truth is that developing our full potential allows us to better help others. When I grow my skills as an educator, I expand the possibilities for my students. When I nurture a talent, whether it's becoming a master chef or a classical singer or a medevac helicopter pilot, it helps contribute to the quality of others' lived experience. When I develop my inner world so that I'm more engaged and alive, I'll bring that vibrancy to everyone I come into contact with. Meeting our own needs is a gift to the world.

CHAPTER 8

BECOMING OUR BEST SELVES

When we truly choose to care about something,
change always happens.

—Megan Rapinoe, captain of the USA Women's Soccer Team

If we care about ourselves and don't want to suffer, we'll naturally be motivated to achieve our dreams and let go of behaviors that don't serve us anymore. A major impediment to practicing self-compassion is the fear that we'll be lazy and unmotivated if we're not incredibly hard on ourselves. This fear stems from misunderstanding the yin and yang of self-compassion. It's true that the tender side of self-compassion helps us accept ourselves in all our glorious imperfection. It reminds us that we don't need to be flawless to be lovable. We don't need to fix ourselves. We're good enough just as we are now to be worthy of care and kindness.

But does this mean that we don't try to change unhealthy habits, to reach our goals, or fulfill our destiny? Absolutely not. The desire to alleviate our suffering drives us forward to attain what we want in life not out of a sense of insufficiency or inadequacy, but out of love. Instead of harshly criticizing ourselves every time we make a mistake or fail at something important to us, we focus on what we can learn from the situation. When we use fierce self-compassion to motivate ourselves, we experience it as encouraging, wise vision.

ENCOURAGEMENT

The word *encourage* comes from the Old French "to take heart," and with self-compassion we take heart as we guide ourselves on the path of growth and change. Rather than threatening to punish ourselves if we don't achieve our goals, we're kind and supportive, affirming our inherent potential. Encouragement doesn't mean lying to ourselves or using positive affirmations such as "Every day in every way I am getting stronger and stronger" because that may not be the case. Once we get past a certain age, we *don't* keep getting stronger and stronger (at least physically). Also, research shows that positive affirmations don't help if you doubt yourself. They ring hollow, backfire, and just make you feel worse. But encouragement allows us to take the journey as far as we're able to go, even if it doesn't turn out to be as far as we'd hoped. When I can trust that even if I blow it, I won't cruelly turn on myself but will instead be supportive, it establishes the sense of safety needed to take risks. I'll draw inspiration and energy from my own loving heart, and try harder because I want to, not because I have to in order to be acceptable.

Mark Williamson, who runs the Action for Happiness organization in the United Kingdom, said that he was radically changed after hearing me give a talk on self-compassion and motivation. He realized that he was always berating himself whenever he made a mistake. "You f***ing idiot" was a common refrain—as if swearing at himself would make him try harder next time. The voice was so habitual it almost operated outside of his awareness, but it still negatively impacted him and undermined his self-confidence. So he started doing an intentional practice whenever he noticed he was beating himself up for some perceived failure, redirecting his instinct to swear at himself with an acronym: Friendly, Useful, Calm, Kind. It's much more constructive and motivating than verbal abuse!

Kindness doesn't mean condoning anything we do, of course, because that's also not helpful. Sometimes we have to use tough love, to be fierce with ourselves to stop unhealthy behavior. If we're really harming ourselves—addicted to alcohol or drugs, or stuck in a toxic relationship—we may need to say no quite firmly. Tough love is strong but ultimately kind. It gives clear messages like "You need to leave because if you stay you will continue to be depressed." Encouragement makes it clear that the desire for change comes from a place of care and commitment, rather than blame or judgment, which is why it's ultimately more effective.

WISDOM

The wisdom of common humanity allows us to see the complex conditions that lead to success or failure, so we can learn from our mistakes. We all know that failure is our best teacher. As Thomas Edison said, "I have not failed. I've just found ten thousand ways that won't work." We understand that there's more information of value in getting it wrong than in getting it right.

So why are we so upset when we get it wrong? It's because we unconsciously believe that we *shouldn't* fail, and that there's something wrong with us when we do. We get so overwhelmed by the feelings of shame and self-blame that go along with failure that we can't see clearly, which inhibits our ability to grow.

Research shows that self-compassionate people are wiser and better able to learn from the situations they find themselves in. When confronted with a problem, they're more likely to consider all relevant information and less likely to get so upset that they can't come up with solutions. Self-compassionate people are also more likely to see failures as learning opportunities rather than dead-ends. They have less fear of failure, and when they do fail, they're less disabled by the experience and more likely to try again. Self-compassion helps us focus on what we can glean from failure instead of fixating on what it might say about our worth as a person. We don't define ourselves by our setbacks. Instead, we see their potential to provide us with the information needed to succeed.

Of course, sometimes the wisest course of action is to move on from a particular goal if we've tried our best and it's just not happening. If you've been trying to make your living as a stand-up comedian for years and your jokes are still met with deafening silence, it might be time to shift gears and try something different. A study in Japan asked people to think about an important but unattained goal they held within the last five years. Not only did individuals with greater self-compassion prove to be less upset by the disappointing outcome, they were more likely to let go of that specific objective and aim elsewhere. Self-compassion gives us greater perspective, so that we can identify the best use of our time and effort.

It's helpful here to distinguish between harsh judgment and discriminating wisdom. Harsh judgment involves a narrow, rigid labeling of ourselves as "good" or "bad." Discriminating wisdom identifies what's working and what isn't, what's healthy or harmful, but does so in full knowledge of the complex, dynamic factors influencing the situation. We can still judge our performances or achievements as good or bad without taking things personally. Just because I failed in this last go-around doesn't mean that I'm destined to fail again or that I am somehow "a failure." By framing our experience in the larger context of what it means to be human, we gain the insight needed to learn and grow.

VISION

Mindfulness allows us to focus and stay true to our vision when we're trying to make a change. Because we care about ourselves and want to be happy, we don't get distracted from what's really important. When we miss the mark, we often get absorbed by our feelings of failure. Instead of being mindful of the steps we need to take to move forward, our awareness gets hijacked by the shame bandits.

Maybe you're trying to launch a new venture—a charity that provides childcare for low-income working mothers, for instance. You apply for funding from several foundations and get rejected. You squeeze your friends who know people for possible connections to wealthy donors and come up dry. If you get distracted by these early setbacks, losing faith in yourself and your ability to pull off such an ambitious project, you'll certainly never succeed. But if you stick to your vision, seeing each challenge as a temporary bump in the road, you have a shot. If you remain clearheaded and determined, you may see opportunities that otherwise would've been missed, like starting a GoFundMe campaign or other creative ways of fundraising.

The ability to keep going after failure, to pick ourselves up and try again, and stay focused on our goals is known as grit. Angela Duckworth, the leading scholar who brought scientific attention to what grit is and what it does, once told me she thought self-compassion was one of the key factors we need to develop this trait. The safety, support, and encouragement provided by self-compassion is what allows us to hold steadfast when the path ahead is full of obstacles. Research confirms that self-compassionate people have more grit and determination to stick with things regardless of the hurdles. At the same time, self-compassion provides the clear vision needed to recognize when we need to shift course in order to reach our destination.

MOTIVATING SELF-COMPASSION BREAK

This version of the Self-Compassion Break is designed to tap into the energy of fierce self-compassion to help motivate us with encouraging, wise vision. (A guided audio version of this practice can be found at FierceSelf-Compassion.org.)

Instructions

Think of a situation in your life that you'd like to change. Maybe you'd like to exercise more but can't seem to get it done. Or maybe you're trapped in a boring job and want to leave, but just can't summon the energy or willpower. Now, try to imagine an alternative reality that would be better for you—doing yoga every morning or working as a freelance writer. What feelings arise when you think about making this change— frustration, disappointment, fear, excitement? Make contact with the emotions as a physical sensation in your body.

Find a comfortable sitting or standing position. Make sure that your posture feels energizing and that you aren't slumping. You are going to say a series of phrases (aloud or silently to yourself) designed to bring in the three components of self-compassion so that you can try to motivate yourself to make a change with encouragement and support. As always, the goal is to find language that makes sense to you and feels natural.

- The first phrase brings in mindfulness, so that you have a clear vision of what needs to change. Remind yourself of the new reality you want to bring into your life. Say to yourself slowly and with conviction, "This is my vision of what I want for myself." Other options are "This is what I want to manifest in the world" or "This is possible for me."

- The second phrase calls upon the wisdom of common humanity. Try to remember that everyone gets stuck or gets things wrong, but we can learn from our experience. Say to yourself, "This is a life learning opportunity." Other options include "Growing pains are part of being human," "We usually get it wrong before we get it right," or "I'm not the only one who has faced a challenge like this."

- Now make some supportive gesture, such as putting one hand on the opposite shoulder or doing a small fist pump to signal encouragement. We want to use kindness to support ourselves to make needed changes: not because we're inadequate as we are, but because we want to alleviate our suffering. Try saying to yourself with warmth and conviction, "I want to help myself reach my goals." Other options might be "I have your back. I will support you," "Yes I can," "Just try your best and see what happens," or "I believe in you."

- If you're having difficulty finding the right words, imagine that someone you really cared about was struggling with the exact same situation you're struggling with, and you wanted to encourage and support them in making a change. What would you say to this person? What would your tone of voice be like? Is there any constructive criticism you would offer? Now, can you offer the same message to yourself?

- Finally, allow the fierce energy of encouraging, wise vision to combine with the tender energy of unconditional self-acceptance. We can try our best to make needed changes, but the bottom line is we're also okay as we are. It's okay to be imperfect. We will try to do what we can to be happy and to alleviate our own suffering because we care, but we can also let go of the need to get it exactly right.

WHY ARE WE SO HARD ON OURSELVES?

Research indicates that the number one reason people are harsh rather than kind toward themselves is because they believe self-compassion will undermine their motivation. They think self-criticism is an effective motivator, and that by calling themselves cruel and belittling names they'll try harder next time. Another reason we pummel ourselves is because it gives us the illusion of control. When we criticize ourselves, we're reinforcing the idea that it's possible to avoid failure as long as we do everything right. A third factor that comes into play is the desire to protect our egos. We console ourselves with the idea that at least we have high standards, even if we can't meet them. We identify with the part of ourselves that knows how we *should* be, even if we're not there yet. As discussed earlier, self-criticism is a basic safety behavior.

You may be wondering, how does calling myself a lazy do-nothing because I'm procrastinating on an important work task make me feel safe? Because some part of me believes it will kick me into gear so that

I won't fail and lose my job or become homeless. How does flagellating myself for snapping at my kids make me feel safe? Because I think it will help me be a better mother in the future so my kids won't hate me and abandon me in my old age. How does hurling insults at my image in the mirror because I think I'm old and unattractive make me feel safe? Because I believe bashing myself first will soften the sting of others' real or imagined judgments: beating them to the punch, so to speak. On some level, our inner critic is constantly trying to ward off dangers that might cause us harm.

First, it must be acknowledged that this strategy *kind of* works. Many a person has gotten through med school or law school or achieved other milestones through relentless self-criticism. But it works the way an old coal-powered steam engine does—it gets you up the hill but spits out a lot of black smoke. Although fear of self-criticism may sometimes motivate us, the scare tactic has a number of maladaptive consequences: it makes us afraid of failure, leads to procrastination, undermines our self-confidence, and causes performance anxiety, all things that work directly against our ability to succeed. Let's face it. Shame doesn't exactly foster a get-up-and-go mindset.

Although our inner critic often undermines us, we need to honor it, despite the pain, because it reflects a natural and wholesome desire to be safe. We don't want to beat ourselves up for beating ourselves up! Self-criticism has a caring, if misdirected, intention. As discussed earlier, sometimes our inner critic is the internalized voice of an early caregiver who wasn't trying to keep us safe—who was harmful or abusive. But the young part of us who internalized that voice was trying to help. We had little choice but to take the blame on ourselves as children in order to survive. Even when the criticism doesn't stem from early caregivers but is merely a frightened part of us that wants to improve and do better (like my son's harsh inner dialogues), it all comes from the innocent desire to be safe. Sometimes we need to use fierce compassion with our inner critic and tell it firmly but kindly to stop its bullying tactics. But we also need to have tender compassion for that part of ourselves, acknowledging that it's trying its best to protect us from danger. Only then can we truly start to feel safe.

When we motivate ourselves with compassion rather than criticism, we achieve our sense of safety through the mammalian care system as opposed to the threat-defense system. This has important implications for our physical as well as mental and emotional well-being. Frequent activation of our sympathetic nervous system through self-criticism elevates cortisol levels, leading to hypertension, cardiovascular disease, and stroke—a closely related trio considered the leading source of death in the United States. Self-criticism is also a major cause of depression. In contrast, self-compassion activates the parasympathetic nervous system, which reduces cortisol and increases heart rate variability. It strengthens our immune function, reduces stress, and has been consistently shown to alleviate depression. Learning to motivate ourselves through compassion rather than criticism is one of the best things we can do for our health and happiness.

LOVE NOT FEAR

When we give ourselves compassion after making a mistake or failing to reach our goals, we feel cared for and supported. It's this feeling of safety and self-worth that gives us the stable platform from which to try again. Self-compassion allows us to motivate ourselves out of love not fear, and it's much more effective. Think about how we motivate children. Not so long ago, people thought the best way was to scare them into achieving their goals: "Spare the rod, spoil the child." The prevailing wisdom was that harsh corporal punishment was the only way to prevent kids from becoming indolent loafers. Although punishment does yield compliance in the short term, it's counterproductive in the long run, undermining self-confidence and achievement. And yet, we still use the rod with ourselves. It's helpful to think about motivation in the context of parenting, because in many ways self-compassion is a way of reparenting ourselves.

To effectively motivate our children, we need to find the right balance between being too accepting and too demanding. I know this from my own experience as a mother. The reason we homeschooled Rowan most of his life was because the public schools in the small town of Elgin couldn't meet his needs. We did give them a try, but when we came to check on him in kindergarten one day, we found all the special needs kids sitting around doing absolutely nothing while the teachers' aides watched TV and drank sodas. So we pulled him out of public school and his father created the New Trails Learning Center, which used horses and nature as the classroom. The staff mainly focused on providing equine therapy for other autistic children, but one person was trained to homeschool Rowan according to the Texas state curriculum. There were many wonderful things about how he was schooled—being outdoors, riding horses, traveling, and doing project-based learning (like our wildlife expedition to Romania).

However, as Rowan grew up, I realized he wasn't being challenged enough. The center had a philosophy of creating a "yes" environment, meaning it was set up so that autistic children wouldn't be told no or have any pressure on them, triggering their especially sensitive anxiety-prone brains in a way that shuts down learning. For instance, instead of taking tests on the material he learned, Rowan would be taken on a treasure hunt where his teacher would assess whether he knew the material by how he answered the clues (e.g., go left if Henry VIII lived in the Middle Ages or right if he lived in the Renaissance). Rowan never had the experience of being explicitly evaluated or graded.

While this approach reduced his anxiety and worked very well when he was younger, as Rowan became an adolescent it stopped serving him. He needed to learn how to deal with failure and pressure. I worried he wouldn't advance academically.

I moved to Austin with Rowan when he was sixteen and enrolled him in an excellent public school known for its autism program. He had to enter as a freshman because he was behind in his studies, but he fit right in. Rowan thrived on being stimulated, having a different teacher in each class, learning new material. The advantage of being homeschooled was that Rowan's spirit had never been crushed. He was happy and self-confident and fully comfortable with his autism. This helped him adapt. The disadvantage came when he took his first set of tests. He was confused and didn't really know how to study. So unsurprisingly, Rowan bombed his first major World Geography test—an unequivocal F.

When he came home and shared the news with me, I could have tried to motivate him with the whip approach I sometimes heard Rowan using with himself. The same approach that many of us use with *ourselves*. "You're a good-for-nothing failure. I'm ashamed of you. You need to do better on your next test or else." I didn't do that, of course. It would've not only been cruel, but completely counterproductive. Such a harsh response would just make him feel worse about failing and cause him overwhelming anxiety on his next test. Labeling him as incompetent would undermine his ability to succeed, perhaps leading him to eventually drop World Geography altogether.

Instead, I gave him a huge hug and reassured him of my love. I had compassion for the pain of his experience, and let him know it was normal and natural to fail when trying something new. I made sure he understood that failing said nothing about his intelligence or worth as a person. But did I stop there? Did I give up and go back to the treasure hunt approach? Of course not! To stop there and merely accept his failure, without helping him to try to overcome it, would have also been cruel.

Instead, I met with all his teachers and looked carefully at how Rowan was studying. We figured out how to support him by creating tailored study materials. I encouraged him to keep trying because I believed in him and knew he could do it. By the end of the semester not only was he getting good grades on his tests, but he was actually enjoying the process of studying and the feeling of accomplishment he gained from succeeding.

We can take a similar approach to motivating ourselves. We don't want to just continue with the status quo because then we won't learn or grow. We need to take risks. But taking risks means we'll inevitably fail. How we react to inevitable moments of failure is pivotal in determining what comes next. Beating ourselves up doesn't move us forward; it just makes us want to stop trying. If we accept ourselves for the continually evolving works-in-progress that we really are, it means we'll get over setbacks more easily. Tender self-compassion allows us to comfort and reassure ourselves when we don't succeed, and fierce self-compassion inspires us to try again.

MOTIVATING CHANGE WITH COMPASSION

This practice draws on encouraging, wise vision to help us change a harmful habit. It's adapted from an exercise we teach in MSC called Finding Your Compassionate Voice that took years to refine. We used to ask people to first look at how their inner critic typically motivated change, then switch directly to a more compassionate approach. Most people had trouble making the switch, however. After becoming more familiar with Internal Family Systems therapy, we added in the step of appreciating our inner critic's efforts to keep us safe. All the pieces clicked into place, and now it's one of the most powerful exercises in the program. Because it involves looking directly at our inner critic, it's good to proceed cautiously if you know this critical voice was internalized from someone abusive in your past. If this is the case, you may want to complete the exercise with the guidance of a therapist. Remember you can also stop if needed. This is a writing exercise, so please take out something to write with.

Instructions

- Think about a behavior that you would like to change—something that is causing problems in your life, and one that you often criticize yourself for. Select a behavior that is mild to moderately problematic, not one that is extremely harmful.

- Examples of such behaviors are "I eat unhealthy food," "I don't exercise enough," "I procrastinate," or "I'm very impatient."

- Don't choose an unchangeable characteristic that you criticize yourself for, like the fact that you have big feet. The focus is on something you *do* that you would like to change.

- Write down the behavior and also write down the problems the behavior is causing.

Finding your inner critic

- Now consider how your inner critic expresses itself when this behavior occurs. Is it through harsh words? If so, write down the typical language you use as close to verbatim as possible. Also, what tone of voice does your inner critic use?

- For some people, the inner critic doesn't use harsh words, but instead conveys a feeling of disappointment or coldness or even numbness. Every person is different. How does your inner critic show up?

Compassion for feeling criticized

- Now switch perspectives, and try to get in touch with the part of yourself that receives this criticism. How does it feel to get this message? What's the impact on you? What are the consequences? Write this down.

- You may want to call up some tender self-compassion to comfort yourself for the fact that it's hard to be the recipient of such harsh treatment. Try writing some warm and supportive words to this part of yourself such as: "This really hurts," "I'm so sorry," "I'm here for you," or "You aren't the only one."

Understanding your inner critic

- Now, see if you can turn toward your inner critic with interest and curiosity. Reflect for a moment on what's motivating your inner critic. Is it trying to protect you in some way, to keep you safe from danger, to help you, even if the result has been unproductive? This critical part of yourself may be young and immature, with a limited understanding of how to help. Its intention may be good, however.

- Write down what you think may be driving your inner critic. If you don't know for sure that's okay, just consider some possibilities.

Thanking your inner critic

- If you were able to identify some way your inner critic might be trying to protect or help you, and if it feels safe to do so, see if you can acknowledge its efforts, perhaps even writing down a few words of thanks. (If you can't find any way your inner critic is trying to help or if you feel it's the internalized voice of someone who abused you in the past, skip this step. You don't want to thank someone who traumatized you. Instead, either go back to giving yourself compassion for the pain of past self-criticism or move on to the next step.)

- Let your inner critic know that even though it may not be serving you very well now, you appreciate its efforts to keep you safe. It was doing its best.

Tapping into wisdom

- Now that your self-critical voice has been heard, perhaps it can step aside and make some space for another voice—the wise and caring voice of self-compassion.

- Unlike our inner critic who sees our behavior as the result of being bad or inadequate, our inner compassionate self understands the complex patterns driving our behavior. It can see the bigger picture and help us learn from our mistakes.

- Can you identify any reasons why you are stuck or factors that contribute to your unhelpful behavior? Maybe you are extremely busy or stressed, or it's a habit you're comfortable with. Are there any lessons to be learned from your past failures to change? Write down any insights.

Finding your compassionate voice

- See if you can get in touch with the part of yourself that wants to encourage you to make a change, not because you're unacceptable as you are, but because it wants the best for you. Clearly this behavior is causing you harm, and your inner compassionate self wants to alleviate your suffering.

- Try repeating a phrase that captures the essence of your compassionate voice. For example: "I deeply care about you, and that's why I'd like to help you make a change" or "I don't want you to keep harming yourself. I'm here to support you."

- Now begin to write a little letter to yourself in a compassionate voice, freely and spontaneously, addressing the behavior you would like to change. Using encouraging, wise vision, what words of motivation emerge?

- Perhaps some words of protective self-compassion are also relevant so that you draw boundaries or stand up to your inner critic.

- If you're having difficulty knowing what to say, you can try writing the words that would flow from your kind heart when speaking to a dear friend struggling with a similar issue as you.

Integrating fierce and tender self-compassion

- Finally, try to combine the encouragement to change with the fact that it's also okay to be where you are, a work in progress. We don't need to be perfect or to get it all right. See if you can allow gentle self-acceptance to coexist with the active drive for self-improvement.

- Write some words of affirmation to remind yourself that whether you are successful at making a change or not, you're still worthy as you are. We can try to do our best, but we can't completely control what happens.

One participant from an MSC workshop I taught commented on how surprised she was to learn that her inner critic and her inner compassionate self actually wanted the same thing for her, even though they expressed themselves very differently. Apparently she struggled with reactive anger at work (similar to my inner bulldog), and wanted to improve her interactions with colleagues. She told the class "my inner critic constantly says to me, 'You bitch.' In this exercise, my inner compassionate self just said, 'Whoa tiger!'" We all laughed, and I could certainly relate. It's also a beautiful illustration of how we need to be encouraging and supportive with ourselves as we do the challenging work of learning to integrate fierce and tender self-compassion.

MOTIVATION FOR THE RIGHT REASONS

In psychology there's often a distinction made between learning and performance goals. People with learning goals are motivated by the desire to develop new skills and master tasks. They tend to view making mistakes as a part of the learning process. People with performance goals are motivated to achieve primarily to defend or enhance their ego. They see failure as an indictment of their self-worth and feel they must do better than others to feel good about themselves. This is self-esteem raising its ugly head: it's not enough to achieve my personal best, I have to do better than everyone else. Research shows that self-compassionate people are less likely to have performance goals for achieving, because their sense of self-worth isn't based on social comparisons with others. They tend to set learning goals instead, transforming failure from a negative ("I can't believe the contract went to Joan instead of me, I'm such a loser") into an opportunity for growth

("I wonder what Joan did to secure the contract? Maybe I'll invite her to coffee and ask her about it").

A study at McGill University in Montreal looked at how self-compassion affected the well-being of incoming college freshmen as they dealt with inevitable failures in their first year. Self-compassionate students displayed more learning goals and fewer performance goals. They were less upset on days when they didn't achieve their objectives and reported being more concerned with whether their goals were personally meaningful than with goal success. Self-compassion helps us focus on *why* we're trying to achieve something. When we do it because we want to develop as people, it doesn't really matter if we succeed or not or what others think of us. What matters is that like the caterpillar spinning her cocoon, we realize our potential by continuing to develop our strengths and talents to the fullest extent possible.

Studies indicate that another gift of self-compassion is that it fosters a growth rather than a fixed mindset. Carol Dweck, a psychology professor at Stanford University, was the first to coin these terms. People with a growth mindset believe that they can improve their abilities and change aspects of their personality. Those with a fixed mindset consider themselves stuck with whatever abilities their DNA and upbringing gave them, with little chance to alter their inherited fate. People with a growth mindset are more likely to try to improve, practice, put in effort to change, and stay positive and optimistic when they encounter challenges.

When we are compassionate toward those aspects of our personality we don't like, we are more likely to adopt a growth mindset and believe we can change. A study by Juliana Breines and Serena Chen at UC Berkeley illustrates the point well. The researchers asked students to identify their biggest weakness—most involved difficulties such as insecurity, social anxiety, or lack of confidence. Students were then randomly assigned to one of three conditions, one in which they wrote about their weakness with self-compassion, one in which they wrote in a way that bolstered their self-esteem, or a control condition in which they didn't write at all.

Next, participants were asked to write about whether or not they thought their weakness was fixed or malleable. Compared to the other two conditions, those told to write self-compassionately about their weakness were more likely to have a growth mindset ("With hard work I know I can change") than a fixed mindset ("It's just inborn—there's nothing I can do"). Ironically, compassion for our weaknesses gives us more confidence in our ability to improve than the rah-rah cheerleading of self-esteem.

WILL I LOSE MY DRIVE?

Self-compassion not only fosters the belief that growth is possible, it also increases our ability to work for it. Although people fear self-compassion will make them lose their edge, the truth is exactly opposite. When people learn to be more self-compassionate, their level of personal initiative—that is, the desire to take charge and fulfill our dreams in life—increases substantially. Self-compassion doesn't mean we sink into passive acceptance the way one might sink into a La-Z-Boy recliner. While we accept the fact that we have weaknesses (who doesn't?), we also try to overcome them.

In another study by Breines and Chen, Berkeley students were given a difficult vocabulary test that they all did poorly on. One group was told to be self-compassionate about the failure ("If you had difficulty with the test you just took, you're not alone. It's common for students to have difficulty with tests like this."), a second was given an ego boost ("Don't worry about it. You must be smart if you got into *this* university."), and a third control group was told nothing. The students were next informed that they would soon be taking a second vocabulary test and were given a list of words and definitions they could study for as long as they wanted before trying again. The researchers then recorded how long the students studied. Those who were encouraged to be self-compassionate after failing the first test spent more time studying than those in the other two conditions, and time spent studying was linked to test performance.

A common reason we don't perform at our best is because we procrastinate. Whether it's hitting the snooze button seven times, putting off that difficult but necessary conversation with an employee who isn't doing an adequate job, or going for your checkup at the dentist, procrastination makes things so much harder. Even though people put things off to avoid the stress and discomfort of doing an unpleasant task, ironically procrastination itself is a major cause of stress and anxiety. Procrastinators often judge themselves and feel incapable of achieving their goals, which just leads to more worry and delay. It can be an endless loop that's extremely difficult to escape. Research shows that self-compassion helps break that cycle, reducing not only procrastination but also the stress associated with it. Tender self-compassion allows us to accept the discomfort of an unwanted task and to be nonjudgmental about our desire to put it off. Fierce self-compassion then propels us to take action so that we do what's needed.

The self-compassionate heart is like rocket fuel for getting things done.

JUST DO IT

Because self-compassion increases motivation and helps us respond productively to failure, it's starting to catch on in the athletic world. The stakes are high for athletes when they make a mistake. A missed field goal or free throw can cost the team a victory and disappoint thousands of fans. But when players beat themselves up, it just keeps them from regaining their stride. Failure is part of playing the game. How athletes respond to their mistakes is key to staying competitive.

The widespread myth that self-compassion hurts motivation is especially pronounced among athletes whose livelihoods may depend on being top performers. In a qualitative study of their beliefs about self-compassion, a young female basketball player said this: "If you are too self-compassionate you are always going to be fine with good enough. You are never going to strive to be better, and for an elite athlete that shouldn't be okay. I need to be hard on myself, because if I'm not, then

I am just going to settle for mediocrity." It breaks my heart to hear athletes say things like this. Cutting yourself down doesn't help you rise above mediocrity, it just keeps you mired in stress and anxiety. You can decide that your performance isn't good enough and strive to do better without harshly judging yourself as a person. This safety net of knowing you're okay even if your performance isn't actually helps you stay on your game.

In fact, a growing body of research shows that self-compassionate athletes have more constructive reactions to failure in emotionally difficult situations in their sport. A study at the University of Saskatchewan found that after performance errors or losses, self-compassionate athletes were less likely to catastrophize ("My life is really screwed up") or take things personally ("Why do these things always happen to me?") and were more likely to maintain equanimity ("Everyone has a bad day now and then"). Another study by the same researchers found that self-compassionate athletes reported feeling more vitality while playing and were more motivated to grow and develop as professionals. When asked about how they reacted to situations like making a mistake that led to a team loss, they were more likely to take responsibility and work on improving their skills.

Self-compassionate athletes report feeling less anxious when playing, more able to concentrate, and less tense in their bodies. This is partly because of self-compassion's effect on the nervous system. Researchers at the University of Manitoba conducted a study of self-compassion in almost one hundred collegiate or national-level athletes. They hooked up the athletes to a biofeedback system to measure their reactions when thinking about a past performance failure. Athletes who were self-compassionate were calmer physiologically and had greater heart rate variability, allowing for more flexibility in responding to sudden changes like those that can occur in speedy sport conditions. Healthy minds create healthy bodies, which is partly how self-compassion helps athletes attain peak performance.

Luckily, some coaches are starting to catch on. A few years ago, Shaka Smart, the head coach for the UT Austin men's basketball team, got interested in self-compassion after reading my first book. He invited me to give a short workshop for his team so they could learn to cope with failure more productively. Because basketball is such an intense game and players are constantly shooting and missing baskets, choking after failure means losing. Shaka thought self-compassion could help.

I figured that the team was probably going to have a negative reaction to the term "self-compassion," so I never used it. Instead, I talked about the importance of inner strength training, since this is what fierce self-compassion provides. I reminded the players that they needed to be mentally as well as physically fit to productively deal with mistakes. To help counter the myth of complacency, I discussed research that shows being supportive to yourself after a mistake increases motivation and persistence. Then I asked, "Which inner coach do you want in your head? A coach that yells at you, cuts you down, and makes you nervous, or a coach that encourages you and has the smarts to tell you what to do differently? Which inner coach is going to be more effective?" The team took to the idea of self-compassion when framed the right way.

I taught the guys some practices, such as creating an image of an ideal coach with encouraging, wise vision to help guide them to play their best (luckily Shaka was a good role model). I showed them how to use the Motivating Self-Compassion Break when they needed a boost and demonstrated supportive touch so they could emotionally ground themselves on and off the court. The team still practices the basic principles of self-compassion today. (Go Longhorns!)

MOTIVATION OR PERFECTIONISM?

Although fierce self-compassion motivates us to improve, if it isn't balanced with self-acceptance, it can easily morph into unhealthy perfectionism. Society puts a lot of pressure on us to get things right. If we spur ourselves to make changes without the self-acceptance of loving, connected presence, we may perpetuate a vicious cycle of relentless self-improvement. We may strive to be smarter or healthier or more successful or even more self-compassionate with a mindset of trying to fix what's broken.

There are two types of perfectionism—adaptive and maladaptive. Adaptive perfectionism means that we adopt high standards for ourselves, and this approach tends to improve achievement and persistence. Maladaptive perfectionism means we criticize ourselves when we don't meet the high standards we've set, so we end up feeling that our honest best isn't good enough. This can cause us to become depressed and, ironically, undermine our ability to achieve.

Compared to self-critical people, those who are self-compassionate aim just as high in terms of performance standards. They dream big and want to achieve as much as anyone else. The difference is how they treat themselves when they don't reach their goals. Self-compassionate people don't tear themselves down when they fail and have much lower levels of maladaptive perfectionism. The balance of yin and yang energizes self-compassionate people to keep pursuing their dreams even when they encounter setbacks. For instance, a study of medical trainees—who tend to set the bar very high—found that interns with more self-compassion were less likely to have maladaptive responses to failure and were more likely to finish their studies.

I encounter a lot of perfectionism among students at a top university like UT Austin. It's typically the students making an A minus in my undergraduate course who come to my office hours to discuss how to earn extra credit. Many graduate students are also perfectionists. And in fact, high standards are often responsible for their academic success. But perfectionism is counterproductive when taking on a challenging task like writing a master's or dissertation thesis. Innovation and creativity are born out of feeling safe enough to make mistakes, to get it wrong.

I had a graduate student named Molly in my research lab who was passionate about studying self-compassion. She'd become familiar with my work as an undergraduate at Texas A&M and said it radically transformed her life. She was a lesbian from a fairly conservative family, and she credited the practice of self-compassion for giving her the courage to come out when she was twenty. Molly used tender self-compassion to fully accept and embrace who she was and fierce self-compassion to tell her parents she was queer, love it or leave it. They were actually more accepting of the news than she'd thought they'd be, although it took some tough conversations to get there.

It was hard not to be charmed by Molly. She was bright, funny, smart as a whip, and a go-getter. She excelled at everything she did, whether it was paragliding (her favorite hobby) or speaking Japanese (she was fluent) or fighting for social justice (she organized a gay pride parade with her LGBTQ+ student group at A&M). She was skeptical of self-compassion at first because she thought it might undermine her drive, but quickly found it made it easier for her to get those As she was used to. She was so intelligent that she hadn't been seriously challenged academically—until she got to graduate school. An exceptionally smart undergraduate is an average graduate student, and although she still got As in most of her classes, she struggled with advanced statistics. She needed specialized statistical skills to conduct her dissertation research (examining how self-compassion helped same-sex couples cope with discrimination). She got extra tutoring, put in late night hours studying, and tried encouraging herself to work harder and do better. But she still got Cs (a C minus is considered a failing grade in grad school).

"I don't know why my grades aren't improving," she told me. "I'm not beating myself up at all. I'm being kind and gently encouraging myself to try harder." Although she wasn't being overtly harsh, I suspected that a part of her just couldn't accept there was something she didn't excel at. There was still an unspoken belief that she needed to be perfect. Being an A student had become such a strong part of her identity that getting a C felt almost like a death to her. I helped her see that the motivation of self-compassion doesn't always mean doing better. While fierceness encourages us to try our best to improve, we also need tenderness to accept our limitations. Would it be the end of the world if she wasn't particularly good at advanced statistics? She could always use a stats consultant for her dissertation. Molly eventually came to be at peace with the fact that this wasn't an area of strength for her, and luckily it didn't keep her from moving forward with her research.

When we balance fierce and tender self-compassion, we not only take action to improve ourselves but also accept our human imperfection. And the more secure we feel in our own unconditional self-acceptance, the more emotional resources we'll have to work hard, challenge ourselves, and do better when possible. Carl Rogers, one of the founders of the humanistic psychology movement in the 1940s, summed it up well when he said, "The curious paradox is that when I accept myself just as I am, then I can change." One of the beautiful things about motivating ourselves with compassion is that it takes the anxiety and stress out of trying to achieve. We stop exhausting ourselves with the need to be perfect or stand out in a crowd. We don't have to outperform others as a measure of success. "Me against the world" becomes "me as part of the world." Personal achievement isn't so personal anymore, meaning we can encourage ourselves to do our best without demanding we always get things right.

THE CHALLENGE FOR WOMEN

It's especially important for women to balance fierce and tender self-compassion as we try to make productive change, in our own lives and the world at large. Perfectionism or striving too hard to achieve without the safety net of unconditional self-acceptance will only add extra pressure on us as we do our work in the world. Harnessing kindness to overcome barriers, on the other hand, with the bottom line being that we'll care for and support ourselves even if we fail, will give us a much better shot.

As women, we have a monumental task in front of us. The planet is warming. The political system is broken. People are dying from starvation in some parts of the world and obesity in others. Entrenched sexism and racism and wealth inequality seem like they'll never end. At her famous speech at the Women's Rights Convention in 1851,

Sojourner Truth reportedly told the gathered attendees, "If the first woman God ever made was strong enough to turn the world upside down all alone, these women together ought to be able to turn it back and get it right side up again! And now they is asking to do it, the men better let them." The old ways of patriarchy aren't working anymore, and it will likely be women who keep the world from going over the edge. As we take on this challenge, it's essential that we have access to all the tools of self-compassion. Loving, connected presence will help hold the pain of it all without being overwhelmed. Brave, empowered clarity will rouse us to protect ourselves and our fellow humans from harm. Fulfilling, balanced authenticity will allow us to carve out a new sustainable way of living in the world. And encouraging, wise vision will inspire us to work for the change that's required. If we can tap into the full power of fierce and tender compassion, aiming to alleviate inner as well as outer suffering, who knows what we could achieve?

PART III

FIERCE SELF-COMPASSION IN THE WORLD

CHAPTER 9

BALANCE AND EQUALITY AT WORK

If you give us a chance, we can perform. After all,
Ginger Rogers did everything that Fred Astaire did.
She just did it backwards and in high heels.

—*Ann Richards, former governor of Texas*

Our great-grandmothers grew up in an era when women couldn't vote. They were expected to stay at home, do domestic work, and care for the children while men held jobs and made the money. Tremendous gains in gender equality have since been made. In the United States, women are now more likely than men to get a college degree at all levels—undergraduate (57 percent), master's (59 percent), and doctoral (53 percent)—and they earn better grades. Women also make up 47 percent of the workforce. They hold approximately 50 percent of all management and professional positions and slightly outnumber men as managers in fields such as education, health care, real estate, finance, human resources, social work, and community service. But we still have a long way to go. In 2018, the average American working woman made 82 cents to the average man's dollar. There are group differences within that figure: Asian women made 90 cents, White women made 79 cents, Black women made 62 cents, and Hispanic women made 54 cents to the average man's dollar. Some of this wage gap is due to plain old discrimination, both sexual and racial. But it's also due to the fact that women are funneled into different professions. Men are more likely to work in higher-paying fields like engineering or computer science, whereas women are more likely to work in lower-paying professions such as nursing or education. And Black and Hispanic women are most likely to work in the worst-paid service jobs.

Also, taking care of home and family is still largely considered a female responsibility. Women are five times more likely to be stay-at-home parents than men. Regardless of their employment status, women spend more time on domestic chores, such as childcare, eldercare, and household work, than men do. Unemployed women spend the most time on domestic labor (roughly thirty-three hours per week), followed by working women (twenty-four hours), unemployed men (twenty-three hours), and working men (sixteen hours). This means that women who work outside the home do more work inside the home than men who don't work at all! And these unequal patterns seem to be consistent across racial and ethnic groups. The fact that even working women are expected to take care of the home means they're more likely to be employed part-time, take parental leave, and require flexible hours—putting us at a disadvantage when it comes to salary and promotion.

Women make up only 23 percent of board seats at Fortune 500 companies, and the number for women of color is a mere 5 percent. In the very top jobs, only 5 percent of Fortune 500 CEOs are women of any ethnicity. According to one recent survey, there are fewer female chief executives than there are male chief executives named James. The glass ceiling appears to be as bulletproof as ever.

The issue of gender equality at work has to be understood in the larger context of stereotypes that portray men as agentic and women as communal. Agency is associated with achievement, displays of skill, competence, ambition, hard work, focus, and self-reliance. It's the ability to take charge and assert oneself forcefully, using rationality and logic to analyze and solve problems. These are the exact qualities needed for effective leaders at the top level.

On the other hand, communion is associated with being warm,

friendly, and cooperative. It's characterized by empathy, emotional sensitivity, and a reliance on intuition as well as logic. It also entails being respectful, self-effacing, and deferent to others. These qualities are more valued in middle managers, secretaries, and service positions.

The fact that the last thirty years have seen almost no shift in agentic and communal gender stereotypes shows the intractability of the predicament we're in. If we ever hope to achieve equity, we need to rethink our views of gender and also expand our ideas of what makes a functional workplace.

IMBALANCE IN THE WORKPLACE

The traditionally masculine world of business emphasizes fierce action. It takes self-protection to make sure bottom lines are safeguarded and competitors don't get the upper hand. It's considered sound business practice to provide for one's needs by continually increasing salaries and profits. And the motivation to be a top performer and reach for excellence is woven into the very fabric of corporate culture. Qualities of kindness, acceptance, and understanding don't carry much weight, creating an imbalance in yin and yang. An analysis of word usage in the *Wall Street Journal* from 1984 through 2000 found that terms such as "win," "advantage," and "beat" appeared in thousands of articles and these appearances had risen more than 400 percent over the seventeen-year time span, whereas terms such as "caring" and "compassion" were practically nonexistent. Concern for the well-being of others is often ignored if it hurts profits, creating a warped lens through which to view the world.

One negative consequence of this imbalance is bullying. People with a one-dimensional view of power try to exercise it by criticizing, ridiculing, belittling, or picking on others. Workplace bullying is more likely to occur in highly competitive environments that emphasize individual achievement. Superiors tend to bully subordinates and men bully more than women do. In other words, when ferocity isn't countered with tenderness, things have the tendency to run amok. Studies have found that the majority of workers in the United States experience bullying at some point in their careers, which leads to higher turnover rates and absenteeism, diminished commitment to work, lower job satisfaction, and mental health issues. Anyone who watched the first presidential debate between Donald Trump and Joe Biden knows how draining and exhausting bullying can be. It makes it hard to get anything done.

Another consequence of this imbalance is rampant greed. Take the pharmaceutical industry: although the field of medicine should be focused on compassion and healing, Big Pharma is often preoccupied with making money for shareholders with little regard for patients. The medicine my brother and I take for our Wilson's disease is a textbook example of this brand of profiteering. Because Wilson's is so rare (affecting less than one in thirty thousand people in the United States), there's almost no market for drugs to treat the disorder. We both take Syprine, a chelating agent developed in the 1960s. In 2015, Valeant Pharmaceuticals bought the patent for the drug and over the course of a few years raised the price 3,500 percent: it used to cost $600 for one month's supply and now costs $21,000. Teva Pharmaceuticals produced a generic version of the drug in 2018 and decided to charge $18,000 for a month's worth (what a bargain!). Luckily my brother and I have good insurance plans and don't have high out-of-pocket costs, but our insurers still have to come up with the half-million-dollar ransom the drug dealers demand each year to cover both of us, an expense passed on to other plan members. The lack of compassion in the marketplace harms everyone.

Fortunately, there is a nascent movement to incorporate values of kindness and connectedness in the business world. Jane Dutton and her colleagues in the Compassion Lab at the University of Michigan Ross School of Business are pioneers studying the influence of compassion in work culture. They argue that the self-serving, profit-at-all-costs business model is unsustainable. Workplaces that don't prioritize the welfare of employees can easily become hostile environments, with self-serving bosses, corrosive office politics, sexual harassment, psychological abuse, even workplace violence. Laboring in uncaring work settings decreases morale, increases stress, and leads to depression. Estimates of economic loss and diminished productivity related to such stress—based on measurable increases in absenteeism and turnover, as well as medical, legal, and insurance costs—can run into the billions each year.

On the other hand, organizations that establish a culture of compassion reap tangible benefits. For example, companies that launch donation drives to help employees in need, reward good deeds, encourage the expression of emotions in the workplace, and have a zero-tolerance policy for bullying have greater employee commitment, team effectiveness, and reduced turnover rates. These programs also increase performance and boost the bottom line. Although this movement provides hope for the future, the current business culture extols fierceness and belittles tenderness, and it will take time before serious reform takes hold.

The imbalance of yin and yang in corporate culture helps explain why women are more likely to take low-paying jobs as teachers, nurses, or social workers. First, male-dominated professions that prioritize greed over caring for others are often unappealing to women. Second, because women have been raised to be skilled nurturers, they tend to be more interested in and feel more qualified for caregiving professions. Others tend to agree and more readily hire women for these roles, resulting in fewer barriers to success in these fields. Unfortunately, the fact that caregiving professions are considered feminine means that employees in those fields also tend to be given less value and status as well as pay.

JUGGLING WORK AND FAMILY

Women's work is often shaped by tradeoffs between work and childcare responsibilities. Among heterosexual partners with children, it's typically the man who works full-time and the woman who works part-time, especially since men tend to be paid more. In a 2018 Center for American Progress survey of a demographically diverse sample of almost five hundred parents, mothers were 40 percent more likely than fathers to report their careers had suffered due to childcare issues. And even when women somehow manage to figure out childcare, they feel more guilt working full-time than men do. Because women are socialized to subordinate their own needs to those of others, we feel it's selfish to prioritize our jobs, a concern not typically shared by men.

The answer here isn't for women to be more like men and prioritize work at the expense of family, but for work opportunities and family responsibilities to be shared more equitably. It can be done, although admittedly it's easier for women with greater resources or a broad circle of family support. Government programs—like universal childcare and paid family leave for fathers—can also make a big difference.

My friend Lin managed to get the balance right. I met her in a yoga class shortly after moving to Austin, and we often got tea together after practice. At the time, Lin was working as a graphic designer in a busy Austin advertising firm, and she was becoming known for her work in the field. However, she was also raised in a traditional Asian American family, so her parents strongly encouraged her to start trying for a baby after turning thirty. Lin wanted a child but wasn't ready yet—she was enjoying her career too much and didn't want to interrupt it. But Lin's husband, David, began to worry about pregnancy complications. He didn't want to wait, so Lin agreed to try for a child. Her firm had an amazing family-leave policy and would hold her job for four months even after her eight weeks of paid maternal leave ran out. She was secretly conflicted when she got pregnant, but assumed the interruption would be six months max.

Lin had a healthy baby girl named Amy, and David proved to be a good father. He was involved and supportive, helping change Amy's diapers, soothing her when she was upset, and taking her for walks in the stroller almost every evening. Lin loved being a mother, but after half a year of full-time mommyhood, she was ready to return to work.

This was pre-COVID-19, and the expectation at Lin's firm was for employees to work in-office, so she needed to figure out childcare.

Although neither set of grandparents lived in town, she managed to find a day-care center that she liked. But Lin's parents were firmly against the idea of her returning to work and laid the guilt on thick: "You don't want to be one of those neglectful absent parents, do you? Your daughter needs you at home. She'll be scarred for life if you abandon her this way." David was also against the idea and didn't like to think of Amy spending the day with strangers at such a young age. Lin was torn, but eventually gave in and decided to work part-time at home for a telemarketing company that offered her flexibility, thinking she could go back to her graphic-design work once Amy was in preschool.

Lin hated being a telemarketer. Still, the money was decent, and she was able to care for Amy between calls. It didn't take long before Lin started to feel aggrieved, however, and she often scowled when David walked through the door after a day of work at his architecture firm. Why did he get to keep the career he enjoyed but she didn't? Lin tried to quell these feelings and focus on all she was grateful for, like a supportive husband and healthy child. Many working mothers didn't have the luxury to stay at home with their kids even if they wanted to. She told herself it would've been selfish to put her own needs first.

By the time Amy was eighteen months old, Lin started to become despondent. David assumed it was postpartum depression caused by hormones, but Lin suspected it was more than that. When we talked about her situation, I encouraged Lin to be curious about what her discontent was signaling. She immediately said that she hated her life and hated herself for hating it. So I suggested she focus on tender self-compassion—treating herself with kindness and acceptance during this difficult time. Lin liked to write, so she wrote in her journal each day. She validated the fact that even though she did have much to be grateful for, her dissatisfaction was real. She reassured herself that it was normal and natural to feel down in her situation, and that in fact many other women felt just as she did. She started being warmer and more supportive toward herself and realized that her needs were important.

After getting on more stable footing, I suggested Lin start to focus on fierce self-compassion and the actions she could take to make a change. She realized how important being a graphic designer was to her; she loved the mix of creativity and pragmatism, where she could integrate both her left and right brain. Doing satisfying work was necessary to her happiness. She wanted to find a way to go back but was torn by her responsibilities as a mother. She was also worried about getting a job after being off the market for so long. I suggested she try writing supportive words of encouragement to herself in her journal, just as she might to a good friend she cared about.

After a couple of months, Lin decided she would try to get her old job back. She relied on fierce self-compassion to approach her former boss, assert herself with her husband, and stand up to her parents. Her boss was easy—Lin was very talented and he said she could come back at any time. Her family was more challenging. Lin told David how she was feeling: their arrangement had made her deeply unhappy. At first, he tried to talk her out of it, but she held firm and said that they needed to place equal priority on both their careers and share the childcare. She suggested that they rethink their job arrangements—maybe they could each split time at the office and home? After some negotiation, David agreed. Their marriage had been suffering, and David did want to see Lin happy again. He also admitted—and this really impressed Lin—that it was the fair thing to do.

Lin's parents remained obstinate, however. Her mother kept saying that Amy would be psychologically harmed if she wasn't with Lin full-time. "I disagree," Lin told her. "When Amy grows up, she will have a strong role model in her mother, someone who values herself and meets her own needs." Her mother didn't approve, but Lin didn't need her mother's approval. She approved of herself! Once Lin was back at work doing what she loved, she found that she could enjoy her time with Amy and David more, and could give more as a wife, mother, and daughter. Although she says finding balance between work and motherhood is a continual struggle, as it is for most women, it's worth the effort.

PERCEPTIONS OF COMPETENCE

It's not only motherhood that poses a barrier for women in the work-place; it's also the pernicious view that women are less competent in the work realm. This bias isn't conscious: when people are asked their opinions of whether men or women are more professionally compe-tent, most respond that they are equally competent or that women are even more competent. But at the unconscious level, the bias is strong. Case in point: a recent study found that virtual assistants with a male voice were rated as more effective than those with a female voice, even though computers aren't even human! Madeline Heilman at New York University is one of the most accomplished researchers in the study of how implicit biases create gendered perceptions at work. In order to be competent, leaders need to have a certain level of aggressiveness and emotional toughness. But information about competence is often a bit vague, so we use gender stereotypes as an unconscious guide to help process information. Because women are stereotyped as having tender communal traits rather than fierce agentic ones, the assumption is that they don't have what it takes to be in charge.

Gender bias puts women at a tremendous disadvantage at work because our behavior is continually being misinterpreted and dis-torted. For instance, defending oneself passionately against criticism by a colleague is seen as a signal of strength in a man but unhinged in a woman. Changing a decision is viewed as a sign of flexibility in a man but is interpreted as erratic or indecisive in a woman. Postponing a decision looks prudent when it's done by a man but is taken as a sign of fear or timidity in a woman.

Experimental research shows that when participants are asked to evaluate the competence of a fictional job applicant, they give higher evaluations of competence and make more job offers to applicants named John versus Jennifer, even if the CV and application letter are identical. These unconscious biases can lead to discriminatory hiring and promotion decisions, even when people believe they're basing deci-sions on objective evaluations. This means that throughout their careers, women are less likely than men to be selected for promotions and prestigious positions. For instance, in academia, female professors of management with qualifications similar to their male counterparts—the same amount of experience, number of publications, and citations by other scholars demonstrating their impact on the field—were significantly less likely to be awarded an endowed chair in their department.

Research repeatedly finds that identical work is evaluated less favorably when it's said to have been performed by a woman, and that women are viewed as less capable unless their performance is extremely robust and rated by clear standards that are unambiguous. This holds true whether the person rating a woman's performance is male or female, a finding that underlines the unconscious nature of these stereotypes. In the leadership sphere, competence means agency means male.

Even when women do display agentic qualities at work, they're still seen as less competent because people believe it's abnormal for women to be fierce. For instance, a series of studies by researchers at Yale found that women who exhibit anger in the workplace are given lower status compared to men who make similar displays. The researchers asked participants to watch videotapes that ostensibly showed professional men and women in a job interview. In the videos, applicants described a situation where they and a colleague lost an important account, and when asked by the interviewer how it made them feel, they said it made them either angry or sad. Participants were then asked to rate the competence of the applicants, make a salary recommendation, and suggest how much status, power, and independence they should be given in a future job.

Study participants rated male applicants who were angry as more competent and deserving of greater salary, status, and independence compared to sad male applicants. They also tended to assume that male applicants were angry because of something relevant to the situation, and that this was an appropriate response. The opposite was true for women. Participants judged professional women who were angry to be less competent because they must have something inherently wrong with them (the situational factors were overlooked), and that they should therefore be given a position with lower prestige, autonomy, and wages.

The degree to which people hold gender stereotypes also influences whether they think gender disparities in the workplace are fair. Those who strongly buy into the view that men are agentic and women are communal use this view as a rationale that explains (or excuses) why so many more high-level managers and executives are male; they assume men are naturally better in leadership positions and therefore get promoted more readily.

These stereotypes have serious, real-life consequences. In a meta-analysis of almost one hundred empirical studies conducted among 378,850 employees in different industries, researchers compared the performance evaluations of male and female employees given by supervisors and found that women's performance was consistently evaluated less favorably than men's. US census data also shows that women entering the labor market with equal qualifications as men and who are employed in similar jobs get paid less at every stage of their careers. Almost half of all working women report having experienced gender discrimination on the job, and one quarter report they've been treated as if they were incompetent.

TEST YOUR LEVEL OF IMPLICIT BIAS ABOUT WOMEN IN THE WORKPLACE

The implicit association test (IAT) measures the degree to which you have unconsciously internalized biases such as the belief that work is a male domain and home is a female domain. An IAT measures how much bias you have by the speed with which you link words together; for instance associating male or female names with work words versus family words.

Three scientists—Tony Greenwald of the University of Washington, Mahzarin Banaji of Harvard, and Brian Nosek of the University of Virginia—have

created a fascinating website called Project Implicit to help people identify their own unconscious biases. You can register at this website for free
and then take a variety of IATs, including one that assesses unconscious
gender-career bias: **https://implicit.harvard.edu/implicit/**.

I got a score indicating that I have a strong gender bias, even though I
consider myself a feminist! Remember to have compassion for yourself if
your results aren't what you'd ideally like. We didn't choose to have implicit biases, but they're within us and color the way we perceive others'
actions and the decisions we make. We need to recognize and clearly
see our biases before we can take action to correct them.

BACKLASH

Given that women are both agentic and communal, many rev up their
yang and tone down their yin in the workplace to be seen as competent. Unfortunately, this makes women vulnerable to a phenomenon
first documented more than twenty years ago: backlash. Backlash refers to the tendency to view women with fierce qualities as socially
deficient—not nice enough—compared to men who display the exact
same behaviors.

Consider the democratic primary debate in December 2019, in
which candidates were essentially interviewing for the highest leadership position in the United States: the office of president. After an
intense couple of hours in which everyone was promoting their qualifications to lead the nation, the seven candidates in that debate—Joe
Biden, Bernie Sanders, Elizabeth Warren, Pete Buttigieg, Amy Klobuchar, Tom Steyer, and Andrew Yang—were asked whether, in the
spirit of the season, they would give a gift to someone else onstage or
ask for forgiveness. The male candidates all offered a gift—mainly of
their ideas: a copy of their book or a policy proposal. The two women
on the stage that night felt compelled to ask for forgiveness. Elizabeth
Warren said, "I will ask for forgiveness. I know that sometimes I get

really worked up. And sometimes I get a little hot. I don't really mean to." Amy Klobuchar said, "Well, I'd ask for forgiveness, anytime any of you get mad at me. I can be blunt, but I am doing this because I think it is so important to pick the right candidates here." In other words, my inner fierceness was on full display, please don't hate me for it. Both felt they had to ask for forgiveness for being forward and assertive, even though they needed to be so in order to be qualified for the position of president. They knew that people would judge them for it, so they felt impelled to apologize, while the men knew they would be admired and respected for the same qualities.

It should come as no surprise that Warren and Klobuchar, both extremely competent and experienced senators, got knocked out of the race. This echoes what happened to Hillary Clinton, who lost the 2016 election to Donald Trump (at least in terms of electoral votes). These strong, competent women who broke gender stereotypes weren't seen as likable enough to be the nation's most powerful leader.

Workplace bias against women is based not only on beliefs that we're communal rather than agentic (called descriptive stereotypes), but also that we *should be* communal rather than agentic (called prescriptive stereotypes). In other words, people don't like agentic women—especially when they're competent—because they automatically assume a fierce woman is *not* communal. And tender qualities of being kind, warm, and nurturing are valued in a woman.

Successful female managers in traditionally male fields are described in negative terms (bitter, quarrelsome, selfish, deceitful, and devious) compared with similarly successful male managers. In one study, Heilman and colleagues examined participants' evaluations of a fictional Assistant Vice President for sales at an aircraft company. The VP was said to be responsible for training and supervising junior executives, breaking into new markets, keeping up with industry trends, and generating new clients. Evaluators read the same information about the characteristics and qualifications of the VPs, but two conditions varied. First, the VP was either given the name Andrea or James. Second, information about the VP's success was either clear (they just underwent an annual performance review and got very high marks) or ambiguous (they were about to undergo an annual performance review). When the information about success was clear, James and Andrea were rated as equally competent. When information was ambiguous, Andrea was rated as less competent, productive, and effective as James. This shows the role of unconscious stereotypes in framing our perceptions, especially when the information we use is vague.

However, what's even more disturbing is that when success was clear and unambiguous according to performance reviews—so both candidates were deemed competent—Andrea was rated as less likable than James. Because her success broke the prescriptive stereotype that women should be communal rather than agentic, she was rated as being more abrasive, conniving, manipulative, pushy, selfish, and untrustworthy. Remember that descriptions of James and Andrea were exactly the same; the only way they differed was in name. Ratings of the two candidates' likability didn't differ when their success was ambiguous, because although people assumed Andrea was incompetent, they also assumed she was nurturing and therefore likable.

A similar phenomenon happens with self-promotion. In order to advance in the workplace, it's often necessary to speak directly about one's strengths, talents, and accomplishments. This is especially true in situations such as being interviewed for a higher-level position. But self-promotion can create backlash for women. A study by Laurie Rudman at Rutgers University examined evaluations of male and female job applicants in videotaped job interviews. The applicants were either modest and self-effacing (looking down and making qualified statements such as "Well, I'm no expert but . . .") or confident and self-promoting (making direct eye contact and statements such as "I am certain I can do it . . ."). Participants preferred self-promoting to self-effacing men, but preferred self-effacing to self-promoting women. The difference was even more extreme for female participants in the study, who really disliked self-promoting women.

Although it might be tempting to dismiss whether or not other people like us, the fact that people dislike agentic women means it's less probable they'll be hired or promoted, given that likability is an influential factor for determining success. One important area in which assertive women face serious backlash is salary negotiations. A woman who aggressively negotiates for a higher salary is disliked, which reduces her chance for a raise. Because women know this, they tend to be less assertive in negotiations and settle for less than their male counterparts. One study from the University of Texas at Austin found that women settled for a full 20 percent less out of fear of backlash. A meta-analysis of 142 studies found that even when male and female employees are rated as equally competent, men are still paid more and promoted more often. In fact, sex differences in pay were fourteen times larger than sex differences in performance evaluations. This is due in no small part to backlash.

So this is the position we're in: we aren't promoted as often or paid as much as men because we aren't considered agentic enough, and we also aren't promoted as often or paid as much because we're considered *too* agentic. And people wonder why there's still a pay gap and so few women obtain top leadership positions!

INTEGRATION AT WORK

Integrating agency and communion at work—in other words, drawing on our fierce and tender sides simultaneously—can help temper backlash. In one experiment, participants saw videotaped interviews of two male and two female applicants for a high-pressure managerial position that required careful listening to clients' concerns. Participants then judged how competent and likable the candidates were and recommended whether they should be hired for the position. All the applicants were highly agentic and self-confident in their interviews, saying things like "I tend to thrive in pressure situations. In high school, I was the editor of the school paper and I had to prepare a weekly column under deadline all the time . . . and I always pulled it off." However, one male and one female applicant piled on the agentic talk, adding comments like "Basically there are two kinds of people, winners and losers.

My goal is to be a winner, the type of person who gets to be in charge and make the decisions." The other two added more communal comments like "To me, life is about being connected to other people . . . If I can help someone out, I feel a real sense of accomplishment."

As in previous studies, the doubly agentic man and woman were both considered competent, but the woman was considered less likable than the man and was therefore less likely to be recommended for the position. However, the woman who combined agency and communion was considered as competent and likable as the man, and was equally likely to be recommended for the position. In a similar study, researchers in Israel found that both males and females are considered more effective leaders when they display both agentic and communal traits, but this difference is particularly pronounced for women. These findings suggest that one effective way for women to reduce gender bias and get ahead in the workplace is by drawing upon caring force to get the job done.

That may take engaging in what Joan Williams, a law professor at the University of California, Hastings, calls gender judo. Judo is a Japanese martial art, and the word means "gentle way." The idea is that you use your opponent's momentum to overpower him, going with the flow rather than fighting directly against it. The term gender judo refers to intentionally bringing in a traditionally feminine quality, such as warmth or care, when we do something masculine and agentic, so that we work within the framework of others' stereotypes. For example, while giving an employee or team member instructions— taking charge the way a leader should—if you smile or ask about the person's well-being, it can soften the negative perception that you're being demanding. The way communal qualities are expressed needs to be authentic and natural, so the style will vary from person to person. But all people have access to yin and yang energies, so intentionally making sure that both are present can help lessen the influence of gender bias.

However, Williams cautions that when we demonstrate warmth and care in these situations, we should avoid any hint of submissiveness, like apologizing and hedging ("Um, I'm really sorry, but would you mind working extra hours this weekend?"), which can undercut the credibility of your leadership. We need to be authoritative and warm at the same time, in whatever way works ("I need you to work extra hours this weekend, but I'll try to make sure it doesn't happen often. How is your family doing by the way?"). By embracing multiple aspects of ourselves simultaneously, we can be authentic and still find a place in the world of business.

Although it's good to know there are ways to work within an unjust system, it's also disheartening that we have to think about these strategies in the first place. I believe that self-compassion has an important role to play in facing and eventually transforming gender bias at work.

HOW TENDER SELF-COMPASSION CAN HELP

It's crucial that, as women, we allow ourselves to experience the pain of discrimination in the workplace. We can draw on loving, connected presence to be with our sadness and frustration—that sinking feeling in the stomach or hollowness in the heart when we realize all the ways in which we still aren't equal. We can acknowledge and turn toward our collective grief over the fact that a woman hasn't yet been elected president and that White males largely continue to run the show in politics and business. Generations of women have seen their talents, skills, and abilities suppressed and denigrated. That's the world we've inherited and, unfortunately, the one we're still basically in right now. We carry that pain inside of us, and it colors the way we relate to other women. We need to be aware of the discomfort that comes from having our more tender side suppressed at work, and the pangs of taking part in a world that hasn't yet opened to the advantages of caring for others as part of its economic mission.

There's also frustration in realizing that our fierce side isn't accepted. It hurts to be reviled and disliked for being competent and assertive. If we pretend the pain isn't there, we won't be able to heal from its damaging effects. However, when we acknowledge the hurt and are loving toward ourselves in response, we can process our grief and also reap the benefits of our own warmth.

When considering the injustice that we face in the workplace, it's especially important to remember that it has nothing to do with us as individuals but is shared with millions of women around the globe. We sometimes internalize societal prejudice in a way that diminishes our self-concept—I'm not good at science, I'm not an effective leader, maybe he's better than I am. But when we see prejudice for what it is, calling out the injustice, we remember that we're not alone. We can connect with people who are also marginalized due to gender or other aspects of their identity—sexual orientation, race, ethnicity, ability, class, religion. The more we let others into our hearts, acknowledging this painful aspect of the human experience, the less isolated we'll feel.

It's also essential that we recognize and forgive the fact that we've contributed to discrimination through our own unconscious bias. As discussed earlier, women are even more likely to dislike competent women than men are. We've all felt the urge to denigrate a successful woman. Many of us have internalized these "bitch" stereotypes without knowing it. We may unconsciously feel threatened by other capable women, fueling our dislike. But we don't have to judge or blame ourselves for this; it happens mostly outside of our awareness. If you're a human being participating in an unjust society, you'll internalize bias against others. Tender self-compassion can give us the sense of safety and unconditional acceptance needed to acknowledge these biases, which is the first step toward changing them.

But do we stop there, feeling comforted but marginalized? Hell no. In order to truly care for ourselves we need to take action and do something about the way we're treated.

HOW FIERCE SELF-COMPASSION CAN HELP

Fierce self-compassion provides the determination needed to correct injustice—not only for women, but for all victims of workplace discrimination. Clarity is crucial for this task. Research shows that one of the most important steps in reducing unconscious gender bias at work is to stare it straight in the face. We can ask ourselves, "Would I form the same impression of this woman's competence or likability if she were a man?" We can ask others to consider the question as well. We can talk to people about the role that unconscious bias plays in our judgments, even for those who are deeply committed to equality. But when we do, it's important that we don't demonize others or they'll just shut us out to protect their egos. We'd also be ignoring their humanity—which is exactly the opposite of what we're trying to accomplish.

When you come upon coworkers talking about a female manager negatively and suspect gender bias is playing a role, you can step in. Perhaps you overhear, "I can't believe Janet was going on and on about herself. Who does she think she is? And did you see how she treated her assistant for being late with the files? She's such a cow." You might respond with something like this: "I'm wondering if Janet would come off that way if she were a man? We're led to believe that women shouldn't promote themselves or be firm with others. Just as a thought experiment, if it were Kevin over in Marketing who said these things, how do you think we'd react?" If it's said in a nonjudgmental way that doesn't shame anyone, using inclusive language (like "we") instead of finger-pointing language (like "you"), there might be a chance to cut through the fog of unconscious bias. Maybe you'll even be lucky enough to hear, "Hmm, I guess I didn't think of that before. Good point." But even if all you get is silence, the point has still been made. As women we can't stay silent anymore. If we're going to move beyond these biases, we need to make the unconscious conscious.

What do we do with our pent-up rage about the unfair treatment of women in the workplace? After all, it's good to be angry. If we're afraid of being angry, things will never move forward. We *must* be angry at injustice so that we can harness this protective energy for social good. But we need to use the power of our anger skillfully, aiming at the harm itself rather than the people causing it. The more we can get our egos and those of others out of the way, the better chance we'll have of getting the outcome we're hoping for. (By the way, I'm not saying this as someone who's incredibly skillful at harnessing her anger for desired outcomes, but as someone who's gotten it wrong so often that she knows what doesn't work.)

If we're asked by a male colleague to make coffee, for instance, take notes for a meeting, make travel arrangements, or help out in other ways that aren't part of our job description, we can stand up for ourselves with caring force. Instead of attacking ("Make your own damn coffee, you pig"), we can say with a wink and a smile something like, "I'm sure you see women as more than just office assistants, don't you?" This gives him the benefit of the doubt so that you don't humiliate him, but also lets him know his request was unreasonable.

Or imagine a scenario where a male colleague takes your idea and promotes it as his own, which research shows is a common phenomenon. Jessica Bennett, author of the *Feminist Fight Club: An Office Survival Manual for a Sexist Workplace,* calls such a man a "bropropriator." She recommends fighting back with a technique she calls "thank and yank." When a man tries to take credit for your idea, you can thank him for liking your idea but make it clear it is your own: "So glad you agree with me on this one. So what are our next steps?" This allows for a positive response to the man while protecting the integrity of your own contribution. She gives similar advice when we encounter a "manterrupter." Studies show that women tend to be interrupted more often than men. Bennett recommends a response of "verbal chicken": just keep talking without pause so that he's forced to stop. You don't shame the manterrupter, but rather wear him down, making it clear you won't be silenced. These are some of the ways we can use our fierceness to protect ourselves in the workplace.

It's also possible to help empower each other at work. Research shows that when one woman speaks up for another, both are liked more. While a female may be disliked if she promotes herself, she doesn't experience backlash if she says something positive about a colleague because her agentic behavior (promotion) is combined with communal behavior (support). And given that women are especially prone to disliking self-promoting women, it's also up to us to change the way we perceive those who take credit for their own success. Rather than feeling threatened by it or succumbing to our unconscious conditioning, we can revel in the success of our sisters, knowing that a gain for one is a gain for all.

Another important benefit that fierce self-compassion can provide in the workplace is guiding us toward careers that are authentic and fulfilling, that balance our individual and professional needs with those of our families. This begins with a simple question: what do I truly want in life? The most satisfying choices will be those that allow us to express both our yin and yang energies so that we feel whole. We don't need to be consumed by runaway greed, and we don't have to choose selfless careers that primarily help others if they're not our calling.

Often work life and home life are portrayed as being in conflict, but in some ways it's a false dichotomy. When we find satisfaction, purpose, and a feeling of competence in our jobs, it enriches our friendships and family life. Conversely, being a well-rounded person outside of our work life helps us reach our full potential within it. In fact, research indicates that self-compassion helps women achieve greater work-life balance. One study of women in fields such as health care, education, and finance found that those with higher levels of self-compassion reported greater work-life balance as well as more satisfaction with their careers and lives in general. Another study found that self-compassionate women had more confidence in their job performance, were more committed to their employees, and experienced lower levels of burnout and exhaustion at work.

A common barrier for working women, especially those in male-dominated fields, is known as the imposter phenomenon. Pauline Clance and Suzanne Imes identified this in 1978 when they realized the highly successful women with Ph.D.s they were studying—all experts in their fields—feared they would be exposed as intellectual impostors. These women were hyper-perfectionists but still blew off their success as being due to luck, meaning they lived in a constant state of anxiety that they'd be unmasked. The imposter phenomenon can hamper our ability to claim our rightful place among men who are no smarter than we are but feel more comfortable as experts because they've been treated from birth as if they belonged to an exclusive males-only club.

Luckily, self-compassion can help. In a study of first-year under-graduates at a prestigious European university, researchers measured the degree to which men and women experienced the imposter phe-nomenon. They also measured the degree to which students had an agentic, communal, or androgynous gender-role orientation along with their level of self-compassion. Researchers found that female stu-dents generally experienced the imposter phenomenon more intensely than males. They also found that agentic and androgynous women were more self-compassionate, and that self-compassionate women were less susceptible to the imposter phenomenon. By unconditionally accepting and supporting ourselves, self-compassion allows us to stake a claim to our own achievements.

Fierce self-compassion is also a potent and stable source of mo-tivation in the workplace, which is key to getting ahead. It provides encouragement, the ability to learn from our missteps, and a clear vi-sion of where we're headed. Self-compassionate individuals have been shown to be more positive and confident when encountering difficul-ties in a job search. They're also more likely to stay calm in the face of challenges, remaining hopeful about their search rather than growing downcast and dejected. Not only that, but self-compassionate em-ployees report higher levels of engagement at work in terms of feeling more energized, enthusiastic, and absorbed. And self-compassion is especially helpful for overcoming failures on the job. Researchers from the Netherlands trained almost one hundred entrepreneurs to be more self-compassionate and found that they became less fearful and better able to cope with situations like a sudden drop in customer demand.

The use of encouragement rather than harsh criticism allows us to stand strong when we fail on the job, so we can summon the grit and determination to keep trying. Serena Chen wrote an article in the

Harvard Business Review unpacking the benefits of self-compassion for the workplace; she pointed out that although the business community has begun to embrace the idea that failure provides an opportunity for learning, it hasn't yet figured out how to help employees make that transformation. Self-compassion—what Chen calls "harnessing the redemptive power of failure"—helps foster precisely the type of growth mindset needed to succeed and thrive at work.

TAKING A SELF-COMPASSION BREAK AT WORK

We all know how important it is to take a break at work. Whether you spend the time getting a cup of coffee or reading a few pages of a good book, a small pause can help you reset. You can also use the time to take a Self-Compassion Break, helping you to cope with any stress, frustration, or difficulty you're facing. The first question to ask yourself is what do I need to care for myself right now? Do I need a Tender Self-Compassion Break (page 121) to calm and comfort myself, providing greater acceptance for what is? Do I need a Protective Self-Compassion Break (page 148) to say no, draw boundaries, or defend myself? Do I need a Providing Self-Compassion Break (page 177) to help me focus on meeting my own needs in an authentic manner? Or do I need a Motivating Self-Compassion Break (page 197) to help encourage a change or to keep going? Perhaps you need some combination of the above. By getting in the habit of tuning in to what you need in the moment, you can greatly enhance your resilience and effectiveness in the workplace.

MY JOURNEY IN ACADEMIA

Like most women, I've encountered gender bias in the workplace. Academia is a yang world. The "scale wars" I discussed earlier are certainly a testament to this, and my academic persona can be quite fierce. However, because this goes against gender norms, it also means that some of my colleagues—including those in my department at UT Austin—don't like me. It's something I've had to contend with over the course of my career. Part of this is a reaction to my bulldog side coming out in inappropriate places like dissertation defenses, which is understandable. But it goes beyond that. If I ask a blunt question without a ton of flowery padding in a department meeting, it's taken as aggressive. When people ask me how I'm doing and I'm honest about my excitement ("Great, thanks! My work was mentioned twice in the *New York Times* last month, isn't that cool?"), it's interpreted as narcissistic and self-promoting. I suspect that none of these behaviors, even my inner bulldog, would raise an eyebrow if I were a man.

At the same time, because the focus of my work is on self-compassion, I've also paid a penalty for being too soft. I was denied promotion from associate to full professor—even though I had 50 percent more citations than the second most highly cited full professor in my department—because my research wasn't deemed "rigorous enough" for an R1 (meaning top tier) research university. Because my classes focus on helping students learn skills of mindfulness and self-compassion, writing papers about the impact of doing such practices in their daily life, my teaching wasn't considered "scholarly enough." And the service I provided in the form of helping to create an international training program in self-compassion wasn't really valued, since it was done outside the bureaucratic system. (I cofounded a nonprofit rather than apply for large federal grants, for instance.)

I already had tenure as an associate professor and the difference in pay between an associate and full professor is minimal, so being denied the promotion was mainly a blow to my ego rather than my livelihood. But to have my life's work be dismissed so lightly felt like a kick in the gut. I'm devoted to the study and teaching of self-compassion because it helps people. I haven't wasted time doing many of the things that are valued in traditional academia—volunteering for extra committee work, organizing and attending scholarly meetings, and writing grants—because this wouldn't actually help anyone. But I operated outside the system, and the academy doesn't like people who go their own way.

Thank goodness for my self-compassion practice. I was dismayed and discouraged after being denied the promotion and needed both tender and fierce self-compassion to get me through. First, I made sure I allowed myself to fully experience the disappointment and grief of being passed over, the feeling of not being appreciated. I remember lying in bed, putting both hands on my heart, and crying all night. I told myself, "This really hurts. I feel so unseen. So unvalued. But I see you, Kristin. I value you and honor how hard you've worked to bring more compassion to this world. I'm so sorry that your department and university have different values. But it has nothing to do with you or the worth of your scholarship." I allowed the storm to arrive, to let loose the deluge of wind, rain, and thunder, and move on.

When I woke up the next morning, I was angry. I felt I'd been treated unfairly. I met with the dean, the university ombudsman, and the chair of the tenure and promotion committee. I created a document comparing the rigor of my scholarship with that of the last two faculty members in similar fields who were promoted to full professor (both males). It was clear that my methods were at least, if not more, rigorous. But the decision was final, and my only option would be to try again in a couple years. However, to do so would require playing the game in a way that was more to the university's liking, and I don't want to do that. I don't want to be distracted from my work in the world and waste time on what the university values but that I see as irrelevant. So I've decided to make a change and am taking early retirement at the end of 2021. I can still conduct research as an associate professor emeritus and am talking with various universities about research appointments, but I will mainly focus on helping the Center for Mindful Self-Compassion bring self-compassion to those who need it around the globe: health-care workers, educators, social-justice advocates, parents, teens, anyone who suffers. Although it's scary to leave a tenured position, I know it's the right thing to do.

As women, we'll need a lot of self-compassion to successfully navigate and transform a sexist workplace. Unfortunately, there are no quick fixes. Our only choice is to forge ahead and be as authentic as possible, honoring both our yin and yang nature. Tender self-compassion allows us to hold the pain of injustice and fierce self-compassion impels us to stand up for ourselves and realize our vision of the future. We can work together to create a workplace in which the value of human kindness is balanced with making profits, each unique voice is given the chance to fully contribute, and all people are on equal footing when climbing the ladder of success.

CHAPTER 10

CARING FOR OTHERS WITHOUT LOSING OURSELVES

Caring for myself is not self-indulgence, it is self-preservation, and that is an act of political warfare.

—*Audre Lorde, author and activist*

A central aspect of the female gender role is the expectation that we will care for and nurture others. But in fulfilling this role we run the risk of being swallowed up, unless there's an equally strong emphasis on meeting our own needs. If not, we may become like those species of spiders who engage in matriphagy—when new spiderlings eat their mother alive as a source of nutrition. But instead of our bodies being devoured, our emotional and psychological reserves will be consumed until we have next to nothing left for ourselves.

There are signs that this may be already happening for some. Currently 80 percent of single parents are women, meaning that mothers are far more likely than fathers to take on the primary responsibility for raising their children. Even in dual-parent households where both parents work full-time—the most common arrangement for today's families—estimates are that working wives do about twice the amount of childcare and housework. This isn't just because men tend to make more money than women. When women start earning more money than their husbands, they actually increase, not decrease, the amount of time spent on housework in order to not undermine their image as good wives. They also spend more time coordinating family activities, planning celebrations, arranging doctor visits, checking in on relatives, and so on. The result is that four in ten working mothers report always feeling rushed, with little to no time left for themselves. By running around taking care of the kids and making appointments and doing the dishes and getting ready for the big meeting the next day, we drain ourselves of precious energy.

Women also shoulder the burden of care for other family members. We're 50 percent more likely than men to be a caregiver for an ill spouse or elderly relative with conditions such Alzheimer's, dementia, or cancer. We are also more likely than men to report negative consequences from caregiving such as anxiety, stress, depression, diminished physical health, and lower quality of life. The simmering resentment many women feel, especially when their domestic burdens aren't shared by their male counterparts, leads to tension and discontent. In fact, married women who work full-time and feel the division of household labor is unfair report being angrier and more distressed, and are also more likely to experience burnout, than those who share their burdens more equally.

While men also provide care for their children, spouses, and relatives, expectations for their contributions are much lower. And when a man does step up, he's often celebrated as if he just volunteered to donate a kidney. A colleague of mine named Stephanie, mother of three children under eight, commented on the absurdity of it all. She told me that she took her two older girls to do some back-to-school clothes shopping at the mall while her husband, Mike, stayed home with their baby boy. Apparently it was quite challenging to make sure neither of the girls wandered off while they trudged from shop to shop, especially since she was carrying multiple bags. In one store, all three of them were squeezed into a little dressing room as the oldest was

trying on clothes. The younger girl somehow managed to crawl unnoticed into the booth next to them, until Stephanie heard a woman's
voice say sharply, "Can you please try to control your children?" She
felt ashamed, like she wasn't up to the task of being a mother. When
she got home, she was exhausted. Mike greeted them as they came
through the door, looking particularly pleased with himself. "How did
your day go?" she asked. "Great!" he said cheerfully. "I put Tyler in the
BabyBjörn and took him grocery shopping, and in the checkout line
an elderly couple told me what a great father I was!" Stephanie told
me she had to keep herself from rolling her eyes. "If only I had it so
easy!"

Stories like Stephanie's are typical. Women can do triple backflips
caring for their children and no one even notices, except when she's
seen to be falling short. A man does half as much and is hailed as a
hero.

While there can be tremendous meaning and satisfaction in caring
for others, it isn't enjoyable if we don't balance it with caring for ourselves too. Whether we're professional caregivers, family caregivers, or
caring for our partners, giving and receiving must be equitable to be
sustainable.

LOPSIDED CARING

One of the most problematic consequences of socializing women to be
tender but not fierce is an overemphasis on helping others—and the
simultaneous underemphasis on helping ourselves. The subordination
of our own needs to those of others is taken to be emblematic of the
admirable self-sacrificing nature that makes women the "nobler sex."
This characterization fuels benevolent sexism because it casts the unequal allocation of resources—with men getting the lion's share—as
somehow due to women's beautiful, generous, and kind nature.

And we often fall for it hook, line, and sinker. Like all human
beings, we want to be loved and approved of. As soon as we discover

that others like us when we sacrifice ourselves, we end up in a strange position: we abandon our own needs to maintain a positive sense of self, even though doing so means there's less of ourselves left over to value.

Vicki Helgeson and Heidi Fritz from Carnegie Mellon University have labeled focusing on the needs of others to the exclusion of personal needs as "unmitigated communion," a state that occurs whenever caring for others isn't tempered by caring for oneself. I call it lopsided caring. It can mean continually agreeing to do what your partner wants (where you vacation, what restaurant you go to, what city you live in) instead of what you want. It might look like spending so much time helping family, friends, or your favorite charity that you have little time to pursue your own interests, leaving you drained and exhausted. Not surprisingly, women register higher levels of lopsided caring than men. While nurturing others does tend to be associated with well-being, doing so at your own expense leads to distress and partially explains why women are more depressed than men.

Sometimes women can't meet their own needs simply because the conditions of daily life give them no chance to do so. A single mother who's working two jobs to support her kids may just not have any time left over for herself. But lopsided caring can also be due to personality type or sense of identity. Some women repeatedly choose to focus on the needs of others to the exclusion of their own because they feel they *should*—they don't think they deserve otherwise. Research indicates that women who are lopsided carers tend to silence themselves and feel inhibited around others because they doubt that what they have to say is worthwhile. They have difficulties expressing their authentic selves or being assertive and standing up for their rights when others are being inconsiderate. This inexpressiveness contributes to challenges with intimacy in romantic relationships. It's hard to share deeply with your partner if you believe what you have to share is inadequate. It also makes it harder to reveal your desires to others or be firm in insisting that your needs be given due consideration.

Women who are lopsided carers don't always do so happily and are often disgruntled about it. They're afraid to ask for what they need, and at the same time begrudge others for not giving them what they want. Of course, waiting for others to spontaneously meet our needs is like waiting for our teenage child to spontaneously take out the trash. Good luck. If we don't ask, it's probably not going to happen.

Losing ourselves in this way can be dangerous, even fatal. Research indicates that lopsided carers tend to neglect their physical health: those with diabetes or breast cancer are less likely to visit the doctor, exercise, eat well, keep up with their prescribed medications, or get adequate rest. One study examined individuals who'd recently been admitted to the hospital for a coronary event such as a heart attack. They found that lopsided carers were more likely to experience continued cardiac symptoms such as chest pain, dizziness, shortness of breath, fatigue, nausea, and heart palpitations because they weren't engaging in enough self-care. We may be literally breaking our hearts by ignoring our own needs.

IS YOUR CARING LOPSIDED?

You can test whether your pattern of caring for yourself and others is out of balance by filling out the Unmitigated Communion Scale, created by Fritz and Helgeson.

Instructions

Please read each statement carefully before answering. For each item, think about whether you agree or disagree with the statement, thinking especially about how accurately it describes the way you relate to the people close to you, friends or family. Respond using a scale of 1 (strongly disagree), 2 (slightly disagree), 3 (neither agree nor disagree), 4 (slightly agree), or 5 (strongly agree).

___ I place the needs of others above my own.

___ I find myself getting overly involved in others' problems.

___ For me to be happy, I need others to be happy.

___ I worry about how other people get along without me when I am not there.

___ I have great difficulty getting to sleep at night when other people are upset.

___ It is impossible for me to satisfy my own needs when they interfere with the needs of others.

___ I can't say no when someone asks me for help.

___ Even when exhausted, I will always help other people.

___ I often worry about others' problems.

After you've made your responses, calculate the total score and divide by 9 to get a mean score. Scores above 3 indicate that your caring is somewhat lopsided. To give you a sense of what is typical, one study of 361 undergraduate students found that the average score for men was 3.05 and the average score for women was 3.32.

A WOMAN'S WORTH

As mentioned, one force driving lopsided caring is the need for external validation. We want others to like and approve of us. Our sense of self-worth often relies on meeting the standards society sets for being a "good" mother (volunteering to bring cupcakes to the PTA dinner), or a "good" wife (taking an interest in our spouse's hobbies), or a "good" daughter (arranging repairs for our elderly parents' home). Many of these actions are authentic expressions of care, but these good deeds become tainted if they are used as a means to gain the approval of others. Instead of balancing acts of generosity with self-care, we start to subordinate what we really want in order to make others happy. This is partly why so many women say yes when they really want to say no; they're afraid no one will love them unless they do.

The problem with this strategy is that it often doesn't work. Others may take our caring for granted and not appreciate us—either because they choose not to or simply because they're too engrossed by their own problems. And even when others do value us, it still may not be enough to counter our feelings of inadequacy. Our partners may say all the right things—"I think you're great, you're so special to me"—but if we don't believe this ourselves, we're likely to just blow off what they say. If we can't value ourselves, we'll never feel good enough. These feelings of unworthiness in lopsided carers directly contribute to their unhappiness and depression.

Instead of looking to others for a sense of worthiness and approval, it's possible to turn inward to our own wellspring of warmth and good-will as the source. It may sound like a tall order, but this is the power of self-compassion. We embrace ourselves, flaws and all, and value ourselves because of, not in spite of, our imperfections. We honor our strengths and our weaknesses. We don't need to do anything to earn this acceptance; we claim it as our birthright. After all, what determines our worth as a person? Is it how nice we are, how useful we are, how attractive we are, how much people like us? Our worth is simply an intrinsic part of being human, doing the best we can with the cards we've been dealt. Our value stems from having a consciousness capable of experiencing the full range of human emotions. When we recognize this, we can learn to give ourselves the love and attention we crave.

This isn't just woo-woo speak. It's backed up by empirical research. Studies show that feelings of self-worth rooted in self-compassion aren't contingent on how much other people like us, or how attractive we are, or how successful we are. Because it comes from the inside rather than the outside, it's more stable and less shaky over time. It's unconditional, there for us in times of praise and blame.

When the bottom line is unconditional self-acceptance, we can give to others because we want to, not because we think we're supposed to. We can say yes when we're feeling resourced. And when our tank is running low, we can say no.

SAYING NO TO OTHERS AND YES TO OURSELVES

Finding the right balance between caring for others and ourselves is crucial for caring to be healthy. Although we have an unlimited pool of love to give to others, we don't have unlimited time or energy. If we give to the point of harming ourselves, we're no longer working in alignment with compassion. Given that compassion is focused on the alleviation of suffering, causing ourselves pain in order to alleviate the suffering of others doesn't work—not only in principle but in practice. If we don't put effort into meeting our own needs so that we feel fulfilled, we'll bankrupt ourselves as caregivers. If we wind up so drained and depleted that we have nothing to give, we won't be much use to anyone.

Veronica learned the importance of caring for herself after she attended one of my weeklong self-compassion intensive workshops. Over lunch, a group of us were talking about cultural expectations placed on women as caregivers. I mentioned that I'd done research comparing norms of self-sacrifice among Mexican American and European American women and found that Mexican American women were especially likely to feel pressure to give up their needs for others in relationships. Veronica, a Mexican American woman in her forties, agreed—in fact, this is why she'd been drawn to the topic of self-compassion. We kept up an acquaintance, and I learned her story.

Veronica grew up in a large, tight-knit, loving family in central California. As the oldest of six kids, she was put in charge of watching over her younger siblings at the age of ten. Her sense of self formed around the notion of being a good caregiver, and she was rewarded for being responsible. This continued into adulthood. She married and had two boys, who were now teenagers, and worked as a manager at a busy accounting firm. She was the main breadwinner in her family because early in her marriage her husband, Juan, had developed multiple sclerosis and couldn't work. After coming home from the office, she would make dinner for her kids and give Juan whatever help he needed, while also making sure the family spent quality time together. She was also a religious woman and volunteered on the weekends at church, cooking at fundraisers and organizing donation drives. If anyone needed help, they'd always ask Veronica.

But inside Veronica was drowning. She worked until she was exhausted and grew resentful of all the people depending on her. It seemed like her life consisted of going from one chore to the next. She rarely had time to do things she enjoyed, like watercolor painting. She'd learned to paint in college and would've loved to become a professional artist but took the safe route and became an accountant instead.

Juan was scheduled to go out of town with the boys to visit his family over a three-day weekend, and she was finally going to get a break. She planned to hole up at home and paint as much as possible. But her parish priest called last minute to ask if she could cover for a sick volunteer at the annual summer camp that weekend. "It would mean so much to the kids," he said. Veronica was about to instinctively say yes, but she paused and said she'd have to think about it. Learning about fierce self-compassion had made a big impression on her, and she knew that she needed more yang. This was an opportunity to practice it.

After she hung up the phone with her priest, the first thing Veronica did was consider what would happen if she said no. She was afraid, she realized. How could she refuse? What would everyone at church think of her? Would they think she was cold, selfish, heartless, unchristian? She later described to me how she used the practices taught in the workshop to help cope with her fears. She first allowed herself to be with the worry, getting in touch with its physical manifestation as a constriction at the back of her throat. It felt almost as if she was choking and couldn't speak. She realized she was frightened that if she asserted herself, she would no longer be worthy of love. So she tried something else that she'd learned, even though it felt awkward. She said out loud to herself, "I love and value you, Veronica. I care about you. I want you to be happy." She said it over and over. At first it felt foreign and awkward. She didn't buy it. But she persisted. Eventually tears started to flow as she began to let it in.

She then tried doing a Providing Self-Compassion Break to call upon the power of fulfilling, balanced authenticity. First, she used mindfulness to validate the fact that what she really wanted was to take a painting retreat instead of volunteering at the camp. She went to the next step, balance, repeating to herself, "My needs are important too." Although she loved her church and wanted to help, she knew she had to start caring for herself in addition to others. Then she took the last step of committing to her own well-being. She cupped her face with both hands and spoke to herself the way she might speak to one of her sons: "I don't want you to feel empty and drained, sweetheart, I want you to feel satisfied and whole. You deserve some time for yourself."

Veronica felt stronger after doing this brief practice and called her priest. "I would love to help you out, but I have plans that weekend. I'm sorry." He was not used to hearing Veronica say no. "Are you sure you can't rearrange things? It would be such a help." She replied warmly but firmly, "No, I can't. I need some time to myself." Her priest had no choice but to accept her decision.

And the world didn't fall apart. Veronica had a thoroughly enjoyable weekend alone painting. She was so proud of herself, she told me afterward. Instead of trying to get love and approval from others as she'd been doing her whole life, she'd found the courage to give herself what she needed.

WHAT DO I NEED NOW?

Self-compassion can be used in so many different ways to meet our needs. Sometimes we need tenderness, sometimes we need fierceness, and other times we need to make a change. You can take inventory of the different aspects of fierce and tender self-compassion and think about what you might need in the moment to care for yourself (maybe you need them all!):

Acceptance. Are you feeling bad about yourself or unworthy in some way? Perhaps you just need to accept yourself with love and understanding, knowing that it's okay to be imperfect.

Comfort. Are you upset about something and need some comfort? Try using some soothing touch to calm your body. Then consider what caring words you might say to a dear friend going through a similar situation. Also consider the tone of voice you might use. Then try saying the same thing, in the same way, to yourself.

Validation. Is there a part of you that feels you don't have the right to complain, or have you been so focused on fixing things you haven't fully acknowledged how much you're struggling in the moment? Try verbalizing your feelings in a way that affirms what is true for you. You might try saying aloud, "This is incredibly hard" or "Of course you're having difficulty. Anyone would in your situation."

Boundaries. Is there someone overstepping boundaries, maybe asking too much of you or making you feel uncomfortable? Try standing tall and drawing on some fierce self-compassion to courageously say no. You don't have to do it in a mean way, but be firm in communicating what is acceptable and what's not.

Anger. Has someone harmed or mistreated you? Do you feel angry about it or are you suppressing your anger in a way that is unhealthy? Give yourself permission to get angry, calling on the power of your inner Momma Bear who's ferocious in her desire to protect those she loves. You'll want to be wise in how you express your anger so that it's constructive rather than destructive, but allow yourself to feel your rage and let it flow freely in your body. This powerful emotion is also a face of love.

Fulfillment. Have you asked yourself what you need to be fulfilled? The first step is identifying what we need, and the second step is taking action to make sure we actually get it. Write down any needs you think aren't being adequately met: emotional support, sleep, laughter? Tell yourself that you deserve to be happy. Also remind yourself that others may not be available to meet your needs. What are some ways that you can meet these needs yourself? For example, if you need touch, can you get a massage? If you need rest, can you set aside two days on your own to just relax? If you need love, can you commit to giving yourself tenderness and affection?

Change. Are you stuck in a situation—like a job or relationship or living situation—that's frustrating you? Do you find yourself repeating a behavior that's harming you in some way, like smoking or procrastinating or watching too much TV? Can you try to motivate a change using kindness and understanding rather than harsh self-criticism? Can you inspire yourself the way a good coach might, pointing out ways you can improve things while demonstrating support and belief in your own capacity to accomplish your goals?

EMPATHIC PAIN

Another challenge that women face as caregivers is feeling the pain of those we care for. Looking after people involves being sensitive to their distress, and women have consistently been shown to be more empathic than men. When those we care for are suffering, we can take on their pain to the point that it becomes overwhelming, interfering with the ability to lead our lives. In order to understand how this happens, we need to take a closer look at the process of empathy.

Carl Rogers defined *empathy* as the ability to "sense another person's world as if it were your own." It involves tuning in to the emotional state of others and underlies our ability to connect. Empathy relies on cognitive perspective-taking to understand what others are thinking and feeling (putting ourselves into their shoes), but it also has a pre-reflective component that operates outside of conscious awareness.

Our brains are designed so that we experience others' emotions directly. We even have specialized neurons called "mirror neurons" whose whole purpose is to resonate with the emotions of others. This capacity is preverbal, meaning it doesn't occur through language. Empathy is what allows us to sense when others are in distress even if they don't explicitly say anything about it. We can feel their pain, literally.

Our brains developed this ability because it helped us cooperate and survive in groups. Although the principle of "survival of the fittest," with its emphasis on winner-take-all competition, is generally attributed to Charles Darwin, he actually considered *cooperation* to be the key factor helping a species survive. Empathy is central to cooperation and also facilitates communication between parents and preverbal infants. This means parents with better mirroring abilities are more able to meet their infants' needs, ensuring the DNA for these skills is passed on.

Empathy isn't always a good thing, however. First of all, sometimes people feel the pain of others but don't care about it. A skilled con artist, for instance, might use the awareness of another's fear or distress as a signal that it's a good moment to make their move. At other times, we may feel so uncomfortable with others' pain that we shut them out, dehumanizing them so we don't have to feel their suffering. Ignoring the plight of the homeless is a good example of this. Neuroscience research indicates that when we're in the presence of someone in pain, the pain centers of our brain become activated. When we're repeatedly in the presence of people experiencing physical, emotional, or mental trauma, it can have serious consequences. First responders such as firefighters or emergency medical technicians may develop secondary traumatic stress disorder, simply through their constant exposure to people in life-threatening situations. The symptoms are very similar to PTSD—hypervigilance to danger, difficulty sleeping, numbness, physical tension, depression, or irritation—even though the trauma is experienced secondhand. People in helping professions, such as nurses, teachers, social workers, and therapists, complain of similar symptoms. It can also affect family caregivers who must continually attend to a suffering child, spouse, or elderly relative.

If we experience empathic pain over a prolonged time, eventually our cup runs dry and we burn out. With burnout comes emotional exhaustion, depersonalization (a numb, hollow feeling), and loss of satisfaction in caring for others. Burnout is a primary cause of turnover among teachers, social workers, and health-care professionals. But family caregivers rarely have the option of quitting. They have to suck it up, resulting in acute stress, anxiety, and depression.

The psychologist Charles Figley originally called the exhaustion of being a caregiver "compassion fatigue," but some argue it should actually be called "empathy fatigue." When we experience empathy, we feel others' pain. When we experience compassion, we feel others' pain, but we also hold that pain with love. This distinction makes all the difference. Compassion generates feelings of warmth and connection that provide a buffer against the negative effects of experiencing someone else's suffering. Compassion is a positive, rewarding, inherently energizing emotion. The more we experience compassion, the better for our minds and bodies. Research shows that compassion reduces depression and anxiety, increases positive mind states like hope and happiness, and enhances immune function.

Neuroscientists Tania Singer from the Max Planck Institute in Berlin and Olga Klimecki from the University of Geneva have extensively studied the difference between empathy and compassion. In one experiment they examined two groups of people who were trained for several days to experience either empathy or compassion and were then showed short news clips depicting suffering—people getting injured, for instance, or enduring a natural disaster. The clips activated distinctly different brain networks in the two groups of trainees. Empathy training led to activation in the amygdala and was associated with negative feelings such as sadness, stress, and fear, while compassion training led to activation in the reward centers of the brain and generated positive emotions such as connection or kindness.

Compassion prevents us from being engulfed by the empathic pain we experience as we tend to others. It's important to not only have compassion for our charges, but to also shine the light of compassion inward. When we have self-compassion for the discomfort of being a caregiver, we're even more resilient.

PREVENTING BURNOUT

One commonly prescribed method of preventing burnout is a form of fierce self-compassion: drawing boundaries. This means placing limits on the amount of time and energy we give to others. Being firm in this way requires protective self-compassion—brave, empowered clarity. Whether it's saying no to your client who asks for your personal phone number to call you over the weekend, or to your elderly Aunt Zelda who asks you to drive her to the store for the third time this week, setting limits is essential to maintaining our sanity and effectiveness.

Another form of boundary-setting involves emotional distancing, so that we're less engaged with others' suffering. Sometimes we simply can't allow ourselves to feel too deeply if it's going to curtail our ability to do our job. When an ER doctor or nurse attends a patient with a life-threatening wound, emotional distance is often needed just to continue working without being overwhelmed. When a criminal defense lawyer goes home, she may have to leave her clients' troubles at the office so they don't intrude on her personal life. As long as we're clear about what we're doing, it can be useful to distance ourselves from the pain of others for a limited time in order to do our jobs effectively. The real problem comes when people distance themselves from their own emotions unconsciously. If we aren't aware that we're shutting down to protect ourselves, we never have the opportunity to process the empathic pain we've experienced. If I get home from work and reach straight for the wine bottle or click the TV on to smooth over the stress I've experienced on my shift, those feelings may stay locked inside me. This can lead to high blood pressure, depression, or substance abuse. But when we shut down consciously, as an act of caring for our well-being in the moment, then we can work through the difficult feelings later when we have more resources.

This is a strategy I use constantly. If I'm teaching a class or workshop and someone shares a heartbreaking story, I may not have the wherewithal to take it in then and there. In order for me to continue teaching without becoming emotionally derailed, I might temporarily compartmentalize my empathic pain so I can continue to teach. However, later that evening, I'll check in with myself to see how I'm doing. If I find I'm still carrying some of the distress from the day, I'll do a practice such as the Tender Self-Compassion Break (page 121) or Being with Difficult Emotions (page 133) to make sure I acknowledge the discomfort and tend to it.

The most commonly prescribed remedy to prevent burnout among caregivers is self-care. This is also a form of fierce self-compassion aimed at providing for ourselves through activities like taking walks, doing yoga, and eating well. Research shows that engaging in regular self-care can make a huge difference in terms of reducing burnout and increasing positive feelings about helping others. Self-care is essential for us to be able to recharge and reset, so that we have the energy to tend to others' needs. Studies indicate that caregivers who are more self-compassionate are more likely to engage in self-care activities such as journaling, exercise, or connecting with friends.

Although these ways of preventing burnout are useful, they have limitations. Sometimes it's not appropriate to draw firm boundaries when caring for others. If the person you're caring for is your child, spouse, or parent, saying no may not be the right thing to do. Strategies like emotional distancing, even when temporary, also have their limitations. Empathy is what allows us to understand the person we're tending to and is necessary to deliver effective care. If, in an effort to protect herself, a doctor or therapist shuts down too much in the presence of her patients, it limits her ability to grasp what is needed to relieve their suffering.

There is also a major limitation to self-care as a way to counter burnout. A common analogy for self-care is putting on your own oxygen mask before helping others in an emergency, as we're advised to do at the beginning of any flight. And yet self-care activities don't happen while the plane is going down; they happen before takeoff or after crashing—in other words, outside of the caregiving setting. If you're a nurse at the bedside of a coronavirus patient on a ventilator, you can't say, "Whoa, man, this is freaking me out! I'm off to do tai chi!" Engaging in self-care in one's free time is crucial, but it's not enough, because it doesn't help when you're in the presence of someone who's suffering and your mirror neurons are buzzing with their pain.

So how do we care for ourselves in the presence of suffering? We bring in tender self-compassion. We learn to be with our empathic pain with loving, connected presence as we engage in the difficult work of caregiving. We acknowledge our distress: "This is so hard. I feel confused and overwhelmed." We recognize that helping others is a challenging but rewarding aspect of the human experience: "I am not alone." And we support ourselves with the type of warm internal dialogue we might naturally use with a friend: "I'm sorry you're struggling. I'm here for you." Holding our empathic pain with compassion in the actual act of caregiving provides tremendous calm, stability, and resilience.

Some may feel it's inappropriate to give ourselves compassion if we're caring for someone who's suffering much more than we are. We might have the thought "Who am I to complain that I've been working for twelve hours straight? This poor guy might not make it through the night!" Although it may feel selfish, it's anything but. We're not giving ourselves care to the exclusion of others, rather we're just including ourselves in the circle of compassion. The idea is that we need to give compassion *both* to ourselves and the person we're caring for. It's not like there's a limited amount of compassion and if I give three units to myself there will only be two left over for someone else. When we open our hearts, we tap into an unlimited pool of compassion. The more it flows inward, the more it can flow outward.

Also, we need to remember that the people we care for resonate with our state of mind too. Empathy goes both ways. If we're frustrated and exhausted, others resonate with these negative feelings, but if we're filled with self-compassion, they tune in to these positive feelings. Just as we can experience secondary traumatic stress, we can also experience secondary loving, connected presence. In this way, giving compassion to ourselves while caring for others is actually a *gift* we give to the world.

CARING FOR ROWAN

I learned a lot about two-way empathy from Rowan. Autistic children can be hypersensitive to the emotions of the people around them, which is one of the reasons they tend to withdraw. When Rowan was a toddler, I started noticing that he was highly affected by my state of mind. If Rowan threw a tantrum and I got upset by it—his screams piercing my brain—the volume and intensity of his outburst would increase. But when I remembered to calm and care for myself because of the pain of his tantrums, the intensity would die down. At times, he was like a clear mirror, reflecting my internal mind state almost instantaneously. The time I really saw this process in action was, yes, on an airplane.

Rowan was about four, at the peak of his autism. He still wasn't toilet-trained, couldn't yet talk, and was incredibly sensitive to the environment. I had to take him on a transatlantic flight from Austin to see his grandparents in London. Needless to say, I was terrified of what might happen on the long ride over. It was a direct flight that left in the evening, so I was hoping he would sleep through most of it. We got through dinner without incident, and I was starting to hope that maybe all would be well. Then the crew dimmed the cabin lights to help everyone get some sleep. That was it. For some inexplicable reason, the change in the lighting set Rowan off: a full-on, screaming, flailing tantrum. I was horrified. It was incredibly loud and disruptive, and I felt terrible for disturbing everyone on the plane, who were now all staring straight at us. I imagined all the horrible things people must be thinking: "What's wrong with that kid? He's way beyond the terrible twos!" Worse than that, I imagined what everyone must be thinking of me: "What's wrong with her? Why can't she quiet her child?"

I was panic-stricken, but jumping out the window wasn't an option. Then I got a brilliant idea. I picked Rowan up and carried him down the aisle to the toilet to let him have his tantrum in there, hoping that would muffle his screams. It felt like the walk of shame. He was crying and flailing and hitting people as we passed. I played the "A card," which is code in autism-parent-speak for telling people their child's autistic in the hope they'll be more understanding. "Terribly sorry. Autistic child coming through. Excuse us." But when I finally made it back to the toilets, they were all occupied. Of course they were. The lesson life had for me in that moment was not how to cleverly escape a difficult situation, but instead how to get through it.

I sunk to the floor in despair. I was out of options, except for one: self-compassion. I made sure Rowan was safe and not harming himself and put 95 percent of my attention on myself. Normally when I give myself compassion in public I do it on the sly—maybe holding my own hand in a casual way while speaking silently to myself. The stakes were so high this time that I didn't care what other people thought. It couldn't get worse anyway. I put both hands over my heart and started rocking back and forth. I whispered to myself, "It's going to be okay, darling. You'll get through this. You're doing the best you can." Almost immediately I felt calmer. I was genuinely moved by my own plight, and my heart opened. Shortly thereafter, Rowan started to calm down. His cries subsided, and I could hold him and rock him. "It's okay, darling. It's okay." We went back to our seats and Rowan slept through the night.

My relationship with Rowan continues to reflect this constant interplay of compassion for him and myself, the back-and-forth nature of our emotions. Rowan is nineteen as I write this and a truly outstanding, kind, caring, charming, responsible, lovely human being. He's passionate about food and has a great sense of humor, often combining the two. (Once when I gasped in horror at the graphic lyrics in the rap music he enjoys, he laughed and said, "Don't worry, Mom, I don't take what they're saying seriously. It just spices up the music like onions on a hotdog." The other day he came up with two more zingers: What food can you eat with your feet? A tostada. What's the most popular food at the North pole? Burritos.) Although he still struggles with anxiety attacks, he no longer has tantrums or acts out.

In fact, Rowan recently got his driver's license. Almost any parent who's taught a child to drive will recognize how our internal mind state affects our kids. If I showed the tiniest quiver of fear when Rowan was merging on the freeway or about to take a left turn across a busy road, he felt it, and it would make him more stressed. The way I dealt with my own fear (sometimes verging on outright terror) made all the difference. I would cross my arms casually—hiding a self-hug—and comfort myself for the stress of the situation. I would remind myself that I wasn't alone, that all parents went through this and somehow survived. This allowed me to feel safer and calmer so that Rowan could feel the same way. Thanks to my son, I've learned firsthand that self-compassion makes us better caregivers.

EQUANIMITY

In order to care for others without losing ourselves, it's also necessary to have equanimity, a type of mental balance that's maintained even in tumultuous circumstances. Equanimity is not cold detachment or a lack of caring, but rather a deep insight into the illusion of control. Although we want to be able to make pain go away, we can't change the reality of the present moment. But we can set our intention to try to help and hope the future takes a turn for the better. Equanimity is at the heart of the Serenity Prayer that's central to twelve-step recovery programs: "God, give us the serenity to accept the things we cannot change, courage to change the things we can, and the wisdom to know the difference."

Equanimity is also one of the gifts that emerges from the integration of yin and yang. It's the dance of being and doing, of acceptance and change, that infuses a compassionate heart. As caregivers, we can use compassion to soothe and comfort, protect from harm, provide for needs, and motivate action. But, ultimately, we aren't in control of what happens, and we must accept that reality. Sometimes we fall into the trap of believing we should be able to make others' pain go away. Our egos become invested, and we think our charges should get better if we're good caregivers. And if they don't, there must be something wrong with us. Doctors have it especially hard because other people collude in this illusion of control—as if doctors had the God-given power of life and death. But the truth is that doctors, like all caregivers, are only human. We can try our best to help those we care for, but in the end the outcome is beyond our control. When equanimity is the space in which caregiving unfolds, we can let go of our attachment to outcomes and focus instead on doing our best to help in the moment.

COMPASSION WITH EQUANIMITY

We teach this practice in the general MSC program, and it's also the highlight of an adaptation aimed at caregivers. This is an informal practice that's designed to be used in the midst of caregiving situations as a self-compassionate response to empathic distress. However, it's helpful to learn how to use the practice by doing it once or twice on your own before applying it in an actual caregiving situation. (A guided audio version of this practice can be found at FierceSelf-Compassion.org.)

Instructions

- Please find a comfortable position and take a few deep breaths to settle into your body and into the present moment. You might put your hand over your heart, or wherever it feels comforting and supportive, as a reminder to infuse your awareness with warmth.

- Bring to mind someone you're caring for who is exhausting you or frustrating you or worrying you—someone who is suffering. Visualize the person and the caregiving situation clearly in your mind and feel the tension in your own body.

- Now say these words silently to yourself, letting them gently roll through your mind:

  Everyone is on their own life journey. I am not the cause of this person's suffering, nor is it entirely within my power to make it go away, even though I wish I could. Moments like these can be difficult to bear, yet I may still try to help if I can.

- Aware of the stress you are carrying in your body, inhale fully and deeply, drawing compassion inside of you and filling every cell of your body with loving, connected presence. If you like, you can also imagine that your body is being filled with a white or golden light. Let yourself be soothed by inhaling deeply, and by giving yourself the compassion you need.

- As you exhale, imagine that you are sending out compassion to the person who you are caring for. You can also imagine that as you breathe out their body is being filled with a white or golden light.

- Continue breathing compassion in and out, allowing your body to gradually find a natural breathing rhythm—letting your body breathe itself: "One for me, one for you. In for me, out for you."

- If you find that you need to focus more on yourself and your distress, feel free to focus more on breathing in. Similarly, if you are drawn to the pain of the person you're caring for, you can focus more on breathing out. You can adjust the ratio as needed, but make sure to always include yourself and the other.

- Notice how your body is being soothed and caressed from the inside as you breathe.

- You might imagine that you are floating effortlessly on a sea of compassion—a limitless ocean that embraces all suffering. More than enough for you and more than enough for the other.

- Continue breathing compassion in and out for as long as you like.

- When you're ready, silently repeat these words once again:

Everyone is on their own life journey. I am not the cause of this person's suffering, nor is it entirely within my power to make it go away, even though I wish I could. Moments like these can be difficult to bear, yet I may still try to help if I can.

- Now let go of the practice and allow yourself to be exactly as you are in this moment.

SELF-COMPASSION AND CAREGIVER RESILIENCE

There's extensive research showing that caregivers who are naturally (or who are trained to be) more self-compassionate are more resilient and have better mental health despite the stressors they face. One study examined how self-compassion helped people cope when caring for a partner diagnosed with lung cancer. Researchers found that self-compassionate caregivers were less distressed by their partner's diagnosis and could talk about it more openly—and their partners were less distressed as well. Professional caregivers such as therapists, nurses, pediatric residents, midwives, and clergy who are self-compassionate report experiencing less fatigue and burnout. They sleep better at night, even after controlling for the stress levels they experience on the job. Self-compassionate caregivers are more engaged and fulfilled in their work. They report greater "compassion satisfaction"—the good feelings associated with being engaged in fulfilling work, such as happiness, excitement, and gratitude for being able to make a difference in the world. They're also more likely to have confidence in their ability to provide calm, compassionate care to others.

I helped to develop a brief training program specifically designed for doctors, nurses, and other health-care professionals called Self-Compassion for Healthcare Communities (SCHC). We developed the program in conjunction with the Center for Resiliency at Dell Children's Medical Center in Austin. The course is adapted from the Mindful

Self-Compassion program, but instead of eight two-and-a-half-hour sessions, it's comprised of six one-hour sessions, which is a much more feasible arrangement for busy health-care professionals. Participants are asked to practice self-compassion on the job using the exercises taught in the course, including the Self-Compassion Break and the Compassion with Equanimity practices. They aren't asked to meditate or do any "homework," which would add to their overfull plates, and this minimal dose seems to be effective. Our research shows that SCHC significantly increased health-care workers' self-compassion, mindfulness, compassion for others, compassion satisfaction, and feelings of personal accomplishment, while also reducing stress, depression, secondary traumatic stress, burnout, and emotional exhaustion.

We interviewed participants who'd completed the program and received glowing feedback. A social worker reported that it helped her to stay connected to her patients: "I'm listening to my patient, but every part of me is here . . . And I listen." A speech therapist said, "I think [self-compassion] helped me create healthier boundaries." A nurse commented, "I think it's so necessary—everybody should do it. It's really, really, really positive and helpful. But it surprises me after going through it that no other hospital I've worked for has ever done anything like this before." Hopefully this won't be true for long and there will be a new self-compassion wave in health care. The hospital where we developed the program has continued to hold SCHC trainings on a regular basis.

The hospital staff also asked us to teach the program to parents of their chronically ill pediatric patients suffering from conditions such as cancer or cerebral palsy. For these parents, the ability to give themselves compassion for the pain of caring for their children proved to be life-changing. It gave them the strength to be present for their kids with open hearts, without feeling drained of their life blood.

Imagine a world in which self-compassion was considered as essential in learning to be a caregiver as taking a temperature or conducting a diagnostic interview or helping a child with behavior problems. The weight of caring for others would become much easier to bear.

One group of caring individuals who particularly need self-compassion are social justice activists fighting for issues like gender equality, sexual expression, racial justice, human rights, or global warming. Social activists are particularly prone to burnout given the intense and daunting task they face trying to change entrenched power structures. While most of us turn away from the devastating consequences of injustice if they don't directly affect us, activists seek it out and confront it by choice. Opening yourself to the suffering of the world can cause tremendous empathic pain, which is made worse by the low pay, high levels of stress, and long working hours the jobs entail. And they also have to deal with the hateful backlash received from those in power who fight their efforts relentlessly. This creates perfect conditions for burnout, causing many people to give up their activism altogether.

Unfortunately, activism can also be accompanied by a belief that care should only go one way. Kathleen Rodgers from the University of Ottawa conducted in-depth interviews with fifty Amnesty International workers and found that a culture of selflessness and self-sacrifice pervaded the organization in a way that directly increased burnout. As one worker commented, "There's a built-in potential for guilt, of not doing enough about the people who are the victims of violation, that 'deserve' or 'need,' or 'must have' the attention, and every bit of attention, and every bit of energy that we can possibly bring to it, so that failing to produce . . . in some ways is sort of like a betrayal of the victims." This view fails to recognize how caring for ourselves is actually the energy source powering our ability to help others.

Self-compassion is crucial to fostering the strength and resilience necessary to take on painful issues like entrenched poverty, sex trafficking, or spousal abuse. If we, as women, are going to bring justice to an inequitable world, we'll need to make sure that our compassion is directed inward as much as outward. The good news is that gender roles have enabled us to be powerful, capable caretakers. We already have the skills and resources to ease suffering; we just need to give ourselves permission to care for ourselves as we do so. We can rely on fierce Momma Bear to fight for what's right and tender Mother to nourish us on our journey.

CHAPTER 11

WHAT WE DO FOR LOVE

There can be no love without justice.

—*bell hooks, author and activist*

One area where the gendering of yin and yang hits hardest is in our romantic relationships. Too often we sell our souls to be with a partner because we've been indoctrinated from birth to believe we're incomplete without one. We start believing that we need to be in a relationship to be happy. Other women often collude in this belief. When you're unmarried and an old friend calls you up to ask how you're doing, often her first question is, a) Are you in a relationship? or b) How's the relationship going? As if this were the most important aspect of our lives.

Common phrases such as "my other half" reinforce the notion that wholeness requires two people in a partnership. Part of what's occurring here is that yin and yang have been split by gender (at least in heterosexual relationships), so that a woman socialized to be yin feels she needs to be with a man socialized to be yang in order for these energies to balance out. Traditionally, a woman is taught to direct her tenderness outward and not inward, and that she needs to feel loved and accepted by a man to experience this tenderness for herself. She learns that loving, connected presence comes from a man who loves her (romantically), is connected to her (emotionally and psychologically), and is in her presence (in a committed relationship). She's also taught that fierce qualities of protecting, providing, and motivating come from outside rather than inside. She needs a man to protect her physically, to help provide for her materially, and to motivate her by giving meaning to her life. Although these traditional norms don't have the same power they once did, they still shade how we feel about relationships.

When the integration of yin and yang occurs in couples but not individuals, it can be unhealthy. Instead of being fulfilled independently, a woman may become codependent, needy, or clingy, forever chasing after a man's attention to feel valuable. She may also become passive, submissive, or uncomfortable with being alone, unable to access power within herself. Colette Dowling famously termed this condition the "Cinderella complex," after the fairy tale whose heroine is helpless and insignificant until she's rescued by Prince Charming. Gender socialization tells us we need to find some prince to make us feel loved and protected—an ideal that gets in the way of learning to love and protect ourselves.

Fortunately, self-compassion provides a way out of this illusion, allowing us to meet our needs directly. It helps us find balance between yin and yang internally rather than externally. Self-compassion also enhances our love life—with or without a relationship. When we truly value ourselves, we're less dependent on someone else to make us feel loved, happy, worthy, or safe. This gives us incredible freedom to enjoy life, be authentic in how we express ourselves, and find meaning and fulfillment whether we're alone, dating, or with a committed partner.

SELF-COMPASSION IN RELATIONSHIPS

When we're in a committed romantic relationship, self-compassion is an invaluable resource to strengthen the partnership. The ability to care for and support yourself when you're having a tough time or are feeling insecure makes it easier to show up and commit to others. If we don't require a partner to meet all our needs exactly as we want, exactly when we want (cuddles one moment and to be left alone the next), then we put less pressure on our partner to always get it right. This makes it easier to find harmony.

The German philosopher Arthur Schopenhauer talked about human relationships using the metaphor of the porcupine dilemma: "One cold winter's day, a number of porcupines huddled together quite closely in order through their mutual warmth to prevent themselves from being frozen. But they soon felt the effect of their quills on one another, which made them again move apart. Now when the need for warmth once more brought them together, the drawback of the quills was repeated so that they were tossed between two evils, until they had discovered the proper distance from which they could best tolerate one another." Like porcupines, we inevitably hurt our romantic partners and experience barriers to intimacy. The more we generate internal warmth through self-compassion, the more we're able to find harmony with our partners and the right balance between space and closeness. Far from being self-focused, this inner resource provides stability and flexibility, enhancing our competence as partners.

This competence is demonstrated in research showing that self-compassionate people have healthier romantic relationships. They're less likely to fight with partners, have more fulfilling interactions, and spend more quality time together. They're also more sexually satisfied. They feel better about who they are in their unions and are happier and less depressed as a result. When conflicts arise, they're more likely to make fair compromises and be honest with their partners when it comes to asking for what they need or want.

A self-compassionate undergraduate in a study we conducted on relationship conflicts talked about how she resolved things with her boyfriend: "I was very busy with school, cheer, sports, music, and work. I put a lot of my time and effort into these things because they were important to me. I know my boyfriend wanted to have more time with me, but there just weren't enough hours in the day." She chose to spend a bit more time with him, but not to the point where she gave up anything that was really important to her. "We have worked things out in this way because we respect each other," she said. "We both had

our own wants and needs, and our relationship was way more important to us than any issue we had at some point in time." This type of
balance was less prevalent in undergrads who lacked self-compassion.
They more often subordinated their needs to those of their partners.
As one young woman said, "I always want to please him and make him
happy. I'm also scared that if I make him mad, he won't want to be
with me. He's very persuasive and usually convinces me to see things
from his point of view." Fierce self-compassion gives us the backbone
to hold our ground when disagreements come up, while tender self-
compassion allows us to be more open-minded, intimate, and loving.

This was apparent in another study we conducted on self-compassion
in romantic relationships. We included over one hundred adult couples who lived in the Austin area and were in committed long-term
partnerships. We assessed each person's level of self-compassion, self-
esteem, their ability to be authentic in the relationship, and how comfortable they felt voicing their opinions. We also asked participants to
report on their partner's behavior. Were partners warm and loving or
cold and distant? Were they accepting and did they give them space
and freedom in the relationship, or were they critical and controlling?
Were their partners ever verbally abusive or aggressive? Finally, we
asked participants how satisfied and secure they felt in the relationship.

People who were more self-compassionate reported being more
authentic and able to speak their minds about important matters,
demonstrating their ability to draw upon inner fierceness to stand up
for themselves. Their capacity for self-care also appeared to translate
into being more caring generally. They were described by their partners as being warmer and more supportive (e.g., "is gentle and kind
toward me"), accepting ("respects my opinions"), and encouraging of
their autonomy ("gives me as much freedom as I want"). They were
less likely to be seen as detached (e.g., "acts as though I'm in the way"),
controlling ("expects me to do everything his/her way"), or aggressive
("yells, stomps out of the room"). Interestingly, we found that it was an
individual's level of self-compassion, not their level of self-esteem, that
determined whether they were described in a positive light by partners.

In other words, people could have high self-esteem, but their partners might still describe them negatively. However, people who were self-compassionate were overwhelmingly described as being more caring in the relationship. Unsurprisingly, the partners of self-compassionate individuals reported feeling more secure and more satisfied. This study offers even more evidence that self-compassion doesn't lead to self-centered or selfish behavior. The more love we're able to give ourselves, the greater reserves we have available for others.

One limitation of our study was that it wasn't very ethnically diverse—the couples were predominantly White—but a dissertation study from Kansas State University of 210 Black heterosexual married couples also found that partners with more self-compassion reported having warmer, more rewarding, and happier relationships. They were less likely to engage in negative behaviors, like belittling each other or getting into confrontations such as accusations, name-calling, or bringing up past hurts. Once again, the findings suggest that treating ourselves with kindness facilitates treating our partners in ways that lead to healthier and more sustainable relationships.

Self-compassion helps us accept that we're flawed human beings doing the best we can. All of us at one point or another have behaved thoughtlessly toward a partner or acted in ways we regret. The more understanding and forgiving we are toward our own all-too-human imperfections, the more understanding and forgiving we're likely to be of our partners' limitations, and this unconditional acceptance in both directions builds stronger relationships. Jia Wei Zhang and Serena Chen from UC Berkeley examined the role of self-compassion and acceptance in romantic relationships. The researchers recruited both undergraduates and older adults and asked them to describe a personal flaw (e.g., I'm messy) and a flaw they perceived in their romantic partner (e.g., he procrastinates). They found that self-compassionate people were more likely to accept their own shortcomings as well as their partner's. Their partners confirmed this and said they felt less judged and more accepted. This mutual acceptance resulted in more overall satisfaction in the relationship.

However, self-compassion isn't just about accepting weaknesses, it also fosters healthy change and growth. A series of three studies by researchers at the University of Tennessee found that self-compassionate women in committed long-term relationships were better able to address difficulties with their partners. The first study found that women with higher levels of self-compassion were more likely to report they were committed to resolving problems (e.g., "I usually try to work things out with my partner right away"). The second study asked women to imagine that they'd done something they regretted, like not supporting their partner in a time of need. Researchers then instructed participants to have compassion for the mistake and found this made them more motivated to put things right. The third study tracked the level of relationship satisfaction among women in their first five years of marriage. Although most people become less satisfied over this period, self-compassionate women were just as happy in their relationship at year five as they were as newlyweds, demonstrating the remarkable power of self-compassion to create and maintain healthy unions.

SELF-COMPASSION FOR RELATIONSHIP CHALLENGES

Romantic relationships are a great source of joy, but also suffering. We can bring both fierce and tender compassion to ourselves when we run up against relationship problems, depending on what we need in the moment. This practice can be done as a written exercise or as an internal reflection, and is designed for people who are currently in a romantic relationship.

Instructions

- Think about a difficulty you are having with your partner. Perhaps you disagreed about something, or are unsatisfied in some way, or feel badly about something you or your partner did. Try to be as

specific as possible, calling the situation vividly to mind. Who said
what to whom, what happened or didn't happen?

- Now see if you can let go of the story line for a moment and check
  in with your emotions. What are you feeling right now? Sad, frustrated, lonely, afraid, ashamed, angry? A combination of feelings?
  Try to locate the feelings in your body. Focus on the physical sensation of the emotion. Use mindfulness to acknowledge the pain
  of what you're feeling. It's hard to feel this way. See if you can allow
  the feelings to be there, without immediately needing to fix them
  or make them go away.

- Next remember the common humanity of the situation. You are
  not alone. Every relationship has challenges. All relationships are
  imperfect. Try to bring some kindness to yourself in the midst of this
  challenge. First, use some sort of soothing and supportive touch
  that feels appropriate—maybe placing a hand on the place in
  your body where you feel the emotions, or putting both hands
  on your heart, or using a gesture of strength like putting your fist on
  your heart with the other placed gently over it.

- Finally, say some words of kindness that are just what you need to
  hear in this moment: maybe some gentle words of acceptance or
  comfort; some fierce words of courage; validation of your needs;
  or encouragement to make a change. If you're having trouble
  finding the right words, you might imagine what you would say to
  a close friend who was experiencing the same relationship difficulty you are. What words would naturally flow toward your friend?
  Can you try saying the same thing to yourself?

I've had many people tell me that once they started practicing self-
compassion, their romantic relationship improved. Michelle, a graduate student who took my advanced seminar in self-compassion, was

one of those people. She told me used to be very self-critical and hard on herself. She was a self-admitted "control freak" who had to get everything right, including her relationship. Michelle was a marathon runner and a health nut, and her glowing skin and trim figure showed it. She'd been seeing Brandon, a firefighter, for about two years, and they loved each other. They had a lot in common: both enjoyed music and hiking and had a similar outlook on life. But there were problems.

Michelle was a punctual person and asked Brandon to text her if he was going to be more than twenty minutes late. He often forgot, especially if he was hanging out with his buddies. Sitting alone at the restaurant table waiting for him, she would fume about how inconsiderate he was. But when he showed up, she would pretend to brush it off as if it didn't matter because she didn't want him to think she was a nag.

Another issue: Brandon wasn't as romantic as she would've liked. She wanted him to communicate his love with more fervor (she was a huge fan of historical romances like *Outlander* and *Poldark* and secretly wanted this intensity). But he was more low-key, and dramatic expressions of emotion felt unnatural to him. His heroes were the strong, silent types whose love was expressed through commitment. Although she appreciated Brandon's stability, she was disappointed by his lack of passion.

She admitted that one of her biggest issues with Brandon was that he liked to eat at fast-food restaurants like Taco Bell and McDonald's. When she found the empty packaging in the back of his car, sometimes she would snap and give him a withering lecture on nutrition. Then she immediately felt ashamed and criticized herself for being so overbearing.

Brandon loved Michelle despite these issues and had asked her to move in with him, but she was hesitant. Was the relationship the problem, or was she just being too picky and demanding? Michelle decided to learn about self-compassion—primarily for herself, but also in hopes that it could help things with Brandon. She read several books and then took my seminar.

Michelle practiced self-compassion diligently (like everything she did), and after a while she started to see changes in herself. She was less anxious, more motivated, and less controlling. Things also started to improve with Brandon. Michelle realized that many of her reactions to him stemmed from her own insecurities. For instance, when Brandon was late, part of her immediately worried it was because he was falling out of love with her and didn't care anymore. That's also why she wanted him to express his affection in a way that made her feel like one of the heroines in the dramas she enjoyed. She wanted to feel 100 percent sure that she was worthy of being loved and adored. Even her focus on health, though generally a positive value in her life, was partly driven by fear of gaining weight or getting sick, and she projected this fear onto Brandon.

Once she learned how to meet these insecurities with self-compassion, they were less debilitating. First, she could accept the fact that these self-doubts were there. She'd done enough therapy to know where they came from—her parents divorced when she was a child and a bitter custody battle followed. She knew that healing would be slow, but she was determined to try. When Brandon was late and she started to go down the path of believing he didn't care, she would become aware of her fear and give herself support and kindness. It was only natural that she would be distressed, and she reassured herself with her own warmth and care. When she wanted Brandon to be more romantic than he was, she'd acknowledge the grief of feeling disappointed. Then she tried to meet her own need for romance by buying herself a huge bouquet of flowers. If she overreacted to Brandon's eating habits, instead of lambasting herself, she tried to understand what was driving her reactions. It was a trigger related to her desire for health, which was actually a good thing.

The more Michelle gave herself tender self-compassion and accepted herself as she was, the more she could do the same for Brandon. Once Michelle took the pressure off and accepted that no relationship was perfect, they started to fight less.

But Michelle didn't stop there. Some of her complaints were

legitimate and needed to be addressed with fierce self-compassion. She realized that lecturing Brandon on his fast-food habits was her issue and that she had no right to tell him what to eat: he was a grown man after all. But the request that he text when late was valid. She told Brandon the truth about how much it upset her, especially when they were meeting in public. Maybe he could set a reminder on his phone if necessary, but this was important to her. She knew his being late didn't mean he didn't love her, but it was still inconsiderate, and she needed him to respect her time.

The more difficult conversations were about Brandon's way of expressing his love. He said he couldn't change who he was, and she shouldn't expect him to act like someone in a romance novel. She acknowledged that. And yet her needs for intimacy weren't being fully met. Buying herself flowers helped, but it wasn't enough. They started having conversations about how she could help him feel safer to open up by demonstrating her support and acceptance of him, which would help him be more vulnerable. They talked about the macho fire service culture, and how this contributed to his discomfort expressing tenderness. Although it was going to feel awkward for him, he was willing to try something different. She learned how to ask Brandon to express his feelings without making him feel judged, and it got more comfortable for him over time.

They even started to have frank discussions about the balance of power in the relationship. Brandon admitted that he sometimes kept her waiting on dates so that his buddies wouldn't think he was "pussy-whipped" and would see him as the one in charge. He was also able to see that his resistance to intimacy was another way to have power, so that she would always be wanting more. These were tough conversations, but they took them on with mutual love, respect, and compassion that helped them actually hear each other. As Michelle modeled self-compassion for her role in their problems, Brandon was able to have compassion for his part and admit his shortcomings more readily. Michelle and Brandon have now been living together for two years—so far, so good.

LOVE AND PATRIARCHY

Gendered power dynamics often play a role in the background of heterosexual relationships. This is because the history of love and marriage was shaped by patriarchy. In the preindustrial era, marriage was seen primarily as an economic arrangement between families, based on status considerations and economic stability. A woman didn't typically choose the man she married; this decision was made by her parents. Love was considered a poor reason to wed. The doctrine of coverture—which continued to be actively enforced until the nineteenth century—basically stated that a man owned his wife, including her body and her services, all her property and wages, and custody of children in the rare case of divorce. Given that a woman was basically considered chattel, she needed a man to physically survive.

But then, with the dawn of the Enlightenment era, the idea of love in marriage as an expression of individual freedom and the pursuit of happiness gained in popularity. Writers such as Jane Austen and Charlotte Brontë glorified romantic love as a source of meaning and fulfillment for women, even though they still didn't have the right to vote or control property. The ideal for a woman, in and out of novels, was to find a man who would love, cherish, adore, and protect her, creating a happy and fulfilling union.

But husbands weren't always loving or safe; sometimes they were emotionally unavailable, negligent, or abusive. Wife beating was legal until 1920. And although romantic love was supposed to be about mutual respect, a wife was expected to submit to her husband's decisions. She needed to downplay her intelligence so as not to threaten his. (As Rita Rudner quipped, "When I eventually met Mr. Right I had no idea that his first name was Always.") Still, being married to a man who made his wife feel special, valued, and protected was society's romantic ideal, even if few marriages lived up to the arrangement. It certainly feels better to be lost in a romantic dream than to wake up and see the truth of your disempowerment.

Women had to bend over backward to preserve these illusions, given that they were financially dependent on men and had no real place in society outside of marriage. Since female power was confined to the home sphere, women had to try to find their satisfaction there. They often looked the other way at infidelities, ignored boorish behavior, and put up with being talked down to. There was nothing to do but put on a brave face in unhappy unions, since divorce wasn't an option. This view of marriage, sustained by the romantic ideal, more or less continued through the Ozzie and Harriet years of the 1950s.

Things started to change from the 1960s through the '80s. Divorce and cohabitation became more common. A greater number of women began working and going to college. The second wave of feminism (the first was the suffragette movement) crashed down upon us. Trailblazing books like Betty Friedan's *The Feminine Mystique*, which questioned the woman-as-wife-and-homemaker ideal, became best sellers. Gloria Steinem cofounded *Ms.* magazine with tremendous success, rejecting the idea that a woman's status is determined by whether she is single (Miss) or married (Mrs.). The very idea of romantic love was called into question, with radical feminists arguing that "Love, in the context of an oppressive male-female relationship, becomes an emotional cement to justify the dominant-submissive relationship." Customs designed to make women attractive to men such as wearing makeup were seen as colluding with patriarchy. A protest at the Miss America pageant included throwing high-heeled shoes and bras into a trash can, which protesters didn't actually burn but nonetheless was described by journalists as bra-burning, similar to draft-card burning, which is how an entire generation of outspoken women came to be called bra-burning feminists.

The following decades saw a cultural backlash to the feminist agenda, and the desire to end female oppression in romantic relationships got rebranded as man-hating. Despite the best efforts of the next wave of feminists who grew up with Title IX and women's studies classes, feminism went relatively quiet—until the tsunami of activism that rose up with #MeToo and the Women's March after Trump's inauguration.

Issues of sexual harassment and the exclusion of women from positions of power were once again dominating headlines. What's been slower to reawaken is the need to question the role of love and romance in our lives. Many high-powered, activist, self-sufficient women I know still believe they need a partner to feel loved, fulfilled, and valued.

Women are skilled at giving their hearts. The problem is that we give away our power with our hearts if we believe that the source of love and safety lies in a relationship with a partner, rather than in a relationship with ourselves. Heterosexual women are so conditioned to feel valued based on whether or not a man loves and commits to us that we sometimes abandon ourselves in order to achieve union. Even when a woman earns good money and is successful and independent, she often believes she *needs* a man to be happy. This can lead too many of us to stay in bad situations longer than we should. Think of all the wealthy female celebrities we hear about who constantly make poor relationship choices. Think of your own friends. Think of yourself. Although it's hard to know if a relationship is healthy when we first enter it, once we're in one, it's partly our belief that we need a partner to be whole that colors our decision-making process. We often ignore red flags because we want so badly for our relationships to succeed.

Women in same-sex relationships don't face quite the same issues as heterosexual women do, because they're less likely to be locked into gendered cultural scripts. A study conducted by researchers at the University of Texas at Austin examined 157 lesbian couples and 115 heterosexual couples who were legally married or cohabitating (for an average of fifteen years), and found that women in heterosexual unions were more likely than those in same-sex ones to say their spouse let them down, acted in an inconsiderate manner, or didn't attentively listen. Lesbian women also reported more psychological well-being in their relationships. Although same-sex couples face increased discrimination and external pressure from society—and this injustice cannot be ignored—within the sphere of their relationship, they're often freed from some of the harmful dynamics of patriarchy.

DO WE NEED TO BE IN A RELATIONSHIP TO BE HAPPY?

Although women no longer need to be married to have status in our society, the drive to be in a relationship is still strong. Even when we leave a bad relationship, the feeling that we aren't complete unless we're coupled can spur us to get involved with someone else too quickly. The perception that unpartnered women are worthless spinsters still persists, even if subtly, and our culture reinforces this view. Men may want to be in relationships and feel loved, but they don't *need* it. Their value and sense of safety isn't dependent on it at the deepest unconscious level the way it is for women. They aren't pitied for being single the way we are. In fact, the media reflects many images of men who are single, happy, and respected. Not so for women.

Wendy Langford's book *Revolutions of the Heart*, though written twenty years ago, still resonates today. She interviewed fifteen women on the place of romantic relationships in their lives. Hannah, who's single and desperately wants a relationship, says, "There feels like there's a gap in my life . . . It's that idea that you're *really* special to one person . . . I yearn for somebody to have the kind of, you know, waking up at three in the morning next to—and just thinking oooh, you know, this is really *intimate* . . . I do wonder if I'll ever find anybody to be intimate with ever again. That worries me."

Another common theme for the women was that they needed a man who loved them in order to feel worthy. Ruth says, "I think perhaps I had it in my mind somewhere, you know, that if I was *really* a desirable person, you know, attractive or whatever, or nice, then there would be a man around." They also looked at romantic love as a way to feel complete. When Diane describes the feeling of falling in love in a past relationship, she says, "It was lovely. It was like a oneness, you know? A feeling of two pieces of a walnut together making a whole." These attitudes toward being in a romantic relationship haven't really changed over the past two decades.

If women are to truly be free, we're going to have to let go of the idea that we need a partner to be whole. We can learn how to feel whole on our own. Many women in their forties and fifties (myself included) are single and divorced. We want to be in a relationship but can't find a partner who can offer what we need—emotional intelligence, spirituality, self-awareness, respect, equality. Some women compromise and get in a relationship with someone who doesn't make them happy or stay single and feel unsatisfied because they don't have a partner. The common denominator here is the belief that we need a partner to be happy. We don't. There are many sources of joy, including friendships, family, career, and spirituality. The most important sources are those that are unconditional and don't depend on circumstances, and one of the most accessible is self-compassion.

A LOVE RELATIONSHIP WITH OURSELVES

Self-compassion not only makes us happier when we're in a romantic relationship, it allows us to be happy without one. A radical gift of self-compassion for women is the realization that we don't need a partner to fulfill us. We can fully develop and access our own yin and yang energies, all within the context of self-compassion. For heterosexual women who fear that cultivating this kind of self-sufficiency somehow translates into becoming a man-hater, it doesn't. We can love men, enjoy their company, live with them, marry them, or raise children with them if we so choose. The point is simply that we don't *need* them. We can draw on tender self-compassion to feel loved and valued and fierce self-compassion to feel safe and provided for.

The ability to be with and accept ourselves with loving, connected presence is central to finding happiness outside of a romantic relationship. We all have a deep need to feel special, adored, worthy, important, and cared for. We can meet these needs directly, because when our heart is fully open, we see our own beauty. This beauty doesn't depend on physical perfection or having it all together. It's the beauty of being a unique individual with a unique history, one of a kind and therefore special. Our worth doesn't come from our accomplishments, nor does it come from finding a partner who tells us we're lovable. It comes from the fact that we're a conscious, feeling, breathing human being who is a part of life unfolding moment to moment, as precious as any another. When we give ourselves the attention we long to receive from others, we become remarkably self-sufficient.

When we're fully in touch with fierce self-compassion, we can provide ourselves with the things that heterosexual women have been told only come from a man. When the energy of brave, empowered clarity flows through our veins, we can call upon our inner warrior when needed. The ability to stand up for ourselves means that we aren't dependent on a man to protect us. If someone insults us or pushes our boundaries, we can face that person head on. There may be some situations where physical strength is needed, or where we are in physical danger, but if we aren't in a relationship we can turn to our friends or family or neighbors or legal authorities to ask for help. And if we have the means, we can hire help to do the things we may have previously relied on our husbands or boyfriends to do. (For instance, there are online services where you can hire someone hourly to move heavy objects, fix things around the house, mow the lawn, and so on.)

We don't need a man to provide for us either. First, we can meet our own financial needs. Although women are paid less and that must change, it's not worth it to be in a relationship with a man we're not happy with just to increase our material comfort. It's a calculus that often doesn't work in our favor. In terms of our emotional needs like support and companionship, many of those can be met by close friends. More and more women are choosing to root their sense of belonging in a circle of friends rather than a man and find that these bonds are deep, fulfilling, and stable. Most important, with self-compassion we can give *ourselves* love, care, and emotional support.

We can also spend our time doing what's fulfilling and authentic. In fact, in some ways we're freer to learn and grow without a partner. It's common for women to give up their interests and focus most of their energy on their relationship, especially in its early stages. I have a good friend who's been wanting to write a book for years. She's very talented, and I know her project would be a great gift to the world.

When she's single, she makes good progress on it, but as soon as she gets into a relationship the book goes on hold. How much of our precious time and energy is consumed by finding a partner, falling in love, worrying about whether or not we should stay, if the relationship is right for us, working through issues? Of course, if we are in an established, solid relationship, that can also provide a lot of freedom and support to accomplish things. But we don't want to throw everything else out the window while looking for that happy ending. When we're single, we have the time and space to pursue our dreams. If we fall into the trap of believing that the only important goal in life is to be partnered, what are we missing out on? Self-compassion can help us grow into our full potential, regardless of our circumstances.

When yin and yang are integrated internally, we are freed from many of the confines of gender roles. Masculine and feminine energies become joined within us. We stop outsourcing one essential part of our being and as a result are able to realize our true selves. Of course, this doesn't mean that we stop wanting or needing others. The desire for romantic love is also an essential part of our nature, and grief naturally arises when we're alone. The dream of meeting Prince Charming isn't just about wanting someone to take care of us, the way it's presented in the Cinderella complex. It's also about wanting to experience love and intimacy and connection through the joining of two souls. It's a deeply spiritual and beautiful experience.

Since the publication of her influential *Ain't I a Woman* in 1981, bell hooks has been a central figure in the feminist movement, calling out the ways that romantic love can trick women into accepting their subordination under the guise of loving and caring for their man. Yet she also acknowledges the importance of the desire for union. In her book *Communion: The Female Search for Love*, she writes, "Powerful, self-loving women know that our ability to take care of our own emotional needs is essential, but this does not take the place of loving fellowship and partnership." When I've said to women that they can meet their needs for romance by telling themselves what they want to hear from others—"I love you, you're beautiful, I respect you, I won't abandon you"—their immediate reaction has been that it's not the same as having a partner tell you this. Correct, it's not the same. We don't want to pretend that it is. Instead, we can fully open to the pain of not having our dream of romantic love fulfilled and hold it with the same tenderness we might use with a child who's frightened and lonely. We can honor that dream and keep the flame of hope alive that someday it may happen.

The problem is that we tend to prioritize this one source of happiness over all others. We believe that this love is the only one that really counts. Even though we're exactly the same person when a partner tells us we're worthy and lovable as when we tell ourselves, we think a partner's perspective is the only one that's valid. When we do this, we give away our power and discount our own ability to love.

We also set ourselves up for heartbreak, since a lasting union is not guaranteed even when we find "true love." We may be lucky enough to experience it for a time, but all too often life gets in the way, things change, people grow apart. Think of all the women you know who are in fulfilling romantic relationships that are likely to last for the rest of their lives. They exist, but they're not the norm. Only about half of all marriages last more than twenty years, and many lasting marriages are still unsatisfying ones. Do we really want to base our happiness on something so fragile, that we have so little control over?

Although providing ourselves with love doesn't replace a romantic relationship, it's actually more important because it's not contingent on circumstances. We're the only ones 100 percent guaranteed to be with us our entire lives. And the love that comes from self-compassion doesn't stem from our small self but instead grows from our connection with something larger. When we're truly present and caring toward ourselves, in times of both joy and sorrow, the sense of being separate from others fades away. We realize that our consciousness is a window into our unique, ever-changing, unfolding experience, but the light of consciousness peering through this window isn't separate from the light coming through other windows. As human beings our experiences are different, and some suffer much more than others, but the light is essentially the same. The reason the union of two people in love is so amazing is because we experience a merging of consciousness. But we don't need to have another person with us to experience that. Merging, union, and oneness can be found within.

MY JOURNEY TO WHOLENESS

After several failed relationships, I've personally come to embrace being alone. I've faced the loneliness and fear of "not counting" if I'm not in a relationship with a man. I've also gained insight into how self-compassion is the key to breaking out of this prison. At this point, I'm proud to say that my happiness is no longer dependent on being in a relationship. Although I'd like to be with someone, I'm not willing to compromise anymore. I can be happy on my own, and I've learned that I'm the only one who can make me feel loved, valued, fulfilled, and safe—not to say it hasn't been a long journey to get here.

Some readers may be familiar with the tale told in my first book, *Self-Compassion,* about meeting my husband, Rupert, in India before moving to Texas and having our son, Rowan. He was a human rights activist and travel writer, and one of the most interesting people I had ever met. Rupert was my Prince Charming. A blond-and-blue-eyed knight-in-shining-armor from Britain who swept me off my feet and seemed to fulfill the dream of love and romance that we're all taught to yearn for as little girls. After Rowan was diagnosed with autism, Rupert—an avid horseman—discovered that Rowan had a mysterious connection with horses and that his autism symptoms were greatly alleviated when he was around them. In a gathering of indigenous healers that took place to raise awareness about the plight of the Bushmen of the Kalahari, Rowan also responded well to contact with shamans. So our family went on a fantastical journey to a land where shamanism is the national religion and where the horse originates: Mongolia. We rode on horseback through the steppe, eventually meeting up with the Reindeer people to get healing for our son. This story was chronicled in the documentary and best-selling book *The Horse Boy*. The stuff of fairy tales. But as more of us are learning, these fairy tales don't serve us, and in fact more often disempower us.

Rupert was my second husband. My first marriage had ended when I had an affair—something that went against every value I hold dear. It was the process of dealing with the shame and self-recrimination for my behavior that largely helped me understand the power of self-compassion to heal and start again. I wanted to get it right when deciding to marry for the second time. Honesty was key for me, and I made a solemn commitment to be honest in my relationship no matter what. I never wanted to feel that internal civil war again. I thought Rupert had made a similar commitment.

However, shortly after Rowan's diagnosis I started to get the feeling that Rupert wasn't telling me everything. I can't tell you precisely why, I just had a gut sense. Because we were struggling to cope with Rowan's autism, however, I put the nagging feeling aside. His diagnosis was one of the hardest things I'd ever gone through, and I didn't have any leftover energy to deal with doubts about my marriage. Without going into the details, let's say that I eventually learned that Rupert had been lying to me, repeatedly, about hidden sexual encounters with other women. When I confronted him, he appeared to be overcome with shame and guilt. He told me how sorry he was, and how he wanted more than anything to save our relationship.

I was devastated. The big confrontation happened just before going on a meditation retreat, and I cried the whole time I was there. However, my mindfulness and self-compassion practice was strong, and I was able to get through it. I tried to sit in a state of loving, connected presence, and I was able to hold the pain without being overwhelmed. Given that we had a young son with special needs, I felt the best choice was to try to make the marriage work. We went to couple's therapy, and I hoped things would get better.

In the meantime, my self-compassion work was taking off. When writing my first book, I primarily recounted the wonderful parts of my relationship with Rupert. I managed to convince myself that he wasn't lying to me anymore. In hindsight, I realize there were signs and red flags that I brushed aside. To be frank, it was easier to assume that everything was okay than to face the truth that it wasn't.

Shortly after the book was published in 2011, I discovered more hidden liaisons—several of them, in fact. I knew beyond a shadow of a doubt that I must end the marriage. Even though I still loved him. Even though we had a young autistic son. I couldn't allow myself to be treated that way. I got support from my friends, who helped me find strength. I didn't know about fierce self-compassion at that point, but I knew it would take tremendous fortitude to leave. Momma Bear was awakened even though I didn't have a name for her yet. I carried a piece of iron in my purse to symbolize the determination I needed.

When I told Rupert that I was leaving, he once again told me how sorry he was, how ashamed he felt, and admitted he probably had a problem with sex addiction. Although I had compassion for him, my internal protector stood up and said no. I wasn't going to wait around to see if he could change or not. I was done. Because we had to co-parent and homeschool Rowan, we remained friendly and both of us tried to make sure our breakup didn't adversely impact him.

Although I was proud of myself for leaving, I remained attached to the idea of having a fulfilling romantic relationship. Maybe my soul-mate was still out there. About a year later I met a Brazilian man. He was kind, intelligent, a serious meditator, and gorgeous. Just one problem: he stated explicitly at the beginning that he didn't want a committed relationship. Because we connected passionately on so many levels—emotionally, spiritually, and sexually—I hung in there for years hoping he'd finally come around. He never did. He was always honest and truthful with me but pulled away whenever he felt we were getting too serious. I tried blaming him for the situation—he must have an attachment disorder, there must be something wrong with him. The reality was that we just wanted different things in life. Fair enough. My self-compassion practice helped me hold the grief and pain of this truth, but the desire for a relationship still burned strongly within me.

More recently I had a brief but intense relationship with another man who seemed to give me everything I'd ever wanted—honesty, passion, love, friendship, support, and, most important, commitment. He told me I was the woman of his dreams and wanted to spend the rest of his life with me. He also got along wonderfully with Rowan and seemed to be a positive male presence in his life. Given that Rupert had by this time formed another family and moved halfway around the world to Germany, I needed the help. The new guy was a musician and revealed that he was an ex-addict, but he was sober now and he was so self-aware. He'd even read my book in AA before we met! I was concerned about his history but tried to be accepting and nonjudgmental. We were madly in love, and he moved in.

But eventually he started regressing, playing video games for hours on end and acting like a moody adolescent. Sometimes when talking to him he would nod off midsentence. I knew it wasn't normal, but I also knew he had insomnia. When I questioned him about it, he swore it was due to lack of sleep. Once again, I ignored that little nagging feeling and turned away from it, because part of me still valued the illusion of love over the truth. After about three months of this, I Googled what it means when someone nods off, and the first thing that popped up was that this is a telltale sign of opiate addiction. I confronted him and asked him to take a drug test. He got angry and said he couldn't be with a woman who didn't trust him, gathered up his clothes, and stormed out of the house. Luckily Rowan was in Europe visiting his dad at the time, and I immediately changed all the locks in my house.

He came back the next day, saying he wanted another chance. I didn't blink an eye. Momma Bear arose, and although I felt compassion for him as I had with Rupert, there was no way in hell I was going to let him anywhere near my son. But I had to sit with the fact that, given his history, I should've been more wary, and I'd put Rowan at risk by allowing him to move in. I sold myself out to pursue the dream of romance, not willing to fully see the truth. Once again, I needed to flood myself with tender self-compassion to forgive my mistakes and hold the pain of it all. My trusting and accepting nature is actually a beautiful quality, but it got out of balance with fierce self-protection.

I had done enough therapy to realize I was being driven by a young, wounded little girl part of me that was trying to gain wholeness through partnership. The source of this wound was obvious: my father left when I was two years old, and I saw him infrequently while growing up. After breaking up with the musician, I went to visit my father in Denmark where he lives. (He'd moved there after marrying a Danish woman and stayed even after they divorced.)

The visit, though painful, gave me new insight into my early history. I'd gathered up the courage to tell my dad about all the inner work I'd done and said that I forgave him for leaving and loved him despite everything. I suppose I was hoping for a "I'm so sorry for hurting you sweetheart, I love you too."

Instead, he got a strange pained expression as he looked down. "I promised myself I would never tell you this. I promised myself!" he muttered.

"What is it?" I asked.

He proceeded to tell me, "When you were a baby, you hated me!"

"What?" I asked, astounded.

"You hated me. You didn't talk to me for the first two years of your life. You wanted me gone so you could have your mother to yourself. I felt leaving was the best thing I could do."

Fortunately, I didn't take it personally. My only thought was, "This man is crazy. He needed to project hate onto an innocent baby to justify his leaving? That's sick." I didn't try to argue him out of it, even though I was dying to say, "Babies don't hate. And don't you know they don't talk to anyone for the first two years?" Instead, I just said I was tired and went to bed. I realized that he was elderly now and loved me as best he could. I was able to attend to my own wounds and accept him as he was. It was his problem, not mine.

Later, when I asked my mom about it, she said that my dad had been jealous of all the love and attention she gave me when I was born, and that was partly why he left. I could see how this was once again the separation of yin and yang playing itself out. My father was cut off from his own tender self-compassion (he'd had a troubled relationship with his parents), and therefore depended on receiving care from my mother. When her nurturing energy was directed toward me, he felt lost and abandoned, and so took off. That left a hole in me, which I was still trying to fill with a romantic relationship.

Now, I'm fully committed to not putting any stock in the fallacy that I'm incomplete. I won't sell myself out anymore, even if that means never having a partner again. Although I'm certainly open to love, I'm focused on finding happiness through inner connection. I realize that when our sense of togetherness is predicated on our sense of separation—when our tender yin energy is separated from our fierce yang energy—we'll never be whole. When we think that intimacy has to occur with someone outside of ourselves, we feel lonely when we're alone. But the notion that connection only occurs between two separate beings is an illusion. Connection is to be found within. Connection comes from the merging and integrating of yin and yang. Connection comes from realizing our true nature, our inherent interrelatedness with all of life. You can call it God, universal consciousness, love, nature, the divine—it doesn't matter what you call it. We can feel it when we let go of the egoic mind's identification with a separate self, which is driving the sense that we aren't enough, that we're incomplete.

My explicit practice over the last year has been to see past this illusion of separation. When feelings of loneliness or yearning for a man arise in me, I notice them with mindfulness. I don't dismiss or belittle the yearning. I honor it and recognize its sacredness. I ask myself what it is that I most long for. Usually it's affirmations of my worthiness as a woman, that I'm desired, beautiful, loved, and valued. That I'm safe and won't be abandoned. Then I make these affirmations out loud to myself (in a private space, of course). As long as I don't get attached to the thought, "I want these words to come from someone else," and say them in an authentic manner, they're surprisingly satisfying. I remember that I'm already whole and don't need anyone else to complete me. I am already connected—to myself, to the world, to consciousness, to love, to Being.

WHAT DO I YEARN FOR?

This exercise draws on several practices in MSC designed to help us get in touch with our deepest needs and meet them directly with self-compassion. It can be done simply as an internal reflection or as a writing exercise, whatever feels right for you.

Instructions

- First, ask yourself: what are your relationship yearnings? If you are currently in a romantic relationship, perhaps you are yearning for something missing—more intimacy, passion, validation, commitment? If you are not in a relationship, do you yearn to have a romantic partner in your life?

- See if you can locate the feeling of yearning in your body as a felt sensation. It may be a burning in your heart, or a hollowness in your stomach, or pressure in your forehead, or an overall achiness. What are the body sensations that let you know that yearning is present? If you can't locate any particular sensation, that's okay; just notice how your body feels.

- Now put a gentle hand over the place in your body where you feel the yearning (if you can't locate a place, just put your hand on your heart or some other comforting place).

- What is it that you think you would gain in your life if your yearning was fulfilled (for example, more connection, excitement, support, stability)?

- How do you think having this yearning fulfilled would make you feel as a person (special, valued, worthy, beautiful, loved, important, happy)?

- Is there anything that you long to hear your relationship partner whisper into your ear (you're amazing, I love you, I respect you, I will never leave you)?

- Now say out loud to yourself the same words that you long to hear from a partner. It may sound awkward, but just let it be so. If thoughts arise that these words feel vain or self-centered, see if you can let these thoughts go. This is what you long to hear, and these longings are valid in their own right. Can you say these words to yourself with meaning?

- Take a few deep breaths, imagining that on the in-breath you are activating fierce self-compassion and on the out-breath you are relaxing with tender self-compassion. Feel these two energies merge and integrate within you.

- Know that your yearning for union and connection is valid. It can be filled within yourself by the merging of yin and yang. It can be expanded by allowing yourself to feel your connection with the larger whole. Use whatever symbol of oneness feels right to you. If you are a spiritual person, it may be God, or Allah, or divine consciousness, or if you are not a spiritual person, it may simply be the planet Earth or the universe. In truth, you are not alone. See if you can sense this connection to something larger than yourself, and stay with this awareness for as long as you are able.

- Finally, try saying some words of gratitude for all the sources of love and connection you have in your life, including yourself.

I do this practice regularly, and it has been transformative for me. At the moment of this writing, I can honestly say that I've found greater love, joy, and fulfillment than I could have ever imagined. Although I haven't given up on finding a man to share my life with, the fact that my happiness isn't dependent on it is a precious gift I've given myself.

BECOMING A COMPASSIONATE MESS

We can still be crazy after all these years. We can still be
angry after all these years . . . The point is not to try to
throw ourselves away and become something better.
It's about befriending who we are already.

—*Pema Chödrön, author and meditation teacher*

I've been practicing self-compassion daily for almost twenty-five years now. Although I'm definitely stronger, calmer, and happier because of it, and my inner bulldog barks less often than it used to, I still struggle. I'm as imperfect as ever, and this is how it should be. Being human isn't about getting it right, it's about opening up your heart—whether you get it wrong or right. I've learned to do this over time, just by moving through all my mistakes and difficult experiences.

I tend to be more yang than yin, but when this gets me into trouble, I'm gentle toward myself in response—restoring balance again. I've learned to love this fierce, brave, sometimes grumpy and reactive side of myself because I know it's partly responsible for so much of what I've accomplished: writing books, conducting research, developing training programs, teaching workshops, and, most important, raising my son, Rowan. These achievements have been powered by ferocity just as much as by tenderness. But even if I hadn't accomplished all this, and even if it all stops tomorrow, I know that I wouldn't be any less worthy as a consequence.

I once heard a meditation teacher say, "The goal of practice is simply to become a compassionate mess." Think about that. If your goal is just to be supportive, helpful, and compassionate toward yourself *whatever* occurs, your goal is always achievable. You learn to embrace the mess as the full expression of experiencing human life. It's not like you reach a state of balance and then stay that way. We constantly fall out of balance, over and over, and it's compassion for stumbling that restores equilibrium. When I'm too blunt with someone I disagree with, as soon as I realize it's occurred (usually in just seconds), I apologize and am kind toward myself. I know that the spark behind my overreaction is a wonderful fierce part of me that's temporarily overridden consideration of the person's feelings. When I let behavior slide (in myself or others) that turns out to be harmful, it doesn't take me long to realize that this over-acceptance stems from a peaceful, loving part of myself that has a vast ability to be with what is, but that I need more corrective fierce action.

By opening my heart to the whole tangled mish-mashed mess, I've found the strength to bear more than I ever thought possible, and I wouldn't change any of it because it's allowed me to be who I am today.

I believe this process is also occurring for women more generally. As we reclaim the fierceness that has been suppressed throughout the ages, we are restoring equilibrium and honoring our true nature. As we learn to be nurturing without being submissive, and angry without being aggressive, we are not only integrating yin and yang within ourselves, but in society as a whole. This journey is challenging, and we'll surely make mistakes along the way. As we call out predators, we may get it wrong in terms of protecting privacy and making sure people are presumed innocent until proven guilty. As we make strides toward gender justice, we may forget to pay enough attention to the needs of other oppressed groups. As we try to find the right balance between work and family, or personal fulfillment and social justice, we may become overwhelmed. We will inevitably fail over and over again on the path to achieving our goals—equal political representation, equal pay, equal treatment. And then we'll pick ourselves up, correct the imbalance, and try again. The feminist movement, like all movements, has been and will continue to be a mess. But because of our caring skills, it has real potential to be a compassionate mess. If we infuse fierce and tender compassion into the entire process of female empowerment, we can stay focused on our ultimate goal—the alleviation of suffering. If we keep our hearts open as we go about the work of change, we will have succeeded.

This needs to happen at the personal and societal level simultaneously. While each of us is the central protagonist in the story of our lives, all our stories are intertwined. When fierce and tender compassion runs through our veins and flows inward as well as outward, we help both society and ourselves. Stumbling and falling down not only becomes an opportunity to learn and grow; it allows us to relate to others who also struggle, strengthening interconnection. The entire heartbreaking drama that is unfolding on the personal, political, and global level may be exactly what is needed to provide essential lessons for our awakening. Who knows which events—difficult as they may be—are necessary to positively shape our individual and collective evolution? At the very least, our struggles give us greater insight into the nature of suffering. By opening to it all with love and compassion, we will be better able to embrace the challenges and work with them productively.

Rowan is finally coming around to this idea, incorporating it into his approach to life. After fighting the reality of pain and imperfection for years, he now realizes how it's all necessary for our transformation. The other day, after forgetting to do an important chore—something that in the past would've led to self-flagellation—he quite spontaneously said, "A life without mistakes would be like a bland meal. Boring and predictable. Imperfection is the spicy sauce that makes the meal tasty." He needed to come to this realization in his own way and in his own time, but it's starting to really make a difference. As he's dealt with all the changes due to the pandemic—sheltering in place, then e-learning on Zoom, now going to class in person but with just a few other students—he's blown me away with his flexibility and resilience. Although his anxiety attacks are still a challenge, now he's likely to put his hand on his heart after one occurs and say, "It's okay, Rowan. You're safe. I'm here for you." It's helping tremendously. He learned at a young age that it's not so much what happens to you in life that determines your health and happiness, but how compassionately you relate to everything that's happening.

As for myself, I'm entering a new phase—the wise woman or "crone" years, as this time is often called. After menopause, women are free from worrying about getting (or not getting) pregnant. Our kids, if we've had them, are typically grown, and we've established ourselves in our careers. It's a time of accumulating wisdom and giving it back to the community. Although there are some aspects of getting older—our skin sags and our vision declines—that we may struggle to accept, it can also be a wonderful time as long as we don't resist the changes and embrace them willingly. It's the time when we really come into our power as women, having shed many of the insecurities and illusions of youth. Although society often devalues older women because sexual attractiveness is no longer our dominant quality, this is a value system imposed by patriarchy, a twisted view easily dismissed with fierce self-compassion. The truth is that we get more beautiful as we get older, because our souls have had the chance to fully blossom. This stage can be exhilarating and radically transformative—I know it has been for me.

For one, I've stopped trying to understand my patterns and heal my wounds. I've realized that my ego and personality are functional enough. I don't need to understand my parts more thoroughly— although I'm grateful to the years of therapy that helped me reach that place. I've gotten to know and appreciate all aspects of myself: the part that's like a warrior with a drawn bow when I perceive someone to be violating the truth; the part that speaks authentically, even if not always diplomatically; the part that's hardworking and keeps going even when things get difficult in life; and the part that can hold it all with love.

Now my work is primarily focused on letting go of the blocks that get in the way of my yin and yang energy flowing freely. When I meditate, I don't even know what I'm letting go of. There's no story line present. I simply repeat, "May I let go of what no longer serves me," and I feel the energy shifting in my body. Because I use my intellect so intensely for my work, I practice being comfortable with not knowing. I don't know what I'm attached to, I don't know why things are the way they are, I don't know what will happen in the future—if I'll ever be in a relationship again, what's going to happen after I retire from UT Austin, what will happen to our society and our planet. I focus on being at peace with not having a clear grasp of what's happening, and trust that I'll accept what needs to be accepted and work to change what needs to be changed when the time comes. It's as if I, "Kristin," am no longer controlling things or making decisions in my life, but am rather just supporting and helping myself as it unfolds moment by moment. By letting go of identification with the self who knows things and controls things, I feel lighter inside—both in terms of feeling less bogged down and feeling more full of light.

As women, we are also letting go of self-identification and freeing ourselves in the process. We're letting go of identification with gender roles that have limited us through the years, through our own lives and our mothers' lives, for generations. As we become less dependent on gender-based social approval for our sense of self-worth, and as we become less dependent on men for our sense of safety, each one of us will be able to uniquely express her own yin and yang energy. This holds true for men, transgender, nonbinary, and gender fluid people as well. Just imagine who each of us, regardless of gender, could become if we jettisoned narrow stereotypes of who we're supposed to be. If we let go of what no longer serves us: self-judgment and feelings of isolation and the story lines of fear and inadequacy that hold us back. If we could honor the fact that getting repeatedly knocked down and springing back up again is not a problem, it is our path. If we celebrated ourselves as the ever-evolving, glorious mess that we are. By claiming fierce and tender compassion as guiding principles in our lives, we might just have a chance to put the world right.

ACKNOWLEDGMENTS

This book was a team effort, and I have many people to thank for its existence. First of all, I'd like to acknowledge Chris Germer, my long-term colleague, good friend, and cocreator of the Mindful Self-Compassion program. We developed many of the ideas about fierce and tender self-compassion together, and most of the practices in this book come from our joint work. I like to joke that Chris represents my most functional adult male relationship, and it truly has been an amazingly wonderful and productive partnership.

There are many MSC teachers, such as Michelle Becker and Cassondra Graf, who contributed their ideas and insights into how the fierce side of self-compassion manifests. I'm so grateful for them and the support of the whole team at the Center for Mindful Self-Compassion, including our brilliant executive director Steve Hickman, for encouraging the practice of self-compassion throughout the world.

The contributions of Kevin Conley were invaluable to writing this book. He acted as my first editor, and worked with me to actually craft the manuscript. His helping hand can be seen on almost every page. His patience and good humor as we bounced around ideas and traded drafts back and forth were greatly appreciated.

Deep gratitude also goes to my editor at Harper Wave, Karen Rinaldi, who helped shape this book in so many ways. She "got" this book from the very beginning and it's wonderful to feel so understood. I am also grateful for the careful editing of Haley Swanson, and the wonderful team at Harper Wave. I feel very taken care of.

I'd like to give thanks to my agent, Elizabeth Sheinkman, who I first sent the book proposal to, and who convinced me it was a book I needed to write. Her feedback about the ideas as a woman were just as helpful as her professional feedback about the book's marketability, and her confidence in me means a lot.

A big debt is owed to the wisdom of teachers in the Insight Meditation tradition who first taught me about fierce compassion, especially Sharon Salzberg and Tara Brach. These two Momma Bears are wonderful exemplars of what the integration of fierce and tender self-compassion looks like, and their guidance and mentorship have been invaluable.

Another spiritual teacher I'd like to thank is Carolyn Silver. I have been working with her for many years now and her hands-on help in my unfolding process is a gift that I will never be able to repay. She keeps me on track when I drift off center and I love her dearly.

I'd like to thank my close friend and colleague Shauna Shapiro, who was the first person other than myself ever to use the self-compassion scale in research, and who over the years has become a dear and trusted confidant.

Also essential to this book has been the love and friendship of Kelley Rainwater, my BFF. She initiated me into the mysteries of the divine feminine, and helped me call upon this source of guidance when I needed it most. Our hours-long talks about womanhood, patriarchy, and history were instrumental to the development of many of the ideas I write about. She has been a constant companion and helped me get through some of the most difficult moments of my life. We have also celebrated many happy moments, and my life would not be the same without her.

Of course, my life wouldn't even exist without my mother. I'm grateful not only for the incredible job she did raising my brother, Parker, and me, but also for her continual friendship. She doesn't take any BS from anyone and taught me a lot about being a fierce woman.

My deepest gratitude goes to my son, Rowan, whose amazing bravery and resilience is an inspiration to me every day. He's taught me so much and I am blessed to have such a kind, loving and delightful son.

Finally, I'd like to thank all the brave women who went through the collective trauma of "George" and who came together to support each other when needed. Hopefully we're stronger because of it and can use our voices to help prevent events like this from happening in the future.

NOTES

INTRODUCTION: CARING FORCE

3 "One thing is certain: if we merge mercy with might": A. Gorman, "The Hill We Climb," poem, read at the presidential inauguration of Joseph Biden on January 20, 2021, https://www.cnbc.com/2021 /01/20/amanda-gormans-inaugural-poem-the-hill-we-climb-full-text .html.

3 Compassion is aimed at alleviating suffering: J. L. Goetz, D. Keltner, and E. Simon-Thomas, "Compassion: An Evolutionary Analysis and Empirical Review," *Psychological Bulletin* 136, no. 3 (2010): 351–74.

4 program called Mindful Self-Compassion: C. Germer and K. D. Neff, "Mindful Self-Compassion (MSC)," in I. Ivtzan, ed., *The Handbook of Mindfulness-Based Programs: Every Established Intervention, from Medicine to Education* (London: Routledge, 2019), 55–74.

5 Marvel Comics writer Jack Kirby: G. Groth, Jack Kirby Interview, Part 6, *Comics Journal* #134, May 23, 2011.

6 "When I speak of love": "Beyond Vietnam: A Time to Break Silence," speech delivered by Dr. Martin Luther King Jr. on April 4, 1967, at a meeting of Clergy and Laity Concerned at Riverside Church in New York City.

6 theoretical paper defining self-compassion: K. D. Neff, "Self-Compassion: An Alternative Conceptualization of a Healthy Attitude toward Oneself," *Self and Identity* 2, no. 2 (2003): 85–102.

6 the Self-Compassion Scale (SCS): K. D. Neff, "Development and Validation of a Scale to Measure Self-Compassion," *Self and Identity* 2 (2003): 223–50.

6   greater levels of well-being: K. D. Neff, K. Kirkpatrick, and S. S.
    Rude, "Self-Compassion and Adaptive Psychological Functioning,"
    Journal of Research in Personality 41 (2007): 139–54.

6   well over three thousand scientific journal articles: Based on a
    Google Scholar search of entries with "self-compassion" in the title
    conducted November 2020.

6   According to Kohlberg's model: L. Kohlberg and R. H. Hersh,
    "Moral Development: A Review of the Theory," *Theory into Practice*
    16, no. 2 (1977): 53–59.

7   Turiel resolved the argument: E. Turiel, *The Culture of Morality:
    Social Development, Context, and Conflict* (Cambridge, UK:
    Cambridge University Press, 2002).

7   Turiel's research also shows that social power: C. Wainryb and E.
    Turiel, "Dominance, Subordination, and Concepts of Personal
    Entitlements in Cultural Contexts," *Child Development* 65, no. 6
    (1994): 1701–22.

11 changes our lives for the better: A. C. Wilson et al., "Effectiveness of
    Self-Compassion Related Therapies: A Systematic Review and Meta-
    Analysis," *Mindfulness* 10, no. 6 (2018): 979–95.

12 study of the effectiveness of MSC: K. D. Neff and C. K. Germer,
    "A Pilot Study and Randomized Controlled Trial of the Mindful
    Self-Compassion Program," *Journal of Clinical Psychology* 69, no. 1
    (2013): 28–44.

13 brief version of the Self-Compassion Scale: F. Raes et al.,
    "Construction and Factorial Validation of a Short Form of the Self-
    Compassion Scale," *Clinical Psychology and Psychotherapy* 18 (2011):
    250–55.

CHAPTER 1: THE FUNDAMENTALS OF SELF-COMPASSION

17 "We need women who": Commencement address given by Kavita
    Ramdas on May 19, 2013, to the graduates of Mount Holyoke
    College.

20 "The point of spiritual practice": J. Kornfield (2017), "Freedom of the
    Heart," *Heart Wisdom*, Episode 11, https://jackkornfield.com/freedom
    -heart-heart-wisdom-episode-11, accessed November 13, 2020.

20 According to my model: K. D. Neff, "Self-Compassion: An

Alternative Conceptualization of a Healthy Attitude toward Oneself," *Self and Identity* 2 (2003): 85–101.

21 interconnected brain regions called the default mode network: L. Mak et al., "The Default Mode Network in Healthy Individuals: A Systematic Review and Meta-analysis," *Brain Connectivity* 7, no. 1 (2017): 25–33.

21 mindfulness deactivates the default mode: J. A. Brewer, "Meditation Experience Is Associated with Differences in Default Mode Network Activity and Connectivity," *Proceedings of the National Academy of Sciences* 108, no. 50 (2011): 20254–59.

24 tend to produce the same findings: M. Ferrari et al., "Self-Compassion Interventions and Psychosocial Outcomes: A Meta-Analysis of RCTs," *Mindfulness* 10, no. 8 (2019): 1455–73.

24 benefits of self-compassion: For a good review of the research literature on self-compassion, see chapters 3 and 4 of C. K. Germer and K. D. Neff, *Teaching the Mindful Self-Compassion Program: A Guide for Professionals* (New York: Guilford Press, 2019).

24 happier, more hopeful, and optimistic: K. D. Neff, S. S. Rude, and K. L. Kirkpatrick, "An Examination of Self-Compassion in Relation to Positive Psychological Functioning and Personality Traits," *Journal of Research in Personality* 41 (2007): 908–16.

24 anxious, depressed, stressed, and fearful: A. MacBeth and A. Gumley, "Exploring Compassion: A Meta-Analysis of the Association between Self-Compassion and Psychopathology," *Clinical Psychology Review* 32 (2012): 545–52.

24 contemplate suicide: S. Cleare, A. Gumley, and R. C. O'Connor, "Self-Compassion, Self-Forgiveness, Suicidal Ideation, and Self-Harm: A Systematic Review," *Clinical Psychology and Psychotherapy* 26, no. 5 (2019): 511–30.

24 abuse drugs and alcohol: C. L. Phelps et al., "The Relationship between Self-Compassion and the Risk for Substance Use Disorder," *Drug and Alcohol Dependence* 183 (2018): 78–81.

24 regulate their emotions more effectively: K. D. Neff et al., "The Forest and the Trees: Examining the Association of Self-Compassion and Its Positive and Negative Components with Psychological Functioning," *Self and Identity* 17, no. 6 (2018): 627–45.

24 develop eating disorders: T. D. Braun, C. L. Park, and A. Gorin,

"Self-Compassion, Body Image, and Disordered Eating: A Review of the Literature," *Body Image* 17 (2016): 117–31.

24 more likely to engage in healthy behaviors: D. D. Biber and R. Ellis, "The Effect of Self-Compassion on the Self-Regulation of Health Behaviors: A Systematic Review," *Journal of Health Psychology* 24, no. 14 (2019): 2060–71.

24 They're physically healthier: W. J. Phillips and D. W. Hine, "Self-Compassion, Physical Health, and Health Behaviour: A Meta-Analysis," *Health Psychology Review* (2019): 1–27.

24 They're more motivated: J. G. Breines and S. Chen, "Self-Compassion Increases Self-Improvement Motivation," *Personality and Social Psychology Bulletin* 38, no. 9 (2012): 1133–43.

24 more responsibility for themselves: J. W. Zhang and S. Chen, "Self-Compassion Promotes Personal Improvement from Regret Experiences Via Acceptance," *Personality and Social Psychology Bulletin* 42, no. 2 (2016): 244–58.

24 resilient when faced with life challenges: A. A. Scoglio et al., "Self-Compassion and Responses to Trauma: The Role of Emotion Regulation," *Journal of Interpersonal Violence* 33, no. 13 (2018): 2016–36.

24 relationships with friends, family, and romantic partners: L. M. Yarnell and K. D. Neff, "Self-Compassion, Interpersonal Conflict Resolutions, and Well-Being," *Self and Identity* 12, no. 2 (2013): 146–59.

24 more sexual satisfaction: J. S. Ferreira, R. A. Rigby, and R. J. Cobb, "Self-Compassion Moderates Associations between Distress about Sexual Problems and Sexual Satisfaction in a Daily Diary Study of Married Couples," *Canadian Journal of Human Sexuality* 29, no. 2 (2020): 182–96.

24 able to take others' perspectives: K. D. Neff and E. Pommier, "The Relationship between Self-Compassion and Other-Focused Concern among College Undergraduates, Community Adults, and Practicing Meditators," *Self and Identity* 12, no. 2 (2013): 160–76.

24 caretake without burning out: Z. Hashem and P. Zeinoun, "Self-Compassion Explains Less Burnout among Healthcare Professionals," *Mindfulness* 11, no. 11 (2020): 2542–51.

24 the quest for high self-regard: K. D. Neff and R. Vonk, "Self-

Compassion Versus Global Self-Esteem: Two Different Ways of Relating to Oneself," *Journal of Personality* 77 (2009): 23–50.

25   "threat-defense response": P. Gilbert, "Social Mentalities: Internal 'Social' Conflicts and the Role of Inner Warmth and Compassion in Cognitive Therapy," in P. Gilbert and K. G. Bailey, eds., *Genes on the Couch: Explorations in Evolutionary Psychotherapy* (Hove, UK: Psychology Press, 2000), 118–50.

25   sympathetic nervous system is activated: S. W. Porges, *The Polyvagal Theory: Neurophysiological Foundations of Emotions, Attachment, Communication, and Self-Regulation* (New York: Norton, 2011).

25   leading to stress, anxiety, and depression: R. J. Gruen et al., "Vulnerability to Stress: Self-Criticism and Stress-Induced Changes in Biochemistry," *Journal of Personality* 65, no. 1 (1997): 33–47.

26   remarkable neuronal plasticity: S. Herculano-Houzel, *The Human Advantage: A New Understanding of How Our Brain Became Remarkable* (Cambridge, MA: MIT Press, 2016).

26   "tend-and-befriend" response evolved: S. E. Taylor, "Tend and Befriend: Biobehavioral Bases of Affiliation Under Stress," *Current Directions in Psychological Science* 15, no. 6 (2006): 273–77.

26   increases feelings of security: C. S. Carter, "Oxytocin Pathways and the Evolution of Human Behavior," *Annual Review of Psychology* 65 (2014): 17–39.

26   reducing sympathetic activity: S. W. Porges, "The Polyvagal Theory: Phylogenetic Contributions to Social Behavior," *Physiology and Behavior* 79, no. 3 (2003): 503–13.

26   respond to physical touch almost immediately: T. Field, *Touch* (Cambridge, MA: MIT Press, 2014).

28   internalize this supportive attitude: P. R. Shaver et al., "Attachment Security as a Foundation for Kindness toward Self and Others," in K. W. Brown and M. R. Leary, eds., *The Oxford Handbook of Hypo-egoic Phenomena* (Oxford: Oxford University Press, 2017), 223–42.

28   more challenging to be self-compassionate: N. D. Ross, P. L. Kaminski, and R. Herrington, "From Childhood Emotional Maltreatment to Depressive Symptoms in Adulthood: The Roles of Self-Compassion and Shame," *Child Abuse and Neglect* 92 (2019): 32–42.

28   our attachment style: R. C. Fraley and N. W. Hudson, "The

Development of Attachment Styles," in J. Specht, ed., *Personality Development across the Lifespan* (Cambridge, MA: Elsevier Academic Press, 2017), 275–92.

28 consequently kinder to themselves: M. Navarro-Gil et al., "Effects of Attachment-Based Compassion Therapy (ABCT) on Self-Compassion and Attachment Style in Healthy People," *Mindfulness* 1, no. 1 (2018): 51–62.

28 scary to give yourself compassion: L. R. Miron et al., "The Potential Indirect Effect of Childhood Abuse on Posttrauma Pathology through Self-Compassion and Fear of Self-Compassion," *Mindfulness* 7, no. 3 (2016): 596–605.

29 label he came up with for it is "backdraft": C. Germer, *The Mindful Path to Self-Compassion: Freeing Yourself from Destructive Thoughts and Emotions* (New York: Guilford Press, 2009).

30 focus our mind on a single object: A. Lutz et al., "Attention Regulation and Monitoring in Meditation," *Trends in Cognitive Sciences* 12, no. 4 (2008): 163–69.

30 practice helps people self-regulate: N. N. Singh et al., "Soles of the Feet: A Mindfulness-Based Self-Control Intervention for Aggression by an Individual with Mild Mental Retardation and Mental Illness," *Research in Developmental Disabilities* 24, no. 3 (2003): 158–69.

31 big *New York Times* article: T. Parker-Pope, "Go Easy on Yourself, a New Wave of Research Shows," *New York Times*, February 29, 2011, https://well.blogs.nytimes.com/2011/02/28/go-easy-on-yourself-a-new-wave-of-research-urges/.

31 Sharon Salzberg talks about it: S. Salzberg, "Fierce Compassion," Omega, 2012, https://www.eomega.org/article/fierce-compassion.

32 "a strong, powerful energy": "Sharon Salzberg + Robert Thurman: Meeting Our Enemies and Our Suffering," *On Being with Krista Tippett*, October 31, 2013, https://onbeing.org/programs/sharon-salzberg-robert-thurman-meeting-our-enemies-and-our-suffering.

32 concept of yin and yang: M. Palmer, *Yin & Yang: Understanding the Chinese Philosophy of Opposites* (London: Piatkus Books, 1997).

35 goddess of compassion, Avalokiteshvara: E. Olson, "The Buddhist Female Deities," in S. Nicholson, ed., *The Goddess Re-Awakening: The Feminine Principle Today* (Wheaton, IL: Quest Books, 1989), 80–90.

38 "Near enemy": J. Kornfield, *Bringing Home the Dharma: Awakening Right Where You Are* (Boston: Shambala, 2012).

CHAPTER 2: WHAT'S GENDER GOT TO DO WITH IT?

43 "grow some balls": B. White, *If You Ask Me (And of Course You Won't)* (New York: Putnam, 2011).

43 females are considered "communal" and males "agentic": A. H. Eagly and V. J. Steffen, "Gender Stereotypes Stem from the Distribution of Women and Men into Social Role," *Journal of Personality and Social Psychology* 46, no. 4 (1984): 735–54.

44 men are harmed by a culture of toxic masculinity: T. A. Kupers, "Toxic Masculinity as a Barrier to Mental Health Treatment in Prison," *Journal of Clinical Psychology* 61, no. 6 (2005): 713–24.

44 hinder male emotional intelligence: Y. J. Wong and A. B. Rochlen, "Demystifying Men's Emotional Behavior: New Directions and Implications for Counseling and Research," *Psychology of Men and Masculinity* 6, no. 1 (2005): 62–72.

44 serve to maintain social inequality: D. D. Rucker, A. D. Galinsky, and J. C. Mage, "The Agentic–Communal Model of Advantage and Disadvantage: How Inequality Produces Similarities in the Psychology of Power, Social Class, Gender, and Race," *Advances in Experimental Social Psychology* 58 (2018): 71–125.

45 three forms of sexism: J. K. Swim and B. Campbell, "Sexism: Attitudes, Beliefs, and Behaviors," in R. Brown and S. Gaertner, eds., *The Handbook of Social Psychology: Intergroup Relations,* vol. 4 (Oxford: Blackwell Publishers, 2001), 218–37.

45 associated with bias and discrimination: P. Glick and S. T. Fiske, "An Ambivalent Alliance: Hostile and Benevolent Sexism as Complementary Justifications for Gender Inequality," *American Psychologist* 56, no. 2 (2001): 109–18.

45 televangelist Pat Robertson: Associated Press, "Robertson Letter Attacks Feminists," *New York Times,* August 26, 1992, https://www .nytimes.com/1992/08/26/us/robertson-letter-attacks-feminists.html.

46 hanged as witches: M. K. Roach, *Six Women of Salem: The Untold Story of the Accused and Their Accusers in the Salem Witch Trials* (Boston: Da Capo Press, 2013).

46 Make Women Great Again conference: The 22 Convention, October 2020, https://22convention.com.

46 MAGA hat for the uterus: K. Fleming, "Mansplaining Conference Hopes to 'Make Women Great Again,'" *New York Post,* January 2,

2020, https://nypost.com/2020/01/02/mansplaining-conference -hopes-to-make-women-great-again/.

46   leaders in the "manosphere": D. Ging, "Alphas, Betas, and Incels: Theorizing the Masculinities of the Manosphere," *Men and Masculinities* 22, no. 4 (2019): 638–57.

46   endorse the myths about rape: A. J. Kelly, S. L. Dubbs, and F. K. Barlow, "Social Dominance Orientation Predicts Heterosexual Men's Adverse Reactions to Romantic Rejection," *Archives of Sexual Behavior* 44, no. 4 (2015): 903–19.

47   glue that holds patriarchy: J. T. Jost and A. C. Kay, "Exposure to Benevolent Sexism and Complementary Gender Stereotypes: Consequences for Specific and Diffuse Forms of System Justification," *Journal of Personality and Social Psychology* 88, no. 3 (2005): 498–509.

47   simply denies that sexism exists: J. K. Swim, "Sexism and Racism: Old-Fashioned and Modern Prejudices," *Journal of Personality and Social Psychology* 68, no. 2 (1995): 199–214.

47   victims of reverse discrimination: J. E. Cameron, "Social Identity, Modern Sexism, and Perceptions of Personal and Group Discrimination by Women and Men," *Sex Roles* 45, nos. 11–12 (2001): 743–66.

48   "Women are likely to prioritize": N. Bowles, "Jordan Peterson, Custodian of the Patriarchy," *New York Times,* May 18, 2018, https:// www.nytimes.com/2018/05/18/style/jordan-peterson-12-rules-for -life.html.

48   Sex-related variability in hormones: K. D. Locke, "Agentic and Communal Social Motives," *Social and Personality Psychology Compass* 9, no. 10 (2015): 525–38.

48   better at empathy and cooperation: M. Schulte-Rüther et al., "Gender Differences in Brain Networks Supporting Empathy," *Neuroimage* 42, no. 1 (2008): 393–403.

48   power increases testosterone: M. L. Batrinos, "Testosterone and Aggressive Behavior in Man," *International Journal of Endocrinology and Metabolism* 10, no. 3 (2012): 563–68.

48   participants in a mock workplace setting: S. M. Van Anders, J. Steiger, and K. L. Goldey, "Effects of Gendered Behavior on Testosterone in Women and Men," *Proceedings of the National Academy of Sciences* 112, no. 45 (2015): 13805–10.

49   caring for infants predicts oxytocin: I. Gordon et al., "Oxytocin and the Development of Parenting in Humans," *Biological Psychiatry* 68, no. 4 (2010): 377–82.

49   slight biological tendency: A. H. Eagly and W. Wood, "The Nature-Nurture Debates: 25 Years of Challenges in Understanding the Psychology of Gender," *Perspectives on Psychological Science* 8, no. 3 (2013): 340–57.

49   amplified by the behavior of parents: E. W. Lindsey and J. Mize, "Contextual Differences in Parent–Child Play: Implications for Children's Gender Role Development," *Sex Roles* 44, nos. 3–4 (2001): 155–76.

49   driver of gender differences: J. S. Hyde, "Gender Similarities and Differences," *Annual Review of Psychology* 65 (2014): 373–98.

49   exaggerated by social factors: K. Bussey and A. Bandura, "Social Cognitive Theory of Gender Development and Differentiation," *Psychological Review* 106, no. 4 (1999): 676–713.

49   affect almost every important area of life: S. Damaske, *For the Family? How Class and Gender Shape Women's Work* (Oxford: Oxford University Press, 2011).

49   known as gender schemas: S. L. Bem, "Gender Schema Theory: A Cognitive Account of Sex Typing," *Psychological Review* 88, no. 4 (1981): 354–64.

49   organized knowledge structures: J. Piaget, *The Language and Thought of the Child*, trans. M. Gabain (London: Lund Humphries, 1959; original work published 1926).

50   known as cognitive dissonance: L. Festinger, "Cognitive Dissonance," *Scientific American* 207, no. 4 (1962): 93–106.

50   boy cooking as a girl cooking: C. L. Martin and C. F. Halverson Jr., "The Effects of Sex-Typing Schemas on Young Children's Memory," *Child Development* 54, no. 3 (1983): 563–74.

50   self-confident about their math ability: F. Hill et al., "Maths Anxiety in Primary and Secondary School Students: Gender Differences, Developmental Changes and Anxiety Specificity," *Learning and Individual Differences* 48 (2016): 45–53.

50   less talented in science: D. Z. Grunspan et al., "Males Under-Estimate Academic Performance of Their Female Peers in Undergraduate Biology Classrooms," *PLOS ONE* 11, no. 2 (2016): e0148405.

50 females are less intelligent than males: J. Herbert and D. Stipek, "The Emergence of Gender Differences in Children's Perceptions of Their Academic Competence," *Journal of Applied Developmental Psychology* 26, no. 3 (2005): 276–95.

50 schemas are often held unconsciously: L. A. Rudman, A. G. Greenwald, and D. E. McGhee, "Implicit Self-Concept and Evaluative Implicit Gender Stereotypes: Self and Ingroup Share Desirable Traits," *Personality and Social Psychology Bulletin* 27, no. 9 (2001): 1164–78.

50 invisible filter of perception: L. A. Rudman, "Sources of Implicit Attitudes," *Current Directions in Psychological Science* 13 (2004): 79–82.

51 designs were considered more innovative: D. Proudfoot, A. C. Kay, and C. Z. Koval, "A Gender Bias in the Attribution of Creativity: Archival and Experimental Evidence for the Perceived Association between Masculinity and Creative Thinking," *Psychological Science* 26, no. 11 (2015): 1751–61.

51 Researchers from New York University: M. E. Heilman and M. C. Haynes, "No Credit Where Credit Is Due: Attributional Rationalization of Women's Success in Male-Female Teams," *Journal of Applied Psychology* 90, no. 5 (2005): 905–16.

51 from 1983 to 2014: E. L. Haines, K. Deaux, and N. Lofaro, "The Times They Are a-Changing . . . or Are They Not? A Comparison of Gender Stereotypes, 1983–2014," *Psychology of Women Quarterly* 40, no. 3 (2016): 353–63.

52 gender stereotypes from early adolescence to early adulthood: K. D. Neff and L. N. Terry-Schmitt, "Youths' Attributions for Power-Related Gender Differences: Nature, Nurture, or God?," *Cognitive Development* 17 (2002): 1185–1203.

52 sense of self forms: D. D. Tobin et al., "The Intrapsychics of Gender: A Model of Self-Socialization," *Psychological Review* 117, no. 2 (2010): 601.

52 first categories infants learn: M. E. Kite, K. Deaux, and E. L. Haines, "Gender Stereotypes," in F. L. Denmark and M. A. Paludi, eds., *Psychology of Women: A Handbook of Issues and Theories*, 2nd ed. (Westport, CT: Praeger, 2007), 205–36.

52 women with communal traits: C. Leaper and C. K. Friedman, "The Socialization of Gender," in J. E. Grusec and P. D. Hastings, eds., *Handbook of Socialization: Theory and Research* (New York: Guilford Press, 2007), 561–87.

53 step down in status: E. F. Coyle, M. Fulcher, and D. Trübutschek, "Sissies, Mama's Boys, and Tomboys: Is Children's Gender Nonconformity More Acceptable When Nonconforming Traits Are Positive?," *Archives of Sexual Behavior* 45, no. 7 (2016): 1827–38.

53 succeed at the dating game: J. P. Hill and M. E. Lynch, "The Intensification of Gender-Related Role Expectations during Early Adolescence," in J. Brooks-Gunn and A. C. Petersen, eds., *Girls at Puberty* (New York: Springer, 1983), 201–28.

53 downplay their competence: A. A. Nelson and C. S. Brown, "Too Pretty for Homework: Sexualized Gender Stereotypes Predict Academic Attitudes for Gender-Typical Early Adolescent Girls," *Journal of Early Adolescence* 39, no. 4 (2019): 603–17.

53 experience social backlash: L. A. Rudman and P. Glick, "Prescriptive Gender Stereotypes and Backlash toward Agentic Women," *Journal of Social Issues* 57, no. 4 (2001): 743–62.

53 mental health among women: B. E. Whitley, "Sex-Role Orientation and Psychological Well-Being: Two Meta-Analyses," *Sex Roles* 12, nos. 1–2 (1985): 207–25.

53 more anxious and depressed: E. C. Price et al., "Masculine Traits and Depressive Symptoms in Older and Younger Men and Women," *American Journal of Men's Health* 12 (2018): 19–29.

53 distressed by the problems of loved ones: J. Taylor, "Gender Orientation and the Cost of Caring for Others," *Society and Mental Health* 5 (2015): 49–65.

54 high in both agency and communion: B. Thornton and R. Leo, "Gender Typing, Importance of Multiple Roles, and Mental Health Consequences for Women," *Sex Roles* 27, no. 5 (1992): 307–17.

54 bounce back from failure: J. S. Nevid and S. A. Rathus, *Psychology and the Challenges of Life*, 13th ed. (New York: Wiley, 2016).

54 two ways of coping: C. Cheng, "Processes Underlying Gender-Role Flexibility: Do Androgynous Individuals Know More or Know How to Cope?," *Journal of Personality* 73 (2005): 645–73.

54 expressing their true selves: S. Harter et al., "Level of Voice among High School Women and Men: Relational Context, Support, and Gender Orientation," *Developmental Psychology* 34 (1998): 1–10.

54 Personal Attributes Questionnaire (PAQ): J. T. Spence and R. L. Helmreich, *Masculinity and Femininity: Their Psychological Dimensions, Correlates, and Antecedents* (Austin, TX: University of

Texas Press, 1978). Note that only the masculine and feminine items of the PAQ are included, and the order and wording of some items have been modified to facilitate scoring. Also, the scoring system differs slightly from the original. This adapted version of the scale should not be used for research purposes.

56 meta-analysis of seventy-one studies: L. M. Yarnell et al., "Meta-Analysis of Gender Differences in Self-Compassion," *Self and Identity* 14, no. 5 (2015): 499–520.

56 we tend to be more self-critical: P. Luyten et al., "Dependency and Self-Criticism: Relationship with Major Depressive Disorder, Severity of Depression, and Clinical Presentation," *Depression and Anxiety* 24, no. 8 (2007): 586–96.

56 more compassionate to others: R. Lennon and N. Eisenberg, "Gender and Age Differences in Empathy and Sympathy," in N. Eisenberg and J. Strayer, eds., *Empathy and Its Development* (Cambridge, UK: Cambridge University Press, 1987), 195–217.

56 gave almost 1,400 adults: K. D. Neff, M. Knox, and O. Davidson, "A Comparison of Self-Compassion and Compassion for Others as They Relate to Personal and Interpersonal Wellbeing among Community Adults" (manuscript in preparation).

56 analogous compassion scale: E. Pommier, K. D. Neff, and I. Tóth-Király, "The Development and Validation of the Compassion Scale," *Assessment* 27, no. 1 (2019): 21–39.

57 are just as self-compassionate as men are: L. M. Yarnell et al., "Gender Differences in Self-Compassion: Examining the Role of Gender Role Orientation," *Mindfulness* 10, no. 6 (2019): 1136–52.

57 less afraid of self-compassion than men: P. Gilbert et al., "Fears of Compassion: Development of Three Self-Report Measures," *Psychology and Psychotherapy: Theory, Research and Practice* 84, no. 3 (2011): 239–55.

CHAPTER 3: ANGRY WOMEN

63 "The truth will set": G. Steinem, *The Truth Will Set You Free, But First It Will Piss You Off!: Thoughts on Life, Love, and Rebellion* (New York: Random House, 2019).

64 anger of girls is treated differently from that of boys: R. L. Buntaine and V. K. Costenbader, "Self-Reported Differences in the Experience

and Expression of Anger between Girls and Boys," *Sex Roles* 36 (1997): 625–37.

64 discouraged from showing the fierce quality of anger: A. H. Eagly and V. Steffen, "Gender and Aggressive Behavior: A Meta-Analytic Review of the Social Psychological Literature," *Psychological Bulletin* 100 (1986): 309–30.

64 acceptable in boys but not in girls: R. S. Mills and K. H. Rubin, "A Longitudinal Study of Maternal Beliefs about Children's Social Behaviors," *Merrill-Palmer Quarterly* 38, no. 4 (1992): 494–512.

64 three times more often than boys: K. A. Martin, "Becoming a Gendered Body: Practices of Preschools," *American Sociological Review* 63, no. 4 (1998): 494–511.

64 our role to keep the peace: J. B. Miller, "The Development of Women's Sense of Self," in J. Jordan et al., eds., *Women's Growth in Connection: Writings from the Stone Center* (New York: Guilford Press, 1991), 11–26.

64 mad if he's a boy: R. Fivush, "Exploring Differences in the Emotional Content of Mother-Child Conversations about the Past," *Sex Roles* 20 (1989): 675–91.

64 abnormal for girls: T. M. Chaplin, P. M. Cole, and C. Zahn-Waxler, "Parental Socialization of Emotion Expression: Gender Differences and Relations to Child Adjustment," *Emotion* 5, no. 1 (2005): 80–88.

64 conducted a pioneering: S. P. Thomas, ed., *Women and Anger* (New York: Springer, 1993).

64 "I believe that I have been socialized": S. P. Thomas, "Women's Anger: Causes, Manifestations, and Correlates," in C. D. Spielberger and I. G. Sarason, eds., *Stress and Emotion*, vol. 15 (Washington, DC: Taylor and Francis, 1995), 53–74.

65 "My husband tells me": S. P. Thomas, C. Smucker, and P. Droppleman, "It Hurts Most around the Heart: A Phenomenological Exploration of Women's Anger," *Journal of Advanced Nursing* 28 (1998): 311–22.

65 interpreted as deviant: L. Brody, *Gender, Emotion, and the Family* (Cambridge, MA: Harvard University Press, 2009).

66 in-depth interviews with some of the Black participants: S. P. Thomas, "Women's Anger, Aggression, and Violence," *Health Care for Women International* 26, no. 6 (2005): 504–22.

66 Black women are actually no more angry: J. C. Walley-Jean, "Debunking the Myth of the 'Angry Black Woman': An Exploration of Anger in Young African American Women," *Black Women, Gender and Families* 3, no. 2 (2009): 68–86.

66 the Sapphire stereotype: D. C. Allison et al., eds., *Black Women's Portrayals on Reality Television: The New Sapphire* (Lanham, MD: Rowman and Littlefield, 2016).

66 justify the mistreatment of Black women: M. V. Harris-Perry, *Sister Citizen: Shame, Stereotypes, and Black Women in America* (New Haven, CT: Yale University Press, 2011).

66 one study of almost three hundred White undergraduates: C. W. Esqueda and L. A. Harrison, "The Influence of Gender Role Stereotypes, the Woman's Race, and Level of Provocation and Resistance on Domestic Violence Culpability Attributions," *Sex Roles* 53, nos. 11–12 (2005): 821–34.

67 police tend to take the accounts of Black victims: S. Shernock and B. Russell, "Gender and Racial/Ethnic Differences in Criminal Justice Decision Making in Intimate Partner Violence Cases," *Partner Abuse* 3, no. 4 (2012): 501–30.

67 mock jury deliberation about a murder case: J. M. Salerno and L. C. Peter-Hagene, "One Angry Woman: Anger Expression Increases Influence for Men, but Decreases Influence for Women, during Group Deliberation," *Law and Human Behavior* 39, no. 6 (2015): 581–92.

68 judge ourselves for getting angry: A. Campbell and S. Muncer, "Sex Differences in Aggression: Social Representation and Social Roles," *British Journal of Social Psychology* 33 (1994): 233–40.

68 lower levels of self-compassion than men: L. M. Yarnell et al., "Gender Differences in Self-Compassion: Examining the Role of Gender Role Orientation," *Mindfulness* 10, no. 6 (2019): 1136–52.

68 as men to be depressed: G. Parker and H. Brotchie, "Gender Differences in Depression," *International Review of Psychiatry* 22, no. 5 (2010): 429–36.

68 caused by sympathetic nervous system activation: E. Won and Y. K. Kim, "Stress, the Autonomic Nervous System, and the Immune-Kynurenine Pathway in the Etiology of Depression," *Current Neuropharmacology* 14, no. 7 (2016): 665–73.

68 such as panic attacks: I. Jalnapurkar, M. Allen, and T. Pigott, "Sex

Differences in Anxiety Disorders: A Review," *Journal of Psychiatry, Depression and Anxiety* 4 (2018): 1–9.

68 eating disorders such as anorexia: C. A. Timko, L. DeFilipp, and A. Dakanalis, "Sex Differences in Adolescent Anorexia and Bulimia Nervosa: Beyond the Signs and Symptoms," *Current Psychiatry Reports* 21, no. 1 (2019): 1–8.

68 which also contributes to depression: P. Gilbert et al., "An Exploration into Depression-Focused and Anger-Focused Rumination in Relation to Depression in a Student Population," *Behavioural and Cognitive Psychotherapy* 33, no. 3 (2005): 273–83.

68 sample of 1,125 Americans: R. W. Simon and K. Lively, "Sex, Anger and Depression," *Social Forces* 88, no. 4 (2010): 1543–68.

69 making us ill: S. Nolen-Hoeksema, "Emotion Regulation and Psychopathology: The Role of Gender," *Annual Review of Clinical Psychology* 8 (2012): 161–87.

69 anger can be a helpful emotion: R. W. Novaco, "Anger and Psychopathology," in M. Potegal, G. Stemmler, and C. Spielberger, eds., *International Handbook of Anger* (New York: Springer, 2010), 465–97.

70 effective as a pain reliever: R. Stephens, J. Atkins, and A. Kingston, "Swearing as a Response to Pain," *Neuroreport* 20, no. 12 (2009): 1056–60.

70 constructive and destructive: J. P. Tangney et al., "Relation of Shame and Guilt to Constructive Versus Destructive Responses to Anger across the Lifespan," *Journal of Personality and Social Psychology* 70, no. 4 (1996): 797–809.

71 including verbal and physical attacks: T. A. Cavell and K. T. Malcolm, eds., *Anger, Aggression, and Interventions for Interpersonal Violence* (Mahwah, NJ: Lawrence Erlbaum, 2007).

71 lead to hypertension: S. A. Everson et al., "Anger Expression and Incident Hypertension," *Psychosomatic Medicine* 60, no. 6 (1998): 730–35.

71 immune system dysfunction: R. M. Suinn, "The Terrible Twos—Anger and Anxiety: Hazardous to Your Health," *American Psychologist* 56, no. 1 (2001): 27–36.

71 coronary heart disease: T. W. Smith et al., "Hostility, Anger, Aggressiveness, and Coronary Heart Disease: An Interpersonal

Perspective on Personality, Emotion, and Health," *Journal of Personality* 72 (2004): 1217–70.

71 defends her rights without hostility or aggression: A. Pascual-Leone, et al., "Problem Anger in Psychotherapy: An Emotion-Focused Perspective on Hate, Rage and Rejecting Anger," *Journal of Contemporary Psychotherapy* 43, no. 2 (2013): 83–92.

71 study of almost two thousand adult men and women: K. Davidson et al., "Constructive Anger Verbal Behavior Predicts Blood Pressure in a Population-Based Sample," *Health Psychology* 19, no. 1 (2000): 55–64.

72 violations of rights or fairness: E. Halperin, "Group-Based Hatred in Intractable Conflict in Israel," *Journal of Conflict Resolution* 52 (2008): 713–36.

72 conflicts in a balanced manner: M. R. Tagar, C. M. Federico, and E. Halperin, "The Positive Effect of Negative Emotions in Protracted Conflict: The Case of Anger," *Journal of Experimental Social Psychology* 47, no. 1 (2011): 157–64.

72 Israeli support for compromise: E. Halperin et al., "Anger, Hatred, and the Quest for Peace: Anger Can Be Constructive in the Absence of Hatred," *Journal of Conflict Resolution* 55, no. 2 (2011): 274–91.

72 "The truth is that anger": S. Chemaly, *Rage Becomes Her: The Power of Women's Anger* (New York: Simon and Schuster, 2018), xxiii.

73 study by Diana Leonard and colleagues: D. J. Leonard et al., "We're Mad as Hell and We're Not Going to Take It Anymore: Anger Self-Stereotyping and Collective Action," *Group Processes and Intergroup Relations* 14, no. 1 (2011): 99–111.

73 collective action is defined: D. M. Taylor et al., "Disadvantaged Group Responses to Perceived Inequity: From Passive Acceptance to Collective Action," *Journal of Social Psychology* 127 (1987): 259–72.

73 "Rage Moms": L. Lerer and J. Medina, "The 'Rage Moms' Democrats Are Counting On," *New York Times*, August 17, 2020, https://www.nytimes.com/2020/08/17/us/politics/democrats-women-voters-anger.html.

73 MomsRising: "About MomsRising," MomsRising, https://www.momsrising.org/about.

73 Moms Demand Action: "Our Story," Moms Demand Action, https://momsdemandaction.org/about/.

73   Black Lives Matter movement: "Herstory," Black Lives Matter, https://blacklivesmatter.com/herstory/.

74   anger in over two hundred undergraduates: A. Fresnics and A. Borders, "Angry Rumination Mediates the Unique Associations between Self-Compassion and Anger and Aggression," *Mindfulness* 8, no. 3 (2016): 554–64.

75   Internal Family Systems (IFS) therapy: R. C. Schwartz and M. Sweezy, *Internal Family Systems Therapy* (New York: Guilford Press, 2019).

77   decrease depression and self-criticism: N. A. Shadick et al., "A Randomized Controlled Trial of an Internal Family Systems-Based Psychotherapeutic Intervention on Outcomes in Rheumatoid Arthritis: A Proof-of-Concept Study," *Journal of Rheumatology* 30, no. 11 (2013): 1831–41.

78   Hindu goddess Kali: S. Kempton, *Awakening Shakti: The Transformative Power of the Goddesses of Yoga* (Boulder, CO: Sounds True, 2013).

80   "Anger is the deepest form": D. Whyte, *Consolations: The Solace, Nourishment and Underlying Meaning of Everyday Words* (Edinburgh: Canongate Books, 2019).

80   health, well-being, and contentment: "What Is Qi? (and Other Concepts)," Taking Charge of Your Health and Wellbeing, University of Minnesota, https://www.takingcharge.csh.umn.edu/explore -healing-practices/traditional-chinese-medicine/what-qi-and-other -concepts.

80   "Anger is considered a poison": B. Glassman and R. Fields, "Instructions to the Cook," *Tricycle Magazine*, Spring 1996.

82   SCS as a measure of self-compassion: P. Muris, "A Protective Factor against Mental Health Problems in Youths? A Critical Note on the Assessment of Self-Compassion," *Journal of Child and Family Studies* 25, no. 5 (2015): 1461–65.

82   data to validate the scale: K. D. Neff et al., "Examining the Factor Structure of the Self-Compassion Scale Using Exploratory SEM Bifactor Analysis in 20 Diverse Samples: Support for Use of a Total Score and Six Subscale Scores," *Psychological Assessment* 31, no. 1 (2019): 27–45.

82   one scholar dismissed the data: P. Muris and H. Otgaar, "The Process of Science: A Critical Evaluation of More Than 15 Years

of Research on Self-Compassion with the Self-Compassion Scale," *Mindfulness* 11, no. 6 (2020): 1469–82.

82   wrote a comprehensive response: K. D. Neff, "Commentary on Muris and Otgaar: Let the Empirical Evidence Speak on the Self-Compassion Scale," *Mindfulness* 11, no. 6 (May 23, 2020): 1900–9.

CHAPTER 4: #METOO

89   There is inherent strength: E. Brockes, "#MeToo Founder Tarana Burke: 'You Have to Use Your Privilege to Serve Other People,'" *Guardian*, January 15, 2018, https://www.theguardian.com/world/2018/jan/15/me-too-founder-tarana-burke-women-sexual-assault.

90   2018 large-scale study: "The Facts behind the #MeToo Movement: A National Study on Sexual Harassment and Assault," conducted by Stop Street Harassment, February 2018, http://www.stopstreet harassment.org/wp-content/uploads/2018/01/Full-Report-2018 -National-Study-on-Sexual-Harassment-and-Assault.pdf.

90   subjected to harassment at work: ABC News/*Washington Post* poll on sexual harassment released October 17, 2017.

90   According to one study: H. McLaughlin, C. Uggen, and A. Blackstone, "Sexual Harassment, Workplace Authority, and the Paradox of Power," *American Sociological Review* 77, no. 4 (2012): 625–47.

90   experienced coerced sexual contact at some point in their lives: "Statistics," National Sexual Violence Resource Center, https://www .nsvrc.org/statistics, accessed November 14, 2020.

91   attempted rape in her lifetime: M. C. Black et al., *National Intimate Partner and Sexual Violence Survey: 2010 Summary Report*, retrieved from the Centers for Disease Control and Prevention, National Center for Injury Prevention and Control, 2011, http://www.cdc .gov/ViolencePrevention/pdf/NISVS_Report2010-a.pdf.

91   tiny fraction result in a conviction: Department of Justice, Office of Justice Programs, Bureau of Justice Statistics, "National Crime Victimization Survey, 2010–2016," 2017.

92   difficulties with trust: D. K. Chan et al., "Examining the Job-Related, Psychological, and Physical Outcomes of Workplace Sexual Harassment: A Meta-Analytic Review," *Psychology of Women Quarterly* 32, no. 4 (2008): 362–76.

93 worsened mental and physical health: C. R. Willness, P. Steel, and K. Lee, "A Meta-Analysis of the Antecedents and Consequences of Workplace Sexual Harassment," *Personnel Psychology* 60, no. 1 (2007): 127–62.

93 consequences of sexual assault are even worse: E. R. Dworkin et al., "Sexual Assault Victimization and Psychopathology: A Review and Meta-Analysis," *Clinical Psychology Review* 56 (2017): 65–81.

93 reckon with the truth and heal: A. O'Neil et al., "The #MeToo Movement: An Opportunity in Public Health?," *Lancet* 391, no. 10140 (2018): 2587–89.

93 viewed as sexual objects: L. M. Ward et al., "Sexuality and Entertainment Media," in D. Tolman et al., eds., *APA Handbook of Sexuality and Psychology*, 2nd ed. (Washington, DC: American Psychological Association, 2014): 373–423.

93 defined as a macho attitude: D. L. Mosher and S. S. Tomkins, "Scripting the Macho Man: Hypermasculine Socialization and Enculturation," *Journal of Sex Research* 25, no. 1 (1988): 60–84.

93 feeds directly into sexual harassment and abuse: R. C. Seabrook, L. Ward, and S. Giaccardi, "Why Is Fraternity Membership Associated with Sexual Assault? Exploring the Roles of Conformity to Masculine Norms, Pressure to Uphold Masculinity, and Objectification of Women," *Psychology of Men and Masculinity* 19, no. 1 (2018): 3–13.

93 men's likelihood to commit sexual assault: S. K. Murnen, C. Wright, and G. Kaluzny, "If 'Boys Will Be Boys,' Then Girls Will Be Victims? A Meta-Analytic Review of the Research That Relates Masculine Ideology to Sexual Aggression," *Sex Roles* 46, nos. 11–12 (2002): 359–75.

99 malignant narcissist: S. K. Huprich et al., "Are Malignant Self-Regard and Vulnerable Narcissism Different Constructs?," *Journal of Clinical Psychology* 74, no. 9 (2018): 1556–69.

99 to assert control: A. Arabi, *Becoming the Narcissists' Nightmare: How to Devalue and Discard the Narcissist While Supplying Yourself* (New York: SCW Archer Publishing, 2016).

103 in businesses with fewer than fifteen employees: "Facts About Sexual Harassment," US Equal Employment Opportunity Commission, https://www.eeoc.gov/fact-sheet/facts-about-sexual-harassment, accessed February 18, 2021.

105 "You really can't give yourself love": L. McLean, M. Bambling, and S. R. Steindl, "Perspectives on Self-Compassion from Adult Female Survivors of Sexual Abuse and the Counselors Who Work with Them," *Journal of Interpersonal Violence* (2018): 1–24, advance online publication, DOI: 0886260518793975.

105 difficult emotions like shame: A. A. Scoglio et al., "Self-Compassion and Responses to Trauma: The Role of Emotion Regulation," *Journal of Interpersonal Violence* 33, no. 13 (2015): 2016–36.

105 role of self-compassion in recovering from abuse: J. M. Dicks, "Sexual Assault Survivors' Experiences of Self-Compassion" (unpublished doctoral dissertation, University of Alberta, 2014).

105 "I have realized that": Dicks, "Sexual Assault Survivors' Experiences of Self-Compassion," 75.

106 highly effective if done on a regular basis: L. B. Shapira and M. Mongrain, "The Benefits of Self-Compassion and Optimism Exercises for Individuals Vulnerable to Depression," *Journal of Positive Psychology* 5 (2010): 377–89.

110 occurs within the family: "Child Sexual Abuse Statistics," Darkness to Light, https://www.d2l.org/the-issue/statistics/, accessed October 15, 2020.

CHAPTER 5: HOLDING OURSELVES TENDERLY

113 The way out of our cage: T. Brach, *Radical Acceptance: Embracing Your Life with the Heart of a Buddha* (New York: Bantam, 2004).

116 tone is a primary means: A. Blasi et al., "Early Specialization for Voice and Emotion Processing in the Infant Brain," *Current Biology* 21, no. 14 (2011): 1220–24.

116 independent of their meaning: D. Büring, *Intonation and Meaning* (Oxford: Oxford University Press, 2016).

119 the more we aggravate it: F. J. Ruiz, "A Review of Acceptance and Commitment Therapy (ACT) Empirical Evidence: Correlational, Experimental Psychopathology, Component and Outcome Studies," *International Journal of Psychology and Psychological Therapy* 10, no. 1 (2010): 125–62.

119 "Suffering = Pain × Resistance": S. Young, "Break through Pain," 2017, https://www.shinzen.org/wp-content/uploads/2016/12/art_painprocessingalg.pdf, accessed January 8, 2021.

123 evaluation of self-worth: K. D. Neff, "Self-Compassion, Self-Esteem, and Well-Being," *Social and Personality Compass* 5 (2011): 1–12.

123 feeling special and above average: J. D. Brown, "Evaluations of Self and Others: Self-Enhancement Biases in Social Judgments," *Social Cognition* 4, no. 4 (1986): 353–76.

123 feel competitive with others: S. M. Garcia, A. Tor, and T. M. Schiff, "The Psychology of Competition: A Social Comparison Perspective," *Perspectives on Psychological Science* 8, no. 6 (2013): 634–50.

123 physical bullying: M. R. Di Stasio, R. Savage, and G. Burgos, "Social Comparison, Competition and Teacher–Student Relationships in Junior High School Classrooms Predicts Bullying and Victimization," *Journal of Adolescence* 53 (2016): 207–16.

123 relational aggression: S. M. Coyne and J. M. Ostrov, eds., *The Development of Relational Aggression* (Oxford: Oxford University Press, 2018).

123 lead to prejudice: J. Crocker et al., "Downward Comparison, Prejudice, and Evaluations of Others: Effects of Self-Esteem and Threat," *Journal of Personality and Social Psychology* 52, no. 5 (1987): 907–16.

123 standards we set for ourselves: J. Crocker and K. M. Knight, "Contingencies of Self-Worth," *Current Directions in Psychological Science* 14, no. 4 (2005): 200–3.

123 most common domains: J. Crocker and L. E. Park, "The Costly Pursuit of Self-Esteem," *Psychological Bulletin* 130 (2004): 392–414.

124 it can vacillate wildly: M. H. Kernis and B. M. Goldman, "Assessing Stability of Self-Esteem and Contingent Self-Esteem," in M. H. Kernis, ed., *Self-Esteem Issues and Answers: A Sourcebook of Current Perspectives* (Hove, UK: Psychology Press, 2006), 77–85.

125 directly compared the impact of self-esteem and self-compassion: K. D. Neff and R. Vonk, "Self-Compassion versus Global Self-Esteem: Two Different Ways of Relating to Oneself," *Journal of Personality* 77 (2009): 23–50.

126 enhances well-being: For an overview of the research, see chapter 2 of C. K. Germer and K. D. Neff, *Teaching the Mindful Self-Compassion Program: A Guide for Professionals* (New York: Guilford Press, 2019).

126 to imagine receiving compassion: H. Rockliff et al., "A Pilot
     Exploration of Heart Rate Variability and Salivary Cortisol Responses
     to Compassion-Focused Imagery," *Clinical Neuropsychiatry: Journal
     of Treatment Evaluation* 5, no. 3 (2008): 132–39.

126 recruited participants on Facebook: L. B. Shapira and M. Mongrain,
     "The Benefits of Self-Compassion and Optimism Exercises for
     Individuals Vulnerable to Depression," *Journal of Positive Psychology* 5
     (2010): 377–89.

127 uniquely problematic emotion: J. P. Tangney and R. L. Dearing,
     Shame and Guilt (New York: Guilford Press, 2003).

127 University of Manitoba: E. A. Johnson and K. A. O'Brien, "Self-
     Compassion Soothes the Savage Ego-Threat System: Effects on
     Negative Affect, Shame, Rumination, and Depressive Symptoms,"
     Journal of Social and Clinical Psychology 32, no. 9 (2013): 939–63.

128 without being overwhelmed: A. Allen and M. R. Leary, "Self-
     Compassion, Stress, and Coping," *Social and Personality Psychology
     Compass* 4, no. 2 (2010): 107–18.

128 Researchers asked divorcing adults: D. A. Sbarra, H. L. Smith, and
     M. R. Mehl, "When Leaving Your Ex, Love Yourself: Observational
     Ratings of Self-Compassion Predict the Course of Emotional
     Recovery Following Marital Separation," *Psychological Science* 23
     (2012): 261–69.

128 diabetes: A. M. Friis, N. S. Consedine, and M. H. Johnson, "Does
     Kindness Matter? Diabetes, Depression, and Self-Compassion: A
     Selective Review and Research Agenda," *Diabetes Spectrum* 28, no. 4
     (2015): 252–57.

128 spina bifida: M. R. Hayter and D. S. Dorstyn, "Resilience, Self-
     Esteem and Self-Compassion in Adults with Spina Bifida," *Spinal
     Cord* 52, no. 2 (2013): 167–71.

128 multiple sclerosis: M. Nery-Hurwit, J. Yun, and V. Ebbeck,
     "Examining the Roles of Self-Compassion and Resilience on Health-
     Related Quality of Life for Individuals with Multiple Sclerosis,"
     Disability and Health Journal 11, no. 2 (2017): 256–61.

128 helped women cope with chronic physical pain: A. Barnes et al.,
     "Exploring the Emotional Experiences of Young Women with
     Chronic Pain: The Potential Role of Self-Compassion," *Journal of
     Health Psychology* (2018): 1–11, advance online publication, DOI:
     1359105318816509.

129 conditions such as cancer: L. Zhu et al., "The Predictive Role of Self-Compassion in Cancer Patients' Symptoms of Depression, Anxiety, and Fatigue: A Longitudinal Study," *Psycho-Oncology* 28, no. 9 (2019): 1918–25.

129 or HIV: J. M. Brion, M. R. Leary, and A. S. Drabkin, "Self-Compassion and Reactions to Serious Illness: The Case of HIV," *Journal of Health Psychology* 19, no. 2 (2014): 218–29.

129 parents of autistic children: K. D. Neff and D. J. Faso, "Self-Compassion and Well-Being in Parents of Children with Autism," *Mindfulness* 6, no. 4 (2014): 938–47.

129 addicted to alcohol: C. L. Phelps et al., "The Relationship between Self-Compassion and the Risk for Substance Use Disorder," *Drug and Alcohol Dependence* 183 (2018): 78–81.

129 drugs: S. Basharpoor et al., "The Role of Self-Compassion, Cognitive Self-Control, and Illness Perception in Predicting Craving in People with Substance Dependency," *Practice in Clinical Psychology* 2, no. 3 (2014): 155–64.

129 food: J. C. Rainey, C. R. Furman, and A. N. Gearhardt, "Food Addiction among Sexual Minorities," *Appetite* 120 (2018): 16–22.

129 sex: Y. Kotera and C. Rhodes, "Pathways to Sex Addiction: Relationships with Adverse Childhood Experience, Attachment, Narcissism, Self-Compassion and Motivation in a Gender-Balanced Sample," *Sexual Addiction and Compulsivity* 26, 1–2 (2019): 54–76.

129 addicted to chocolate: A. E. Diac et al., "Self-Compassion, Well-Being and Chocolate Addiction," *Romanian Journal of Cognitive Behavioral Therapy and Hypnosis* 4, no. 1–2 (2017): 1–12.

129 helps people recover: M. Brooks et al., "Self-Compassion amongst Clients with Problematic Alcohol Use," *Mindfulness* 3, no. 4 (2012): 308–17.

129 Alcoholics Anonymous: S. R. Newcombe, "Shame and Self-Compassion in Members of Alcoholics Anonymous" (unpublished doctoral dissertation, Wright Institute, 2015).

130 study tracked Chinese adolescents: Y. Jiang et al., "Buffering the Effects of Peer Victimization on Adolescent Non-suicidal Self-Injury: The Role of Self-Compassion and Family Cohesion," *Journal of Adolescence* 53 (2016): 107–15.

130 People who cut themselves often use physical pain: P. Wilkinson and

I. Goodyer, "Non-suicidal Self-Injury," *European Child & Adolescent Psychiatry* 20, no. 2 (2011): 103–8.

130 who had attempted suicide within the last year: D. LoParo et al., "The Efficacy of Cognitively-Based Compassion Training for African American Suicide Attempters," *Mindfulness* 9, no. 6 (2018): 1941–54.

138 University of California, Berkeley: J. G. Breines and S. Chen, "Self-Compassion Increases Self-Improvement Motivation," *Personality and Social Psychology Bulletin* 38, no. 9 (2012): 1133–43.

138 University of Pittsburgh: A. Vazeou-Nieuwenhuis and K. Schumann, "Self-Compassionate and Apologetic? How and Why Having Compassion toward the Self Relates to a Willingness to Apologize," *Personality and Individual Differences* 124 (2018): 71–6.

139 helps them feel less overwhelmed: K. D. Neff et al., "Caring for Others without Losing Yourself: An Adaptation of the Mindful Self-Compassion Program for Healthcare Communities," *Journal of Clinical Psychology* 76 (2020): 1543–62.

CHAPTER 6: STANDING STRONG

142 inner strength in over two hundred women: O. Stevenson and A. B. Allen, "Women's Empowerment: Finding Strength in Self-Compassion," *Women and Health* 57, no. 3 (2017): 295–310.

142 echoed in other research: J. A. Christman, "Examining the Interplay of Rejection Sensitivity, Self-Compassion, and Communication in Romantic Relationships" (unpublished doctoral dissertation, University of Tennessee, 2012).

143 when a mother is protecting her young: B. L. Mah et al., "Oxytocin Promotes Protective Behavior in Depressed Mothers: A Pilot Study with the Enthusiastic Stranger Paradigm," *Depression and Anxiety* 32, no. 2 (2015): 76–81.

143 "tend and *defend*" response: C. K. De Dreu et al., "The Neuropeptide Oxytocin Regulates Parochial Altruism in Intergroup Conflict among Humans," *Science* 328, no. 5984 (2010): 1408–11.

143 put "mental defectives" into orphanages: S. R. Kaler and B. J. Freeman, "Analysis of Environmental Deprivation: Cognitive and Social Development in Romanian Orphans," *Journal of Child Psychology and Psychiatry* 35, no. 4 (1994): 769–81.

144 "I raise up my voice": M. Yousafzai, *I Am Malala: The Girl Who*

Stood Up for Education and Was Shot by the Taliban (New York: Little, Brown, 2013).

145 "Group identity and influence": J. S. Turner, "Explaining the Nature of Power: A Three-Process Theory," *European Journal of Social Psychology* 35, no. 1 (2005): 1–22.

145 complexity of intersectionality: E. R. Cole, "Intersectionality and Research in Psychology," *American Psychologist* 64, no. 3 (2009): 170–80.

145 Researchers in Italy: G. Fuochi, C. A. Veneziani, and A. Voci, "Exploring the Social Side of Self-Compassion: Relations with Empathy and Outgroup Attitudes," *European Journal of Social Psychology* 48, no. 6 (2018): 769–83.

146 "I felt I had a right to stay where I was": Interview with Rosa Parks, *Scholastic*, January/February 1997 http://teacher.scholastic.com/rosa /interview.htm.

148 "strong back and soft front": J. Halifax, *Being with Dying: Cultivating Compassion and Fearlessness in the Presence of Death* (Boulder, CO: Shambhala Publications, 2009).

150 people won't like us if we say no: W. Wood and A. H. Eagly, "Gender Identity," in M. R. Leary and R. H. Hoyle, eds., *Handbook of Individual Differences in Social Behavior* (New York: Guilford Press, 2009), 109–25.

151 responses she suggests: J. de Azevedo Hanks, *The Assertiveness Guide for Women: How to Communicate Your Needs, Set Healthy Boundaries, and Transform Your Relationships* (Oakland, CA: New Harbinger, 2016).

152 is often the most dangerous: J. C. Campbell et al., "Intimate Partner Homicide: Review and Implications of Research and Policy," *Trauma, Violence and Abuse* 8 (2007): 246–69.

153 women in a domestic violence shelter: A. B. Allen, E. Robertson, and G. A. Patin, "Improving Emotional and Cognitive Outcomes for Domestic Violence Survivors: The Impact of Shelter Stay and Self-Compassion Support Groups," *Journal of Interpersonal Violence* (2017), advance online publication, DOI: 0886260517734858.

153 who has experienced trauma: C. Braehler and K. D. Neff, "Self-Compassion for PTSD," in N. Kimbrel and M. Tull, eds., *Emotion in PTSD* (Cambridge, MA: Elsevier Academic Press, 2020). 567–596.

153 severe psychological shock: R. Yehuda, "Post-Traumatic Stress

Disorder," *New England Journal of Medicine* 346, no. 2 (2002): 108–14.

153 less likely to develop PTSD: B. L. Thompson and J. Waltz, "Self-Compassion and PTSD Symptom Severity," *Journal of Traumatic Stress* 21 (2008): 556–58.

153 function better in daily life: K. Dahm et al., "Mindfulness, Self-Compassion, Posttraumatic Stress Disorder Symptoms, and Functional Disability in US Iraq and Afghanistan War Veterans," *Journal of Traumatic Stress* 28, no. 5 (2015): 460–64.

153 less likely to attempt suicide: J. K. Rabon et al., "Self-Compassion and Suicide Risk in Veterans: When the Going Gets Tough, Do the Tough Benefit More from Self-Kindness?," *Mindfulness* 10, no. 12 (2019): 2544–54.

153 Department of Veterans Affairs: R. Hiraoka et al., "Self-Compassion as a Prospective Predictor of PTSD Symptom Severity among Trauma-Exposed US Iraq and Afghanistan War Veterans," *Journal of Traumatic Stress* 28 (2015): 1–7.

154 recent study of 370 cisgender women: M. A. Cherry and M. M. Wilcox, "Sexist Microaggressions: Traumatic Stressors Mediated by Self-Compassion," *The Counseling Psychologist* 49, no. 1 (2021), 106–137.

154 suicidal ideation in LGBTQ+ youths: J. P. Robinson and D. L. Espelage, "Bullying Explains Only Part of LGBTQ–Heterosexual Risk Disparities: Implications for Policy and Practice," *Educational Researcher* 41, no. 8 (2012): 309–19.

154 self-compassion helped LGBTQ+ teens: A. J. Vigna, J. Poehlmann-Tynan, and B. W. Koenig, "Does Self-Compassion Facilitate Resilience to Stigma? A School-based Study of Sexual and Gender Minority Youth," *Mindfulness* 9, no. 3 (2017): 914–24.

154 LGBTQ+ youth of color: A. J. Vigna, J. Poehlmann-Tynan, and B. W. Koenig, "Is Self-Compassion Protective among Sexual- and Gender-Minority Adolescents across Racial Groups?," *Mindfulness* 11, no. 3 (2020): 800–15.

154 lead to "post-traumatic": C. C. Y. Wong and N. C. Yeung, "Self-Compassion and Posttraumatic Growth: Cognitive Processes as Mediators," *Mindfulness* 8, no. 4 (2017): 1078–87.

155 secure attachment as adults: M. Navarro-Gil et al., "Effects of Attachment-Based Compassion Therapy (ABCT) on

Self-Compassion and Attachment Style in Healthy People,"
Mindfulness 11, no. 1 (2020): 51–62.

155 sexually or physically abused in childhood: A. A. Scoglio et al.,
"Self-Compassion and Responses to Trauma: The Role of Emotion
Regulation," *Journal of Interpersonal Violence* 33, no. 13 (2015):
2016–36.

155 Compassion Focused Therapy (CFT): P. Gilbert, "The Origins and
Nature of Compassion Focused Therapy," *British Journal of Clinical
Psychology* 53, no. 1 (2014): 6–41.

156 Research shows this approach: P. Gilbert and S. Procter,
"Compassionate Mind Training for People with High Shame and
Self-Criticism: Overview and Pilot Study of a Group Therapy
Approach," *Clinical Psychology and Psychotherapy: An International
Journal of Theory and Practice* 13, no. 6 (2006): 353–79.

156 "It's made me feel like I've put on": E. Ashfield, C. Chan, and
D. Lee, "Building 'A Compassionate Armour': The Journey to
Develop Strength and Self-Compassion in a Group Treatment
for Complex Post-traumatic Stress Disorder," *Psychology and
Psychotherapy: Theory, Research and Practice* (2020), advance online
publication, DOI: 10.1111/papt.12275/.

156 this approach is highly effective: C. Craig, S. Hiskey, and
A. Spector, "Compassion Focused Therapy: A Systematic Review of
Its Effectiveness and Acceptability in Clinical Populations," *Expert
Review of Neurotherapeutics* 20, no. 4 (2020), 385–400.

166 "Power without love": M. L. King Jr., *Where Do We Go from Here:
Chaos or Community?*, vol. 2 (Boston: Beacon Press, 2010).

166 a form of nonviolent resistance called *satyagraha:* M. A.
Mattaini, *Strategic Nonviolent Power: The Science of Satyagraha*
(Athabasca, Canada: Athabasca University Press, 2013).

166 he argued may come from fear: M. K. Gandhi, "Letter to Mr.–
(25 January 1920)," *The Collected Works of Mahatma Gandhi*, vol. 19
(Delhi, India: Publications Division, Ministry of Information and
Broadcasting, Government of India, 1958).

166 "'Hate the sin and not the sinner,'" M. K. Gandhi, *My Experiments
with the Truth* (New York: Simon and Schuster, 2014; original work
published 1928).

167 co-opted by certain fundamentalists: P. Valera and T. Taylor,
"Hating the Sin but Not the Sinner: A Study about Heterosexism

and Religious Experiences among Black Men," *Journal of Black Studies* 42, no. 1 (2011): 106–22.

167 "You know I'm automatically attracted to beautiful": D. A. Fahrenthold, "Trump Recorded Having Extremely Lewd Conversation about Women in 2005," *Washington Post*, October 8, 2016, https://www.washingtonpost.com/politics/trump-recorded -having-extremely-lewd-conversation-about-women-in-2005/2016 /10/07/3b9ce776-8cb4-11e6-bf8a-3d26847eeed4_story.html.

167 the goal of the organizers: A. Jamieson, "Women's March on Washington: A Guide to the Post-inaugural Social Justice Event," *Guardian*, December 27, 2016, https://www.theguardian .com/us-news/2016/dec/27/womens-march-on-washington-dc-guide.

167 largest single-day protest in US history: M. Broomfield "Women's March against Donald Trump Is the Largest Day of Protests in US History, Say Political Scientists," *Independent*, January 23, 2017, https://www.independent.co.uk/news/world/americas/womens -march-anti-donald-trump-womens-rights-largest-protest -demonstration-us-history-political-scientists-a7541081.html.

168 no arrests reported anywhere in the United States: K. Capps, "Millions of Marchers, Zero Arrests," *Citylab*, https://www .bloomberg.com/news/articles/2017-01-22/millions-gather-for -women-s-march-none-arrested.

168 has been rightly criticized: N. Caraway, *Segregated Sisterhood: Racism and the Politics of American Feminism* (Knoxville, TN: University of Tennessee Press, 1991).

168 fully supported White supremacy: V. Ware, *Beyond the Pale: White Women, Racism, and History* (London: Verso Books, 2015).

168 feminists often supported Jim Crow: G. E. Gilmore, *Gender and Jim Crow: Women and the Politics of White Supremacy in North Carolina, 1896–1920*, 2nd ed. (Chapel Hill, NC: UNC Press Books, 2019).

168 "an African-American man is threatening me": T. Closson, "Amy Cooper's 911 Call, and What's Happened Since," *New York Times*, July 8, 2020, https://www.nytimes.com/2020/07/08/nyregion/amy -cooper-false-report-charge.html.

168 without even mentioning race: b. hooks, *Black Women and Feminism* (London: Routledge, 1981).

168 intersectional invisibility theory: V. Purdie-Vaughns and R. P. Eibach, "Intersectional Invisibility: The Distinctive Advantages

and Disadvantages of Multiple Subordinate-Group Identities," *Sex Roles* 59, nos. 5–6 (2008): 377–91.

CHAPTER 7: MEETING OUR NEEDS

171 "I am my own muse": H. Grant, *Pocket Frida Kahlo Wisdom* (London: Hardie Grant Publishing, 2018).

171 Women do the majority of household work: "Global Gender Gap Report," World Economic Forum, 2018.

172 sacrificing our own needs: J. H. Shih and N. K. Eberhart, "Gender Differences in the Associations between Interpersonal Behaviors and Stress Generation," *Journal of Social and Clinical Psychology* 29, no. 3 (2010): 243–55.

172 A University of Maryland study: M. J. Mattingly and S. M. Blanchi, "Gender Differences in the Quantity and Quality of Free Time: The US Experience," *Social Forces* 81, no. 3 (2003): 999–1030.

173 report experiencing greater meaning: W. J. Phillips and S. J. Ferguson, "Self-Compassion: A Resource for Positive Aging," *Journals of Gerontology Series B: Psychological Sciences and Social Sciences* 68, no. 4 (2012): 529–39.

173 experience more "harmonious passion": B. J. Schellenberg, D. S. Bailis, and A. D. Mosewich, "You Have Passion, but Do You Have Self-Compassion? Harmonious Passion, Obsessive Passion, and Responses to Passion-related Failure," *Personality and Individual Differences* 99 (2016): 278–85.

174 how college undergraduates resolve conflicts: L. M. Yarnell and K. D. Neff, "Self-Compassion, Interpersonal Conflict Resolutions, and Well-being," *Self and Identity* 12, no. 2 (2013): 146–59.

176 authenticity cultivated by self-compassion: J. W. Zhang et al., "A Compassionate Self Is a True Self? Self-Compassion Promotes Subjective Authenticity," *Personality and Social Psychology Bulletin* 45, no. 9 (2019): 1323–37.

179 process of self-actualization: A. H. Maslow, *A Theory of Human Motivation* (New York: Simon and Schuster, 2013).

179 creators of Self-Determination Theory: R. M. Ryan and E. L. Deci, *Self-Determination Theory: Basic Psychological Needs in Motivation, Development, and Wellness* (New York: Guilford Press, 2017).

179 healthy development can be defined: E. L. Deci and R. M. Ryan,

"The 'What' and 'Why' of Goal Pursuits: Human Needs and the Self-Determination of Behavior," *Psychological Inquiry* 11, no. 4 (2000): 227–68.

179 leads to optimal well-being: E. L. Deci and R. M. Ryan, eds., *Handbook of Self-Determination Research* (Rochester, NY: University Rochester Press, 2004).

179 self-compassion helps us do so: K. D. Neff, "Development and Validation of a Scale to Measure Self-Compassion," *Self and Identity* 2 (2003): 223–50.

179 examined a group of undergraduates: K. E. Gunnell et al., "Don't Be So Hard on Yourself! Changes in Self-Compassion during the First Year of University Are Associated with Changes in Well-Being," *Personality and Individual Differences* 107 (2017): 43–8.

181 duty-based morality: R. A. Shweder, M. Mahapatra, and J. G. Miller, "Culture and Moral Development," in J. Kagan and S. Lamb, eds., *The Emergence of Morality in Young Children* (Chicago: University of Chicago Press, 1987), 1–83.

181 Elliot Turiel argued against: E. Turiel, *The Culture of Morality: Social Development, Context, and Conflict* (Cambridge, UK: Cambridge University Press, 2002).

181 self-sacrifice (termed *sewa*): N. Desai and M. Krishnaraj, *Women and Society in India* (Delhi, India: Ajanta Press, 1987).

182 education than males: R. Batra and T. G. Reio Jr., "Gender Inequality Issues in India," *Advances in Developing Human Resources* 18, no. 1 (2016): 88–101.

182 female leaders like Indira Gandhi: I. Malhotra, *Indira Gandhi: A Personal and Political Biography* (Carlsbad, CA: Hay House, 2014).

182 Hindu youths for my study: K. D. Neff, "Judgments of Personal Autonomy and Interpersonal Responsibility in the Context of Indian Spousal Relationships: An Examination of Young People's Reasoning in Mysore, India," *British Journal of Developmental Psychology* 19, no. 2 (2001): 233–57.

183 "Suma should go to the dance class": K. D. Neff, "Reasoning about Rights and Duties in the Context of Indian Family Life," (unpublished doctoral dissertation, University of California, Berkeley, 1998), 128.

184 bar in Elgin made national news: C. Clarke, "Texas Bar Owner Prohibits Customers from Wearing Masks," CBS News, May 28,

2020, https://www.cbsnews.com/news/texas-bar-liberty-tree-tavern
-bans-masks-customers/.

185 "If you want to identify me": T. Merton, *My Argument with the
Gestapo: A Macaronic Journal* (New York: New Directions Books,
1969), 160–61.

186 Acceptance and Commitment Therapy: S. C. Hayes, K. D. Strosahl,
and K. G. Wilson, *Acceptance and Commitment Therapy: The Process
and Practice of Mindful Change* (New York: Guilford Press, 2011).

189 self-compassionate people engage in self-care: K. J. Homan and
F. M. Sirois, "Self-Compassion and Physical Health: Exploring the
Roles of Perceived Stress and Health-Promoting Behaviors," *Health
Psychology Open* 4, no. 2 (2017): 1–9.

189 Elderly people who are self-compassionate: A. B. Allen, E. R.
Goldwasser, and M. R. Leary, "Self-Compassion and Well-Being
among Older Adults," *Self and Identity* 11, no. 4 (2012): 428–53.

189 study of individuals living with HIV/AIDS: C. Dawson Rose et al.,
"Self-Compassion and Risk Behavior Among People Living with HIV/
AIDS," *Research in Nursing and Health* 37, no. 2 (2014): 98–106.

189 more willing to engage in self-care behavior: M. L. Terry et al., "Self-
Compassionate Reactions to Health Threats," *Personality and Social
Psychology Bulletin* 39, no. 7 (2013): 911–26.

190 compassionate goals in their close relationships: J. Crocker and
A. Canevello, "Creating and Undermining Social Support in
Communal Relationships: The Role of Compassionate and Self-
Image Goals," *Journal of Personality and Social Psychology* 95, no. 3
(2008): 555–75.

190 more caring and giving in their relationships: K. D. Neff and S. N.
Beretvas, "The Role of Self-Compassion in Romantic Relationships,"
Self and Identity 12, no. 1 (2013): 78–98.

190 flaws and shortcomings of others: J. W. Zhang, S. Chen, and T. K.
Tomova, "From Me to You: Self-Compassion Predicts Acceptance of
Own and Others' Imperfections," *Personality and Social Psychology
Bulletin* 46, no. 2 (2020): 228–41.

191 link between self-compassion and compassion for others: K. D.
Neff and E. Pommier, "The Relationship between Self-Compassion
and Other-Focused Concern among College Undergraduates,
Community Adults, and Practicing Meditators," *Self and Identity* 12,
no. 2 (2013): 160–76.

191 found that participation in MSC: K. D. Neff and C. K. Germer,
     "A Pilot Study and Randomized Controlled Trial of the Mindful
     Self-Compassion Program," *Journal of Clinical Psychology* 69, no. 1
     (2013): 28–44.

191 without draining ourselves: M. C. Delaney, "Caring for the
     Caregivers: Evaluation of the Effect of an Eight-Week Pilot Mindful
     Self-Compassion (MSC) Training Program on Nurses' Compassion
     Fatigue and Resilience," *PLOS ONE* 13, no. 11 (2018): e0207261.

191 University of Waterloo: K. Miller and A. Kelly, "Is Self-Compassion
     Contagious? An Examination of Whether Hearing a Display of Self-
     Compassion Impacts Self-Compassion in the Listener," *Canadian
     Journal of Behavioural Science/Revue Canadienne des Sciences du
     Comportement* 52, no. 2 (2020): 159–70.

CHAPTER 8: BECOMING OUR BEST SELVES

193 "When we truly choose to care": Megan Rapinoe, "Why I Am
     Kneeling" (blog), *Players Tribune*, October 2016, https://www.the
     playerstribune.com/articles/megan-rapinoe-why-i-am-kneeling.

193 impediment to practicing self-compassion: K. J. Robinson et al.,
     "Resisting Self-Compassion: Why Are Some People Opposed to
     Being Kind to Themselves?," *Self and Identity* 15, no. 5 (2016):
     505–24.

194 positive affirmations don't help: J. V. Wood, W. Q. Perunovic,
     and J. W. Lee, "Positive Self-Statements: Power for Some, Peril for
     Others," *Psychological Science* 20, no. 7 (2009): 860–66.

195 self-compassionate people are wiser: K. D. Neff, S. S. Rude, and
     K. Kirkpatrick, "An Examination of Self-Compassion in Relation to
     Positive Psychological Functioning and Personality Traits," *Journal of
     Research in Personality* 41 (2007): 908–16.

195 failures as learning opportunities: Y. Miyagawa, Y. Niiya, and J.
     Taniguchi, "When Life Gives You Lemons, Make Lemonade: Self-
     Compassion Increases Adaptive Beliefs about Failure," *Journal of
     Happiness Studies* 21, no. 6 (2020): 2051–68.

195 less fear of failure: K. D. Neff, Y-P Hsieh, and K. Dejitthirat,
     "Self-Compassion, Achievement Goals, and Coping with Academic
     Failure," *Self and Identity* 4 (2005): 263–87.

195 more likely to try again: M. E. Neely et al., "Self-Kindness When

Facing Stress: The Role of Self-Compassion, Goal Regulation, and Support in College Students' Well-Being," *Motivation and Emotion* 33 (2009): 88–97.

196 A study in Japan: Y. Miyagawa, J. Taniguchi, and Y. Niiya, "Can Self-Compassion Help People Regulate Unattained Goals and Emotional Reactions toward Setbacks?," *Personality and Individual Differences* 134 (2018): 239–44.

196 harsh judgment and discriminating wisdom: J. Goldstein and J. Kornfield, *Seeking the Heart of Wisdom: The Path of Insight Meditation* (Boston: Shambhala, 1987).

197 is known as grit: A. Duckworth and J. J. Gross, "Self-Control and Grit: Related but Separable Determinants of Success," *Current Directions in Psychological Science* 23, no. 5 (2014): 319–25.

197 self-compassionate people have more grit: K. D. Neff et al., "The Forest and the Trees: Examining the Association of Self-Compassion and Its Positive and Negative Components with Psychological Functioning," *Self and Identity* 17, no. 6 (2018): 627–45.

199 number one reason people are harsh: Robinson, "Resisting Self-Compassion," 505–24.

200 a number of maladaptive consequences: T. A. Powers, R. Koestner, and D. C. Zuroff, "Self-Criticism, Goal Motivation and Goal Progress," *Journal of Social and Clinical Psychology* 26 (2007): 814–28.

200 who was harmful or abusive: B. E. Gibb, "Childhood Maltreatment and Negative Cognitive Styles: A Quantitative and Qualitative Review," *Clinical Psychology Review* 22, no. 2 (2002): 223–46.

201 as opposed to the threat-defense system: P. Gilbert, "Social Mentalities: Internal 'Social' Conflicts and the Role of Inner Warmth and Compassion in Cognitive Therapy," in P. Gilbert and K. G. Bailey, eds., *Genes on the Couch: Explorations in Evolutionary Psychotherapy* (Hove, UK: Psychology Press, 2000), 118–50.

201 through self-criticism elevates cortisol levels: D. Hering, K. Lachowska, and M. Schlaich, "Role of the Sympathetic Nervous System in Stress-Mediated Cardiovascular Disease," *Current Hypertension Reports* 17, no. 10 (2015): 80–90.

201 major cause of depression: U. Dinger et al., "Interpersonal Problems, Dependency, and Self-Criticism in Major Depressive Disorder," *Journal of Clinical Psychology* 71, no. 1 (2015): 93–104.

201 activates the parasympathetic nervous system: H. Kirschner et al.,

"Soothing Your Heart and Feeling Connected: A New Experimental Paradigm to Study the Benefits of Self-Compassion," *Clinical Psychological Science* 7, no. 3 (2019): 545–65.

201 strengthens our immune function: W. J. Phillips and D. W. Hine, "Self-Compassion, Physical Health, and Health Behaviour: A Meta-Analysis," *Health Psychology Review* (2019): 1–27.

201 shown to alleviate depression: A. M. Ehret, J. Joormann, and M. Berking, "Examining Risk and Resilience Factors for Depression: The Role of Self-Criticism and Self-Compassion," *Cognition and Emotion* 29, no. 8 (2015): 1496–504.

201 "Spare the rod": L. D. Eron, "Spare the Rod and Spoil the Child?," *Aggression and Violent Behavior* 2, no. 4 (1997): 309–11.

201 undermining self-confidence and achievement: E. T. Gershoff, "Corporal Punishment by Parents and Associated Child Behaviors and Experiences: A Meta-Analytic and Theoretical Review," *Psychological Bulletin* 128, no. 4 (2002): 539–79.

208 less likely to have performance goals: M. Shimizu, Y. Niiya, and E. Shigemasu, "Achievement Goals and Improvement Following Failure: Moderating Roles of Self-Compassion and Contingency of Self-Worth," *Self and Identity* 15, no. 1 (2015): 107–15.

209 A study at McGill University: N. Hope, R. Koestner, and M. Milyavskaya, "The Role of Self-Compassion in Goal Pursuit and Well-Being among University Freshmen," *Self and Identity* 13, no. 5 (2014): 579–93.

209 fosters a growth rather than a fixed mindset: R. Chu, "The Relations of Self-Compassion, Implicit Theories of Intelligence, and Mental Health Outcomes among Chinese Adolescents" (unpublished doctoral dissertation, San Francisco State University, 2016).

209 first to coin these terms: C. W. Dweck, *Self-Theories: Their Role in Motivation, Personality, and Development* (Hove, UK: Psychology Press, 2000).

209 identify their biggest weakness: J. G. Breines and S. Chen, "Self-Compassion Increases Self-Improvement Motivation," *Personality and Social Psychology Bulletin* 38, no. 9 (2012): 1133–43.

210 level of personal initiative: I. Dundas et al., "Does a Short Self-Compassion Intervention for Students Increase Healthy Self-Regulation? A Randomized Control Trial," *Scandinavian Journal of Psychology* 58, no. 5 (2017): 443–50.

210 difficult vocabulary test: J. G. Breines and S. Chen, "Self-Compassion Increases Self-Improvement Motivation," *Personality and Social Psychology Bulletin* 38, no. 9 (2012): 1133–43.

211 major cause of stress and anxiety: D. M. Tice and R. F. Baumeister, "Longitudinal Study of Procrastination, Performance, Stress, and Health: The Costs and Benefits of Dawdling," *Psychological Science* 8, no. 6 (1997): 454–58.

211 self-compassion helps break that cycle: F. M. Sirois, "Procrastination and Stress: Exploring the Role of Self-Compassion," *Self and Identity* 13, no. 2 (2014): 128–45.

211 "If you are too self-compassionate": L. M. Sutherland et al., "Narratives of Young Women Athletes' Experiences of Emotional Pain and Self-Compassion," *Qualitative Research in Sport, Exercise and Health* 6, no. 4 (2014): 499–516.

212 University of Saskatchewan: N. A. Reis et al., "Self-Compassion and Women Athletes' Responses to Emotionally Difficult Sport Situations: An Evaluation of a Brief Induction," *Psychology of Sport and Exercise* 16 (2015): 18–25.

212 study by the same researchers: L. J. Ferguson et al., "Self-Compassion and Eudaimonic Well-Being during Emotionally Difficult Times in Sport," *Journal of Happiness Studies* 16, no. 5 (2015): 1263–80.

212 less anxious when playing: Z. Huysmans and D. Clement, "A Preliminary Exploration of the Application of Self-Compassion within the Context of Sport Injury," *Journal of Sport and Exercise Psychology* 39, no. 1 (2017): 56–66.

212 University of Manitoba: L. Ceccarelli et al., "Self-Compassion and Psycho-Physiological Recovery from Recalled Sport Failure," *Frontiers in Psychology* 10 (2019): 1564.

214 adaptive and maladaptive: J. Stoeber and K. Otto, "Positive Conceptions of Perfectionism: Approaches, Evidence, Challenges," *Personality and Social Psychology Review* 10 (2006): 295–319.

214 undermine our ability to achieve: S. B. Sherry et al., "Self-Critical Perfectionism Confers Vulnerability to Depression after Controlling for Neuroticism: A Longitudinal Study of Middle-aged, Community-Dwelling Women," *Personality and Individual Differences* 69 (2014): 1–4.

214 aim just as high: K. D. Neff, "Development and Validation of a

Scale to Measure Self-Compassion," *Self and Identity* 2 (2003): 223–50.

214 lower levels of maladaptive perfectionism: M. Ferrari et al., "Self-Compassion Moderates the Perfectionism and Depression Link in Both Adolescence and Adulthood," *PLOS ONE* 13, no. 2 (2018): e0192022.

214 study of medical trainees: C. M. Richardson et al., "Trainee Wellness: Self-Critical Perfectionism, Self-Compassion, Depression, and Burnout among Doctoral Trainees in Psychology," *Counselling Psychology Quarterly* 33, no. 2 (2018): 1–12.

216 "The curious paradox": C. Rogers, *On Becoming a Person: A Therapist's View of Psychotherapy* (Boston: Houghton Mifflin, 1995; original work published 1960), 17.

217 "If the first woman": Francis Gage's version of Sojourner Truth's "Ain't I a Woman" speech, April 23, 1863, https://www.the sojournertruthproject.com/compare-the-speeches/.

CHAPTER 9: BALANCE AND EQUALITY AT WORK

221 "If you give us a chance": "Transcript of the Keynote Address by Ann Richards, the Texas Treasurer," July 1988 Democratic Convention, *New York Times*, July 19, 1988, https://www.nytimes .com/1988/07/19/us/transcript-of-the-keynote-address-by-ann -richards-the-texas-treasurer.html.

221 college degree at all levels: National Center for Education Statistics, "Table 318.30. Bachelor's, Master's, and Doctor's Degrees Conferred by Postsecondary Institutions, by Sex of Student and Discipline: 2015–16," *Digest of Education Statistics* (2017), https://nces.ed.gov /programs/digest/d17/tables/dt17_318.30.asp?current=yes.

221 they earn better grades: A. R. Amparo, G. Smith, and A. Friedman, "Gender and Persistent Grade Performance Differences between Online and Face to Face Undergraduate Classes," in *EdMedia+ Innovate Learning* (Amsterdam: Association for the Advancement of Computing in Education, June 2018): 1935–39.

221 make up 47 percent of the workforce: M. DeWold, "12 Stats About Working Women," *US Department of Labor Blog*, March 6, 2017, https://www.ishn.com/articles/105943-stats-about-working-women.

221 outnumber men as managers: US Bureau of Labor Statistics, March

2017, https://www.bls.gov/careeroutlook/2017/data-on-display /women-managers.htm.

221 group differences within that figure: R. Bleiweis, "Quick Facts about the Gender Wage Gap," Center for American Progress, March 24, 2020, https://www.americanprogress.org/issues/women/reports /2020/03/24/482141/quick-facts-gender-wage-gap/.

222 funneled into different professions: N. Graf, A. Brown, and E. Patten, "The Narrowing, but Persistent, Gender Gap in Pay," Pew Research Center, March 22, 2019, https://www.pewresearch.org /fact-tank/2019/03/22/gender-pay-gap-facts/.

222 Women are five times: G. Livingston, "Stay-at-Home Moms and Dads Account for About One-in-Five US Parents," Pew Research Center, September 24, 2018, https://www.pewresearch.org /fact-tank/2018/09/24/stay-at-home-moms-and-dads-account-for -about-one-in-five-u-s-parents/.

222 more time on domestic chores: "Global Gender Gap Report," World Economic Forum, 2018.

222 Unemployed women spend: D. Kanal and J. T. Kornegay, "Accounting for Household Production in the National Accounts," *Survey of Current Business* 99, no. 6 (June 2019), https://apps.bea .gov/scb/2019/06-june/0619-household-production.htm.

222 putting us at a disadvantage: Y. van Osch and J. Schaveling, "The Effects of Part-time Employment and Gender on Organizational Career Growth," *Journal of Career Development* 47, no. 3 (2020): 328–43.

222 23 percent of board seats: Alliance for Board Diversity, "Missing Pieces Report: The 2018 Board Diversity Census of Women and Minorities on Fortune 500 Boards," 2018, https://www2.deloitte .com/us/en/pages/center-for-board-effectiveness/articles/missing -pieces-fortune-500-board-diversity-study-2018.html.

222 male chief executives named James: C. C. Miller, K. Quealy, and M. Sanger-Katz, "The Top Jobs Where Women are Outnumbered by Men Named John," April 24, 2018, *New York Times*, https://www .nytimes.com/interactive/2018/04/24/upshot/women-and-men -named-john.html.

222 understood in the larger context of stereotypes: M. E. Heilman and E. J. Parks-Stamm, "Gender Stereotypes in the Workplace: Obstacles to Women's Career Progress," *Advances in Group Processes* 24 (2007): 47–77.

223 almost no shift in agentic and communal gender stereotypes: E. L. Haines, K. Deaux, and N. Lofaro, "The Times They Are a-Changing . . . or Are They Not? A Comparison of Gender Stereotypes, 1983–2014," *Psychology of Women Quarterly* 40, no. 3 (2016): 353–63.

223 masculine world of business: M. E. Heilman and E. J. Parks-Stamm, "Gender Stereotypes in the Workplace: Obstacles to Women's Career Progress," in S. J. Correll, ed., *Social Psychology of Gender: Advances in Group Processes*, vol. 24 (Bingley, UK: Emerald Group Publishing, 2007), 47–77.

223 word usage in the *Wall Street Journal*: J. P. Walsh, K. Weber, and J. D. Margolis, "Social Issues and Management: Our Lost Cause Found," *Journal of Management* 29, no. 6 (2003): 859–81.

223 highly competitive environments: D. Salin, "Bullying and Organisational Politics in Competitive and Rapidly Changing Work Environments," *International Journal of Management and Decision Making* 4, no. 1 (2003): 35–46.

224 workers in the United States experience bullying: A. K. Samnani and P. Singh, "20 Years of Workplace Bullying Research: A Review of the Antecedents and Consequences of Bullying in the Workplace," *Aggression and Violent Behavior* 17, no. 6 (2012): 581–89.

224 shareholders with little regard for patients: M. R. Reiff., "The Just Price, Exploitation, and Prescription Drugs: Why Free Marketeers Should Object to Profiteering by the Pharmaceutical Industry," *Review of Social Economy* 77, no. 2 (2019): 108–42.

224 produced a generic version: A. Keown, "Price of Teva's Generic Drug to Treat Wilson's Disease Sparks Outrage," BioSpace, February 26, 2018, https://www.biospace.com/article/price-of-teva-s-generic-drug-to-treat-wilson-s-disease-sparks-outrage/.

224 influence of compassion in work culture: M. C. Worline and J. E. Dutton, *Awakening Compassion at Work: The Quiet Power that Elevates People and Organizations* (Oakland, CA: Berrett-Koehler, 2017).

225 economic loss and diminished productivity: P. J. Rosch, "The Quandary of Job Stress Compensation," *Health and Stress* 3, no. 1 (2001): 1–4.

225 companies that launch donation drives: J. E. Dutton et al., "Leading in Times of Trauma," *Harvard Business Review* 80, no. 1 (2002): 54–61.

225 boost the bottom line: K. Cameron et al., "Effects of Positive Practices on Organizational Effectiveness," *Journal of Applied Behavioral Science* 47, no. 3 (2011): 266–308.

225 unappealing to women: J. A. Kennedy and L. J. Kray, "Who Is Willing to Sacrifice Ethical Values for Money and Social Status? Gender Differences in Reactions to Ethical Compromises," *Social Psychological and Personality Science* 5, no. 1 (2014): 52–59.

225 more qualified for caregiving professions: K. McLaughlin, O. T. Muldoon, and M. Moutray, "Gender, Gender Roles and Completion of Nursing Education: A Longitudinal Study," *Nurse Education Today* 30, no. 4 (2010): 303–7.

225 given less value and status as well as pay: P. England, M. Budig, and N. Folbre, "Wages of Virtue: The Relative Pay of Care Work," *Social Problems* 49, no. 4 (2002): 455–73.

225 man who works full-time: Pew Research Center, "Raising Kids and Running a Household: How Working Parents Share the Load," November 4, 2015, https://www.pewsocialtrends.org/2015/11/04 /raising-kids-and-running-a-household-how-working-parents-share -the-load/.

226 American Progress survey: J. Halpin, K. Agne, and M. Omero, "Affordable Child Care and Early Learning for All Families," Center for American Progress, September 2018, https://cdn.american progress.org/content/uploads/2018/09/12074422/ChildCarePolling -report.pdf.

226 guilt working full-time than men do: J. L. Borelli et al., "Bringing Work Home: Gender and Parenting Correlates of Work-Family Guilt among Parents of Toddlers," *Journal of Child and Family Studies* 26, no. 6 (2017): 1734–45.

229 women are even more competent: A. H. Eagly, C. Nater, D. L. Miller, M. Kaufmann and S. Sczesny, "Gender Stereotypes Have Changed: A Cross-Temporal Meta-Analysis of US Public Opinion Polls from 1946 to 2018," *American Psychologist* 75, no. 3 (2020): 301.

229 than those with a female voice: C. P. Ernst and N. Herm-Stapelberg, "Gender Stereotyping's Influence on the Perceived Competence of Siri and Co.," *Proceedings of the 53rd Hawaii International Conference on System Sciences* (January 2020).

229 Madeline Heilman at New York University: M. E. Heilman,

"Gender Stereotypes and Workplace Bias," *Research in Organizational Behavior* 32 (2012): 113–35.

229 stereotyped as having tender communal traits: Heilman, "Gender Stereotypes and Workplace Bias," 113–35.

229 applicants named John versus Jennifer: C. A. Moss-Racusin et al., "Science Faculty's Subtle Gender Biases Favor Male Students," *Proceedings of the National Academy of Sciences* 109, no. 41 (2012): 16474–79.

230 female professors of management: L. J. Treviño et al., "Meritocracies or Masculinities? The Differential Allocation of Named Professorships by Gender in the Academy," *Journal of Management* 44, no. 3 (2018): 972–1000.

230 identical work is evaluated less favorably: H. K. Davison and M. J. Burke, "Sex Discrimination in Simulated Employment Contexts: A Meta-Analytic Investigation," *Journal of Vocational Behavior* 56, no. 2 (2000): 225–48.

230 series of studies by researchers at Yale: V. L. Brescoll and E. L. Uhlmann, "Can an Angry Woman Get Ahead? Status Conferral, Gender, and Expression of Emotion in the Workplace," *Psychological Science* 19, no. 3 (2008): 268–75.

231 disparities in the workplace are fair: J. L. Cundiff and T. K. Vescio, "Gender Stereotypes Influence How People Explain Gender Disparities in the Workplace," *Sex Roles* 75, nos. 3–4 (2016): 126–38.

231 one hundred empirical studies: A. Joshi, J. Son, and H. Roh, "When Can Women Close the Gap? A Meta-Analytic Test of Sex Differences in Performance and Rewards," *Academy of Management Journal* 58, no. 5 (2015): 1516–45.

231 women entering the labor market: C. Buffington et al., "STEM Training and Early Career Outcomes of Female and Male Graduate Students: Evidence from UMETRICS Data Linked to the 2010 Census," *American Economic Review* 106, no. 5 (2016): 333–38.

231 experienced gender discrimination: K. Parker and C. Funk, "Gender Discrimination Comes in Many Forms for Today's Working Women," Pew Research Center, December 14, 2017, https://www.pewresearch.org/fact-tank/2017/12/14/gender-discrimination-comes-in-many-forms-for-todays-working-women/.

232 backlash: L. A. Rudman and P. Glick, "Feminized Management and Backlash toward Agentic Women: The Hidden Costs to Women of

a Kinder, Gentler Image of Middle Managers," *Journal of Personality and Social Psychology* 77, no. 5 (1999): 1004–10.

232 democratic primary debate in December 2019: A. Linskey, "The Women Asked for Forgiveness. The Men Tried to Sell Their Books: How a Democratic Debate Moment Put a Spotlight on Gender," *Washington Post*, December 20, 2019, https://www.washingtonpost .com/politics/seek-forgiveness-or-give-a-gift-how-a-democratic -debate-moment-put-gender-in-the-spotlight/2019/12/20/6b77450c -22db-11ea-a153-dce4b94e4249_story.html.

233 described in negative terms: M. E. Heilman, C. J. Block, and R. Martell, "Sex Stereotypes: Do They Influence Perceptions of Managers?," *Journal of Social Behavior and Personality* 10 (1995): 237–52.

234 Laurie Rudman at Rutgers University: L. A. Rudman, "Self-Promotion as a Risk Factor for Women: The Costs and Benefits of Counter-Stereotypical Impression Management," *Journal of Personality and Social Psychology* 74, no. 3 (1998): 629–45.

235 women settled for a full 20 percent less: E. T. Amanatullah and M. W. Morris, "Negotiating Gender Roles: Gender Differences in Assertive Negotiating Are Mediated by Women's Fear of Backlash and Attenuated When Negotiating on Behalf of Others," *Journal of Personality and Social Psychology* 98, no. 2 (2010): 256–67.

235 paid more and promoted more often: A. Joshi, J. Son, and H. Roh, "When Can Women Close the Gap? A Meta-Analytic Test of Sex Differences in Performance and Rewards," *Academy of Management Journal* 58, no. 5 (2015): 1516–45.

235 In one experiment: L. A. Rudman and P. Glick, "Prescriptive Gender Stereotypes and Backlash toward Agentic Women," *Journal of Social Issues* 57, no. 4 (2001): 743–62.

236 researchers in Israel: R. Kark, R. Waismel-Manor, and B. Shamir, "Does Valuing Androgyny and Femininity Lead to a Female Advantage? The Relationship between Gender-Role, Transformational Leadership and Identification," *Leadership Quarterly* 23, no. 3 (2012): 620–40.

236 calls gender judo: J. C. Williams, "Women, Work and the Art of Gender Judo," *Washington Post*, January 24, 2014, https://www .washingtonpost.com/opinions/women-work-and-the-art-of-gender -judo/2014/01/24/29e209b2-82b2-11e3-8099-9181471f7aaf _story.html.

236 help lessen the influence of gender bias: J. C. Williams and R. Dempsey, *What Works for Women at Work: Four Patterns Working Women Need to Know* (New York: NYU Press, 2018).

238 first step toward changing them: J. L. Howell and K. A. Ratliff, "Not Your Average Bigot: The Better-Than-Average Effect and Defensive Responding to Implicit Association Test Feedback," *British Journal of Social Psychology* 56 (2017): 125–45.

239 reducing unconscious gender bias: K. McCormick-Huhn, L. M. Kim, and S. A. Shields, "Unconscious Bias Interventions for Business: An Initial Test of WAGES-Business (Workshop Activity for Gender Equity Simulation) and Google's 're:Work' Trainings," *Analyses of Social Issues and Public Policy* 20, no. 1 (2020): 26–65.

240 research shows is a common phenomenon: M. E. Heilman and M. C. Haynes, "No Credit Where Credit Is Due: Attributional Rationalization of Women's Success in Male-Female Teams," *Journal of Applied Psychology* 90, no. 5 (2005): 905–16.

240 women tend to be interrupted: K. J. Anderson and C. Leaper, "Meta-Analyses of Gender Effects on Conversational Interruption: Who, What, When, Where, and How," *Sex Roles* 39, nos. 3–4 (1998): 225–52.

240 both are liked more: C. A. Moss-Racusin and L. A. Rudman, "Disruptions in Women's Self-Promotion: The Backlash Avoidance Model," *Psychology of Women Quarterly* 34, no. 2 (2010): 186–202.

241 greater work-life balance: J. M. Nicklin, K. Seguin, and S. Flaherty, "Positive Work-Life Outcomes: Exploring Self-Compassion and Balance," *European Journal of Applied Positive Psychology* 3, no. 6 (2019): 1–13.

241 confidence in their job performance: A. Reizer, "Bringing Self-Kindness into the Workplace: Exploring the Mediating Role of Self-Compassion in the Associations between Attachment and Organizational Outcomes," *Frontiers in Psychology* 10 (2019): 1148.

241 the imposter phenomenon: P. R. Clance and S. A. Imes, "The Imposter Phenomenon in High Achieving Women: Dynamics and Therapeutic Intervention," *Psychotherapy: Theory, Research and Practice* 15, no. 3 (1978): 241–49.

242 a prestigious European university: A. Patzak, M. Kollmayer, and B. Schober, "Buffering Impostor Feelings with Kindness: The Mediating

Role of Self-Compassion between Gender-Role Orientation and the Impostor Phenomenon," *Frontiers in Psychology* 8 (2017): 1289.

242 encountering difficulties in a job search: L. M. Kreemers, E. A. van Hooft, and A. E. van Vianen, "Dealing with Negative Job Search Experiences: The Beneficial Role of Self-Compassion for Job Seekers' Affective Responses," *Journal of Vocational Behavior* 106 (2018): 165–79.

242 report higher levels of engagement: Y. Kotera, M. Van Laethem, and R. Ohshima, "Cross-cultural Comparison of Mental Health between Japanese and Dutch Workers: Relationships with Mental Health Shame, Self-Compassion, Work Engagement and Motivation," *Cross Cultural and Strategic Management* 27, no. 3 (2020): 511–30.

242 entrepreneurs to be more self-compassionate: Y. Engel et al., "Self-Compassion When Coping with Venture Obstacles: Loving-Kindness Meditation and Entrepreneurial Fear of Failure," *Entrepreneurship Theory and Practice* (2019): 1–27, advance online publication, DOI: 1042258719890991.

243 *Harvard Business Review*: S. Chen, "Give Yourself a Break: The Power of Self-Compassion," *Harvard Business Review* 96, no. 5 (2018): 116–23.

CHAPTER 10: CARING FOR OTHERS WITHOUT LOSING OURSELVES

247 "Caring for myself": A. Lorde, *A Burst of Light: And Other Essays* (Mineola, NY: IXIA Press, 2017), 130.

247 engage in matriphagy: T. A. Evans, E. J. Wallis, and M. A. Elgar, "Making a Meal of Mother," *Nature* 376, no. 6538 (1995): 299.

247 80 percent of single parents are women: T. Grall, "Custodial Mothers and Fathers and Their Child Support: 2015," US Census Bureau, February 2020, original work published January 2018, https://www.census.gov/library/publications/2018/demo/p60-262.html

247 twice the amount of childcare and housework: S. M. Bianchi et al., "Housework: Who Did, Does or Will Do It, and How Much Does It Matter?," *Social Forces* 91, no. 1 (2012): 55.

248 start earning more money than their husbands: M. Bittman et al., "When Does Gender Trump Money? Bargaining and Time in Household Work," *American Journal of Sociology* 109, no. 1 (2003): 186–214.

248 mothers report always feeling rushed: Pew Research Center, "Who's Feeling Rushed?," February 28, 2016, https://www.pewsocialtrends .org/2006/02/28/whos-feeling-rushed/.

248 50 percent more likely than men: AARP Public Policy Institute, "Caregiving in the US 2015," June 2015, https://www.aarp.org /content/dam/aarp/ppi/2015/caregiving-in-the-us-research -report-2015.pdf.

248 negative consequences from caregiving: Q. P. Li, Y. W. Mak, and A. Y. Loke, "Spouses' Experience of Caregiving for Cancer Patients: A Literature Review," *International Nursing Review* 60, no. 2 (2013): 178–87.

248 report being angrier and more distressed: K. J. Lively, L. C. Steelman, and B. Powell, "Equity, Emotion, and Household Division of Labor Response," *Social Psychology Quarterly* 73, no. 4 (2010): 358–79.

248 more likely to experience burnout: L. Lieke et al., "Positive and Negative Effects of Family Involvement on Work-Related Burnout," *Journal of Vocational Behavior* 73, no. 3 (2008): 387–96.

250 "unmitigated communion": V. S. Helgeson and H. Fritz, "A Theory of Unmitigated Communion," *Personality and Social Psychology Review* 2 (1998): 173–83.

250 women register higher levels of lopsided: D. M. Buss, "Unmitigated Agency and Unmitigated Communion: An Analysis of the Negative Components of Masculinity and Femininity," *Sex Roles* 22, no. 9 (1990): 555–68.

250 leads to distress and partially explains: L. Jin et al., "Depressive Symptoms and Unmitigated Communion in Support Providers," *European Journal of Personality: Published for the European Association of Personality Psychology* 24, no. 1 (2010): 56–70.

250 lopsided carers tend to silence themselves: H. L. Fritz and V. S. Helgeson, "Distinctions of Unmitigated Communion from Communion: Self-Neglect and Overinvolvement with Others," *Journal of Personality and Social Psychology* 75, no. 1 (1998): 121–40.

250 intimacy in romantic relationships: V. S. Helgeson, "Relation of Agency and Communion to Well-Being: Evidence and Potential Explanations," *Psychological Bulletin* 116 (1994): 412–28.

251 often disgruntled about it: S. G. Ghaed and L. C. Gallo, "Distinctions among Agency, Communion, and Unmitigated Agency

and Communion According to the Interpersonal Circumplex, Five-Factor Model, and Social-Emotional Correlates," *Journal of Personality Assessment* 86, no. 1 (2006): 77–88.

251 less likely to visit the doctor: V. S. Helgeson and H. L. Fritz, "The Implications of Unmitigated Agency and Unmitigated Communion for Domains of Problem Behavior," *Journal of Personality* 68, no. 6 (2000): 1031–57.

251 such as a heart attack: H. L. Fritz, "Gender-linked Personality Traits Predict Mental Health and Functional Status Following a First Coronary Event," *Health Psychology* 19, no. 5 (2000): 420–28.

251 Unmitigated Communion Scale: H. L. Fritz and V. S. Helgeson, "Distinctions of Unmitigated Communion from Communion: Self-Neglect and Overinvolvement with Others," *Journal of Personality and Social Psychology* 75, no. 1 (1998): 121–40. Note that a few of the items were changed for this book so that reverse coding would be unnecessary.

252 study of 361 undergraduate students: V. Thornton and A. Nagurney, "What Is Infidelity? Perceptions Based on Biological Sex and Personality," *Psychology Research and Behavior Management* 4 (2011): 51–58.

252 need for external validation: D. C. Jack and D. Dill, "The Silencing the Self Scale: Schemas of Intimacy Associated with Depression in Women," *Psychology of Women Quarterly* 16 (1992): 97–106.

253 contribute to their unhappiness and depression: L. Jin et al., "Depressive Symptoms and Unmitigated Communion in Support Providers," *European Journal of Personality* 24, no. 1 (2010): 56–70.

253 self-worth rooted in self-compassion: K. D. Neff et al., "The Forest and the Trees: Examining the Association of Self-Compassion and Its Positive and Negative Components with Psychological Functioning," *Self and Identity* 17, no. 6 (2018): 627–45.

253 more stable and less shaky over time: K. D. Neff and R. Vonk, "Self-Compassion Versus Global Self-Esteem: Two Different Ways of Relating to Oneself," *Journal of Personality* 77 (2009): 23–50.

254 norms of self-sacrifice among Mexican American: K. D. Neff and M. A. Suizzo, "Culture, Power, Authenticity and Psychological Well-Being within Romantic Relationships: A Comparison of European American and Mexican Americans," *Cognitive Development* 21, no. 4 (2006): 441–57.

258 more empathic than men: A. E. Thompson and D. Voyer, "Sex
    Differences in the Ability to Recognise Non-verbal Displays of
    Emotion: A Meta-Analysis," *Cognition and Emotion* 28, no. 7 (2014):
    1164–95.

258 "sense another person's world": C. Rogers, *On Becoming a Person: A
    Therapist's View of Psychotherapy* (Boston: Houghton Mifflin, 1995;
    original work published 1961), 248.

258 "mirror neurons": M. Iacoboni, "Imitation, Empathy, and Mirror
    Neurons," *Annual Review of Psychology* 60 (2009): 653–70.

259 to be the key factor: D. Keltner, *Born to Be Good* (New York: W. W.
    Norton, 2009).

259 parents with better mirroring abilities: F. B. De Waal, "Putting the
    Altruism Back into Altruism: The Evolution of Empathy," *Annual
    Review of Psychology* 59 (2008): 279–300.

259 our brain become activated: P. L. Jackson, P. Rainville, and J.
    Decety, "To What Extent Do We Share the Pain of Others? Insight
    from the Neural Bases of Pain Empathy," *Pain* 125 (2006): 5–9.

259 secondary traumatic stress disorder: M. Ludick and C. R.
    Figley, "Toward a Mechanism for Secondary Trauma Induction
    and Reduction: Reimagining a Theory of Secondary Traumatic
    Stress," *Traumatology* 23, no. 1 (2017): 112–23.

260 With burnout comes: C. Maslach, "Burnout: A Multidimensional
    Perspective," in W. B. Schaufeli, C. Maslach, and T. Marek,
    eds., *Series in Applied Psychology: Social Issues and Questions.
    Professional Burnout: Recent Developments in Theory and
    Research* (Philadelphia: Taylor and Francis, 1993), 19–32.

260 primary cause of turnover: S. E. Showalter, "Compassion Fatigue:
    What Is It? Why Does It Matter? Recognizing the Symptoms,
    Acknowledging the Impact, Developing the Tools to Prevent
    Compassion Fatigue, and Strengthen the Professional Already
    Suffering from the Effects," *American Journal of Hospice and Palliative
    Medicine* 27, no. 4 (2010): 239–42.

260 resulting in acute stress: M. Ferrara et al., "Prevalence of Stress,
    Anxiety and Depression in with Alzheimer Caregivers," *Health and
    Quality of Life Outcomes* 6, no. 1 (2008): 93.

260 "compassion fatigue": C. R. Figley, ed., *Treating Compassion Fatigue*
    (London: Routledge, 2002).

260 "empathy fatigue": O. Klimecki and T. Singer, "Empathic Distress

Fatigue Rather Than Compassion Fatigue? Integrating Findings from Empathy Research in Psychology and Social Neuroscience," in B. Oakley et al., eds., *Pathological Altruism* (Oxford: Oxford University Press, 2012), 368–83.

260 better for our minds and bodies: E. M. Seppälä et al., eds., *The Oxford Handbook of Compassion Science* (Oxford: Oxford University Press, 2017).

260 difference between empathy and compassion: T. Singer and O. M. Klimecki, "Empathy and Compassion," *Current Biology* 24, no. 18 (2014): R875–78.

261 high blood pressure: M. R. Oreskovich et al., "The Prevalence of Substance Use Disorders in American Physicians," *American Journal on Addictions* 24, no. 1 (2015): 30–38.

262 engaging in regular self-care: A. Salloum et al., "The Role of Self-Care on Compassion Satisfaction, Burnout and Secondary Trauma among Child Welfare Workers," *Children and Youth Services Review* 49 (2015): 54–61.

262 more likely to engage in self-care activities: J. Mills, T. Wand, and J. A. Fraser, "Examining Self-Care, Self-Compassion and Compassion for Others: A Cross-sectional Survey of Palliative Care Nurses and Doctors," *International Journal of Palliative Nursing* 24, no. 1 (2018): 4–11.

266 "God, give us the serenity": J. G. Littleton and J. S. Bell, *Living the Serenity Prayer: True Stories of Acceptance, Courage, and Wisdom* (Avon, MA: Adams Media, 2008), 14.

269 research showing that caregivers: C. Conversano et al., "Mindfulness, Compassion, and Self-Compassion Among Health Care Professionals: What's New? A Systematic Review," *Frontiers in Psychology* 11 (2020): 1–21.

269 examined how self-compassion helped people: M. P. Schellekens et al., "Are Mindfulness and Self-Compassion Related to Psychological Distress and Communication in Couples Facing Lung Cancer? A Dyadic Approach," *Mindfulness* 8, no. 2 (2017): 325–36.

269 Professional caregivers such as therapists: K. Raab, "Mindfulness, Self-Compassion, and Empathy among Health Care Professionals: A Review of the Literature," *Journal of Health Care Chaplaincy* 20, no. 3 (2014): 95–108.

269 They sleep better at night: K. J. Kemper, X. Mo, and R. Khayat,

"Are Mindfulness and Self-Compassion Associated with Sleep and Resilience in Health Professionals?," *Journal of Alternative and Complementary Medicine* 21, no. 8 (2015): 496–503.

269 fulfilled in their work: J. Duarte, J. Pinto-Gouveia, and B. Cruz, "Relationships between Nurses' Empathy, Self-Compassion and Dimensions of Professional Quality of Life: A Cross-sectional Study," *International Journal of Nursing Studies* 60 (2016): 1–11.

269 have confidence in their ability: K. Olson and K. J. Kemper, "Factors Associated with Well-Being and Confidence in Providing Compassionate Care," *Journal of Evidence-Based Complementary and Alternative Medicine* 19, no. 4 (2014): 292–96.

270 SCHC significantly increased: K. D. Neff et al., "Caring for Others without Losing Yourself: An Adaptation of the Mindful Self-Compassion Program for Healthcare Communities," *Journal of Clinical Psychology* 76 (2020): 1543–62.

271 activists are particularly prone to burnout: C. Maslach and M. Gomes, "Overcoming Burnout," in R. MacNair and Psychologists for Social Responsibility, eds., *Working for Peace: A Handbook of Practical Psychology and Other Tools* (Atascadero, CA: Impact Publishers, 2006), 43–59.

271 give up their activism altogether: H. Rettig, *The Lifelong Activist: How to Change the World without Losing Your Way* (New York: Lantern, 2006).

271 University of Ottawa: K. Rodgers, "Anger Is Why We're All Here: Mobilizing and Managing Emotions in a Professional Activist Organization," *Social Movement Studies* 9, no. 3 (2010): 273–91.

271 "There's a built-in potential": Rodgers, "Anger Is Why We're All Here," 280.

CHAPTER 11: WHAT WE DO FOR LOVE

273 "There can be no love": b. hooks, *Communion: The Female Search for Love* (New York: Perennial, 2003), 66.

274 "Cinderella complex": C. Dowling, *The Cinderella Complex: Women's Hidden Fear of Independence* (New York: Pocket Books, 1981).

275 "One cold winter's day": A. Schopenhauer, *Parerga and Paralipomena: Short Philosophical Essays*, volume 2 (Oxford: Oxford University Press, 1851), 651.

275 healthier romantic relationships: E.H.K. Jacobson et al., "Examining Self-Compassion in Romantic Relationships," *Journal of Contextual Behavioral Science* 8 (2018): 69–73.

275 more sexually satisfied: J. S. Ferreira, R. A. Rigby, and R. J. Cobb, "Self-Compassion Moderates Associations between Distress about Sexual Problems and Sexual Satisfaction in a Daily Diary Study of Married Couples," *Canadian Journal of Human Sexuality* 29, no. 2 (2020): 182–196.

275 make balanced compromises: L. M. Yarnell and K. D. Neff, "Self-Compassion, Interpersonal Conflict Resolutions, and Well-being," *Self and Identity* 2, no. 2 (2013): 146–59.

275 "I was very busy with school, cheer, sports": Yarnell and Neff, "Self-Compassion," 156.

276 "I always want to please him": Yarnell and Neff, "Self-Compassion," 156.

276 self-compassion in romantic relationships: K. D. Neff and S. N. Beretvas, "The Role of Self-Compassion in Romantic Relationships," *Self and Identity* 12, no. 1 (2013): 78–98.

277 Kansas State University: Z. Williams, "Relationship Satisfaction in Black Couples: The Role of Self-Compassion and Openness" (unpublished doctoral dissertation, Kansas State University 2019).

277 self-acceptance in romantic relationships: J. W. Zhang, S. Chen, and T. K. Tomova Shakur, "From Me to You: Self-Compassion Predicts Acceptance of Own and Others' Imperfections," *Personality and Social Psychology Bulletin* 46, no. 2 (2020): 228–42.

278 University of Tennessee: L. R. Baker and J. K. McNulty, "Self-Compassion and Relationship Maintenance: The Moderating Roles of Conscientiousness and Gender," *Journal of Personality and Social Psychology* 100, no. 5 (2011): 853.

283 shaped by patriarchy: S. Coontz, "The World Historical Transformation of Marriage," *Journal of Marriage and Family* 66, no. 4 (2004): 974–79.

283 doctrine of coverture: R. Geddes and D. Lueck, "The Gains from Self-Ownership and the Expansion of Women's Rights," *American Economic Review* 92, no. 4 (2002): 1079–92.

283 beating was legal until 1920: "Domestic Violence Facts, Information, Pictures-Encyclopedia.com articles about Domestic violence," *Encyclopedia.com*, retrieved September 6, 2020.

283 "When I eventually met Mr. Right": K. Luppi, "Comedian-Actress
    Rita Rudner Brings a Bit of Real Life to Laguna Playhouse's
    'Act 3' . . .", *Los Angeles Times*, January 8, 2016, https://www.latimes
    .com/socal/coastline-pilot/entertainment/tn-cpt-et-0108-rita-rudner
    -20160108-story.html.

284 "Love, in the context of an oppressive": A. Koedt, E. Levine, and
    A. Rapone, "Politics of the Ego: A Manifesto for New York Radical
    Feminists," in A. Koedt, E. Levine, and A. Rapone, eds., *Radical
    Feminism* (New York: Times Books, 1970), 379–83.

284 bra-burning feminists: N. Greenfieldboyce, "Pageant Protest
    Sparked Bra-Burning Myth," NPR, September 5, 2008, https://
    www.npr.org/templates/story/story.php?storyId=94240375,
    accessed February 6, 2012.

284 the Women's March: K. Boyle, *#MeToo, Weinstein and Feminism*
    (London: Palgrave Pivot, 2019).

285 University of Texas at Austin: M. A. Garcia and D. Umberson,
    "Marital Strain and Psychological Distress in Same-Sex and
    Different-Sex Couples," *Journal of Marriage and Family* 81, no. 5
    (October 2019): 1253–68.

285 same-sex couples face increased discrimination: A. K. Randall et
    al., "Associations between Sexual Orientation Discrimination and
    Depression among Same-Sex Couples: Moderating Effects of Dyadic
    Coping," *Journal of Couple and Relationship Therapy* 16, no. 4 (2017):
    325–45.

285 harmful dynamics of patriarchy: A. M. Pollitt, B. A. Robinson, and
    D. Umberson, "Gender Conformity, Perceptions of Shared Power,
    and Marital Quality in Same-and Different-Sex Marriages, *Gender
    and Society* 32, no. 1 (2018): 109–31.

286 "There feels like there's a gap in my life": W. Langford, *Revolutions
    of the Heart: Gender, Power and the Delusions of Love* (Hove, UK:
    Psychology Press, 1999), 27.

286 "I think perhaps I had it": Langford, *Revolutions of the Heart*, 29.

286 "It was lovely": Langford, *Revolutions of the Heart*, 39.

289 "Powerful, self-loving women": hooks, *Communion*, 152.

290 Only about half of all marriages: C. E. Copen et al., "First Marriages
    in the United States," National Health Statistics Reports, March 22,
    2012, https://www.cdc.gov/nchs/data/nhsr/nhsr049.pdf.

EPILOGUE: BECOMING A COMPASSIONATE MESS

299 "We can still be crazy": P. Chödrön, *The Wisdom of No Escape and the Path of Loving-Kindness* (Boston: Shambhala, 1991), 4.

300 "The goal of practice": R. Nairn, lecture presented at Kagyu Samye Ling Monastery, Dumfriesshire, Scotland, September 2009.

302 the wise woman: J. S. Bolen, *Goddesses in Older Women: Archetypes in Women over Fifty* (New York: Harper Perennial, 2002).

INDEX

happiness:
  finding what brings us, 184–86
  seen as dependent on romantic
    relationship, 286–87
harassment, *see* sexual harassment and
    abuse
harsh judgment, discriminating
    wisdom versus, 196
Harter, Susan, 9
hatred:
  anger and, 71, 72, 80
  "Hate the sin and not the sinner"
    phrase and, 166–67
Hayes, Steven, 186
healing balm of tender self-
    compassion, 126–28, 152,
    160–64
healing from mistreatment, 160–64
  Responding to Harm practice and,
    161–64
health issues:
  disparities and, 11
  lopsided caring and, 251
  self-care behaviors and, 189
  self-compassion and coping with
    pain of, 128–29
  see also well-being
Hegelson, Vicki, 250, 251–52
Heilman, Madeline, 229, 233–34
Helmreich, Robert, 54
helplessness, feelings of, 64
Hinduism, goddess Kali and, 78–79,
    82–83, 96, 103
Hispanic women, wage gap and, 221–22
homelessness, 259
hooks, bell, 273, 289
hormones, sex-related variability and,
    48–49
Horse Boy, The (book and
    documentary), 292
hostile sexism, 45–46, 47
household labor:
  more equitable sharing of, 226, 228
  time spent by women versus men on,
    171–72, 222, 225–26, 247–48

How Do I Treat My Friends and
    Myself in Difficult Times exercise,
    18–19
humanity, *see* common humanity
Human Potential Movement, 178–79
hypermasculinity, 93

idiot compassion, 38
Imes, Suzanne, 241
immigration status, 167
implicit association test (IAT),
    231–32
imposter phenomenon, 241–42
In a Different Voice (Gilligan), 7
Incredible Hulk, 5
inexpressiveness, lopsided caring and,
    250
injustice:
  acknowledging pain of, 237–38
  anger and speaking up in face of,
    72–73
interdependence, 22, 145–46, 170
Internal Family Systems (IFS) therapy,
    75, 77, 204
interruptions by men, "verbal chicken"
    strategy for, 240
"Is Self-Compassion Contagious?,"
    191–92

job interviews, gender bias in
    workplace and, 234, 235–36
Johnson, Edward, 127–28
justice:
  fight for, 5, 6
  moral decision-making and, 7
  see also social justice

Kahlo, Frida, 171
Kali (Hindu goddess), 78–79, 82–83,
    96, 103
Kavanaugh, Brett, 63
Kelly, Megyn, 65
kindness, 20, 23, 115–17
  as antidote to shame, 127, 128
  bravery as manifestation of, 142–44